MASS EFFECT™

EVOLUTION

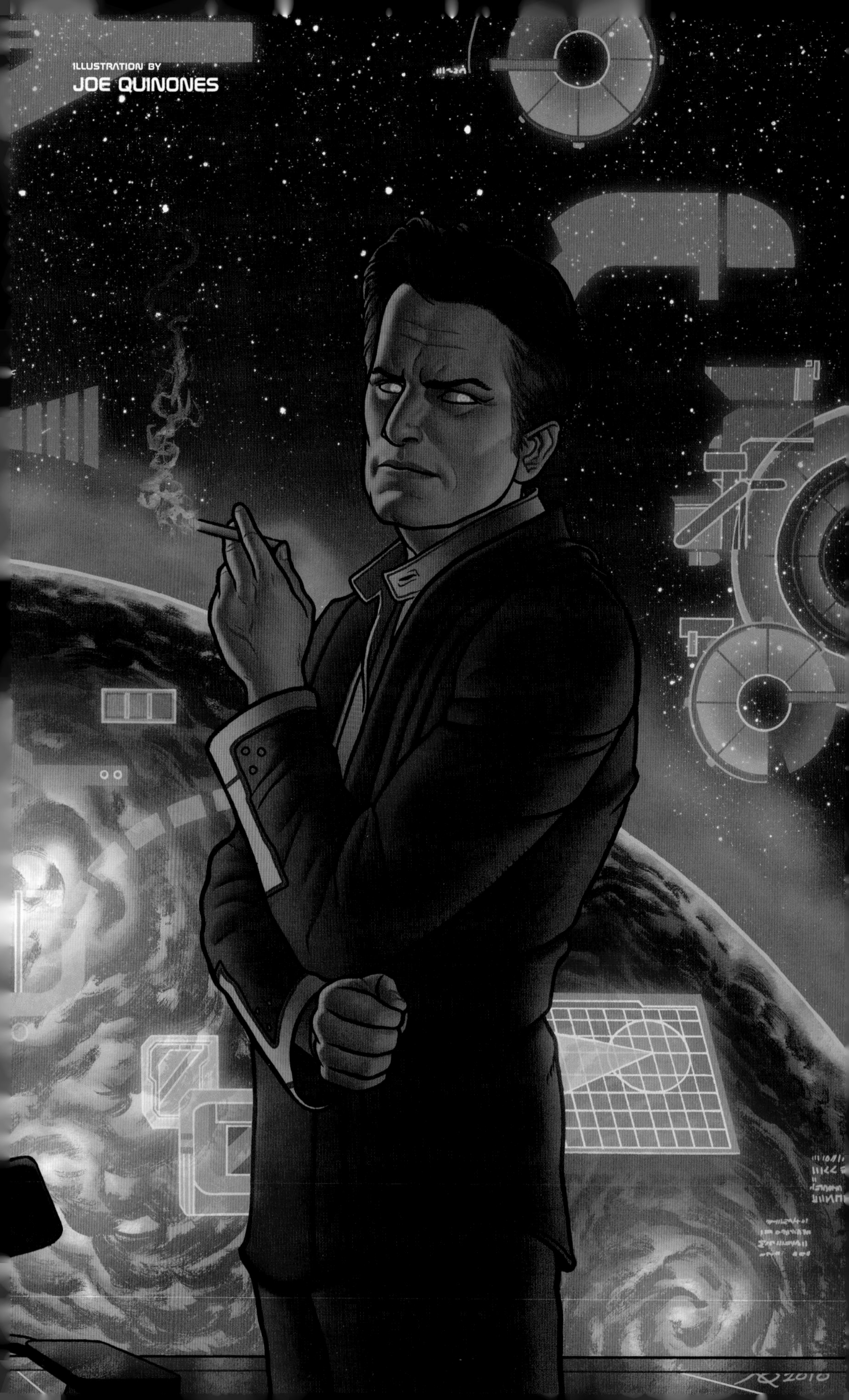

ILLUSTRATION BY
JOE QUINONES

MASS EFFECT
EVOLUTION™

STORY
MAC WALTERS

SCRIPT
JOHN JACKSON MILLER

ART
OMAR FRANCIA WITH **MANUEL SILVA**

COLORS
MICHAEL ATIYEH

LETTERING
MICHAEL HEISLER

DARK HORSE BOOKS®

PUBLISHER
MIKE RICHARDSON

ASSISTANT EDITOR
BRENDAN WRIGHT

EDITOR
DAVE MARSHALL

DESIGNER
STEPHEN REICHERT

MASS EFFECT: EVOLUTION

This volume collects issues one through four of the Dark Horse comic-book series *Mass Effect: Evolution*, as well as short stories from *MySpace Dark Horse Presents #36* and *USAToday.com*.

Thanks to Ray, Greg, and Casey for giving me the opportunity to explore and expand their creations.
—**Mac Walters**

To T. M. Haley, my guide to the galaxy.
—**John Jackson Miller**

I love you so much, Nadia! Thanks to your love and support, my life has changed forever!
My heart and this book are for you, always.
—**Omar Francia**

For David Ingram . . . can't thank you enough for all you have given.
—**Michael Atiyeh**

Special thanks to BioWare, including:
DEREK WATTS, Art Director; CASEY HUDSON, Executive Producer; AARYN FLYNN, Studio GM,
BioWare Edmonton; RAY MUZYKA and GREG ZESCHUK, BioWare Co-Founders

Published by Dark Horse Books
A division of Dark Horse Comics, Inc.
10956 SE Main Street | Milwaukie, OR 97222

DarkHorse.com | MassEffect.com

LIBRARY OF CONGRESS CATALOGING-IN-PUBLICATION DATA

Walters, Mac.
Mass effect : evolution / story, Mac Walters ; script, John Jackson Miller ; art, Omar Francia with Manuel Silva ; colors, Michael Atiyeh ; lettering, Michael Heisler ; cover art, Massimo Carnevale. -- 1st ed.
p. cm.
ISBN 978-1-59582-759-3
1. Graphic novels. I. Miller, John Jackson. II. Francia, Omar. III. Silva, Manuel. IV. Title. V. Title: Evolution.
PN6727.W277M34 2011
741.5'943--dc22
2011012235

First standard edition: October 2011
ISBN 978-1-59582-759-3

Custom hardcover edition: October 2011
ISBN 978-1-59582-858-3

1 3 5 7 9 10 8 6 4 2
Printed at 1010 Printing International, Ltd., Guangdong Province, China

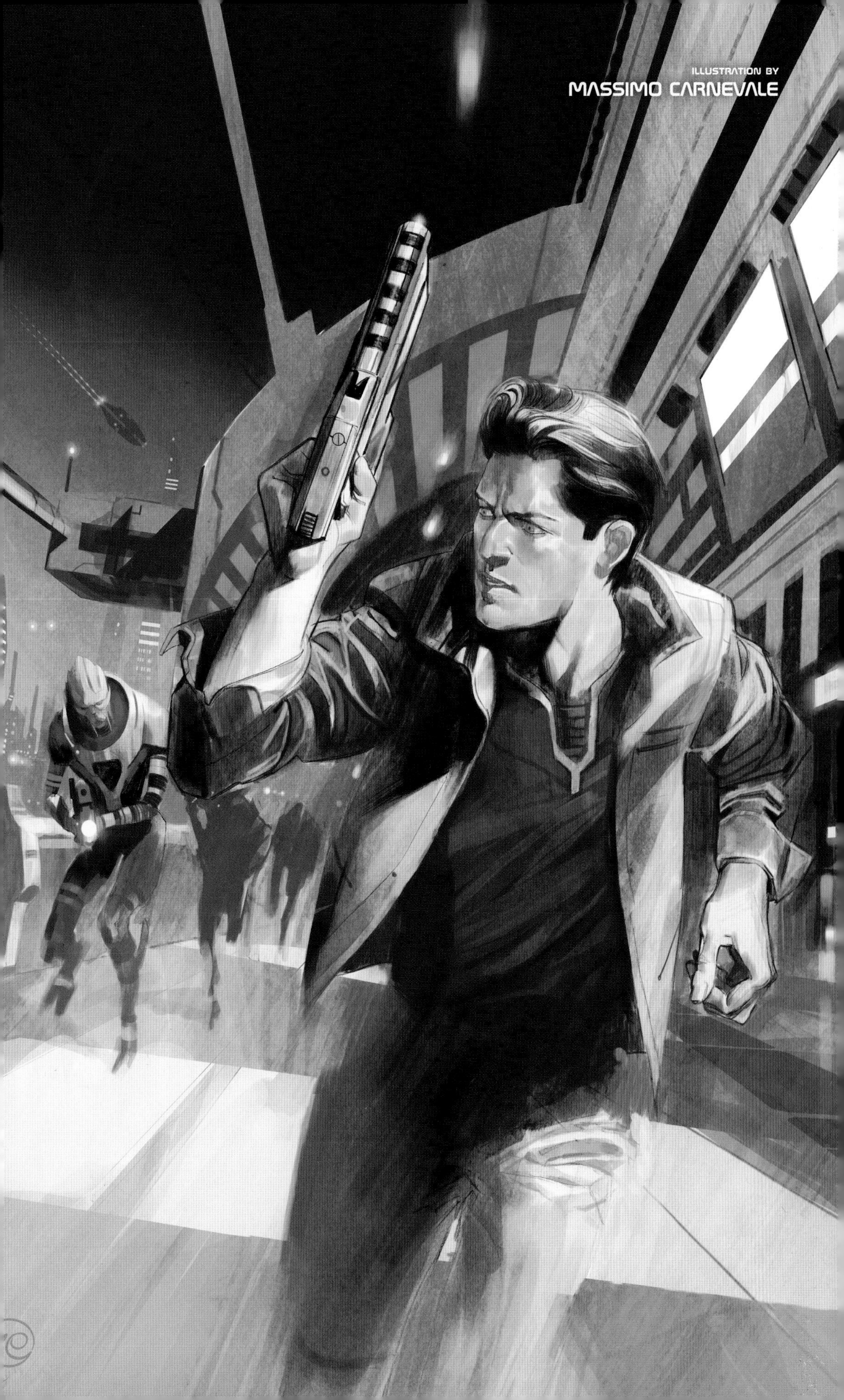
ILLUSTRATION BY
MASSIMO CARNEVALE

In the year 2157, first contact has become humanity's first interstellar war. And maybe its last.

Eight years ago, the people of Earth discovered something astounding near Pluto. Part of a network of ancient devices, the mass relay allowed humans to venture into a galaxy teeming with life.

Others did not welcome the new arrivals. Long established in the galaxy's political scene, the militaristic turians challenged humanity's right to find its destiny in the stars.

But even as Earth's warriors fight the First Contact War, other humans fear harm may come from further exposure to aliens and their strange artifacts. Believing knowledge is the first line of defense, a nascent movement sends its first scouts to the stars—and into the war zone . . .

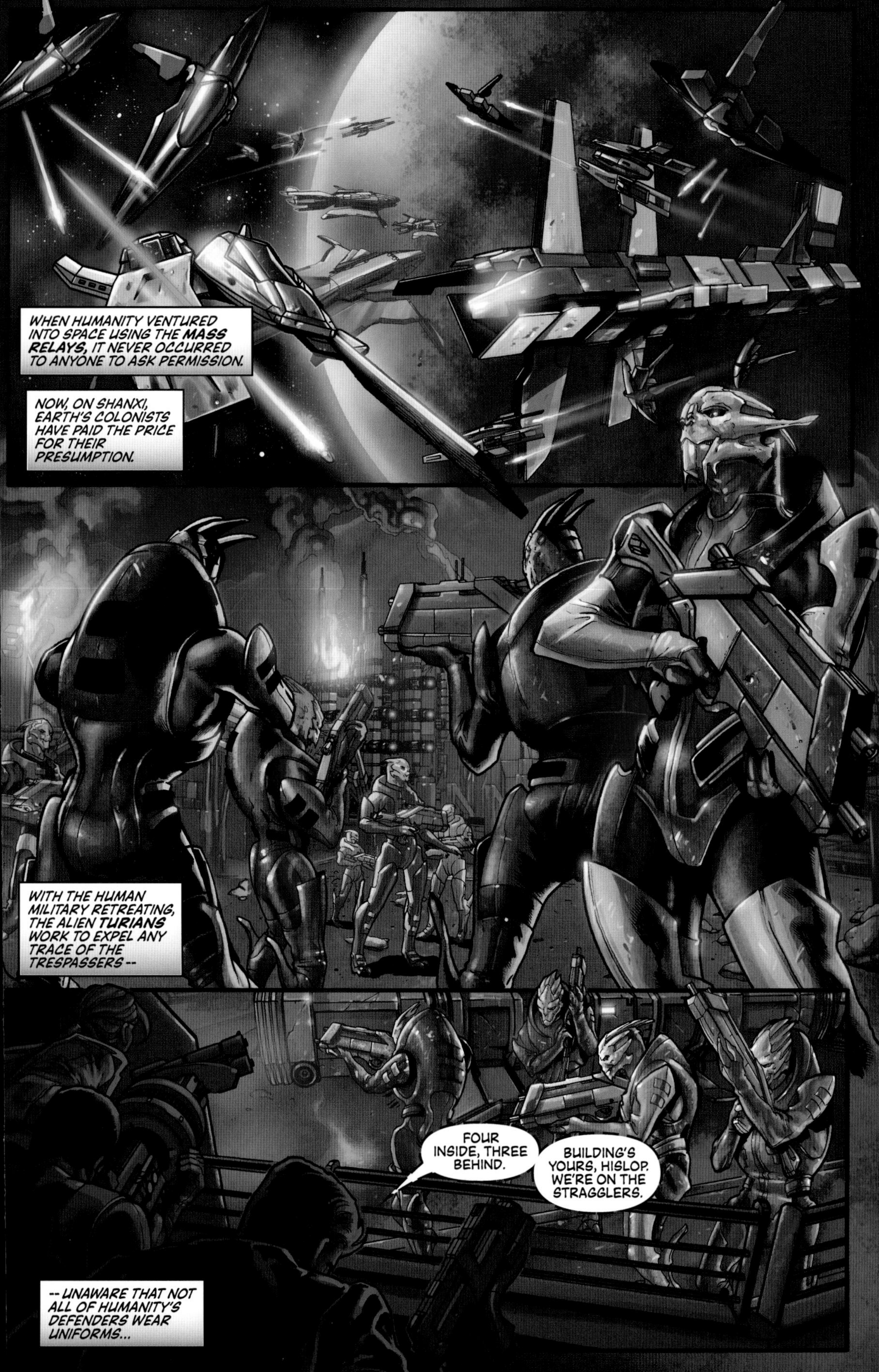
WHEN HUMANITY VENTURED INTO SPACE USING THE MASS RELAYS, IT NEVER OCCURRED TO ANYONE TO ASK PERMISSION.
NOW, ON SHANXI, EARTH'S COLONISTS HAVE PAID THE PRICE FOR THEIR PRESUMPTION.
WITH THE HUMAN MILITARY RETREATING, THE ALIEN TURIANS WORK TO EXPEL ANY TRACE OF THE TRESPASSERS --
FOUR INSIDE, THREE BEHIND.
BUILDING'S YOURS, HISLOP. WE'RE ON THE STRAGGLERS.
-- UNAWARE THAT NOT ALL OF HUMANITY'S DEFENDERS WEAR UNIFORMS...

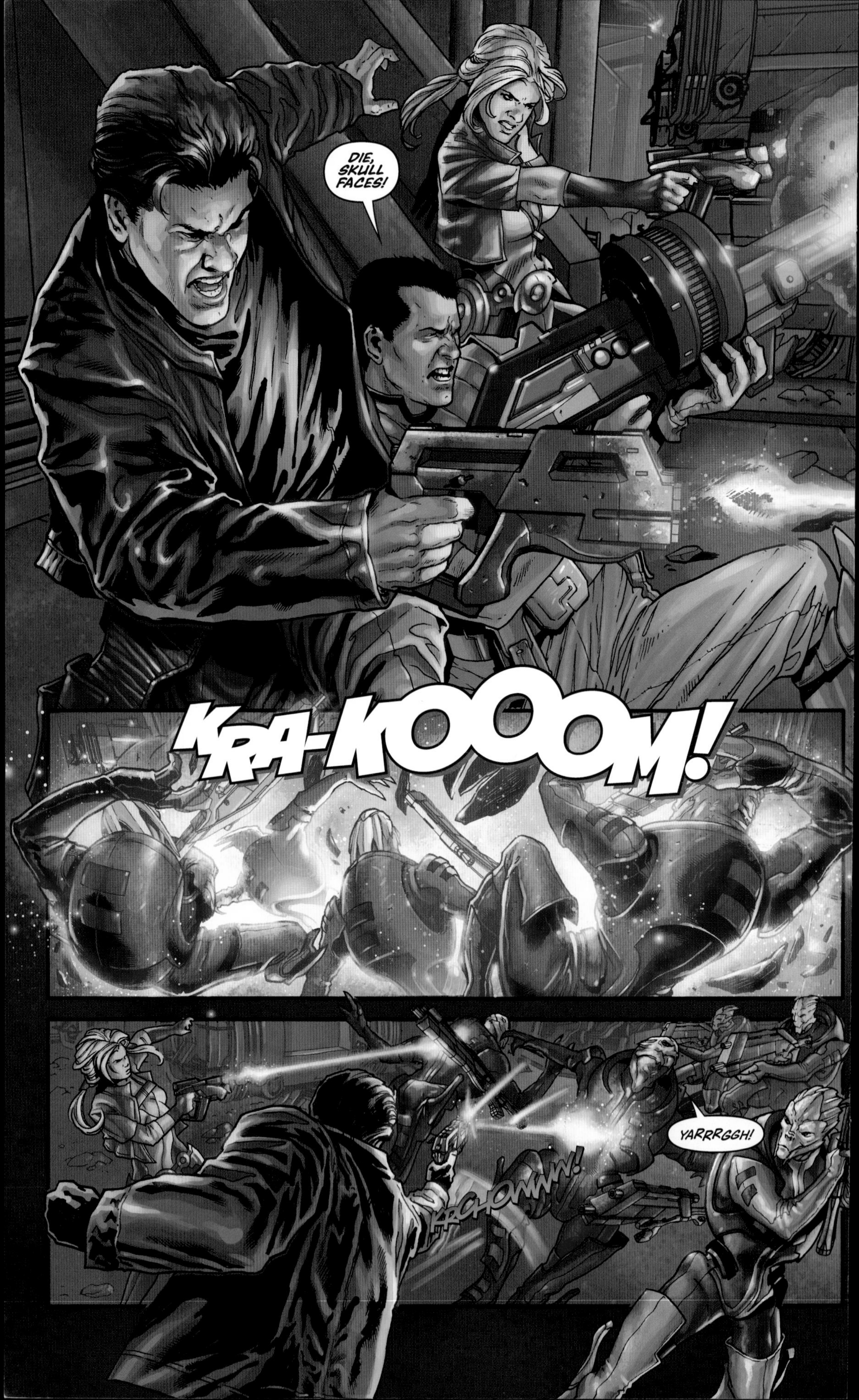
DIE, SKULL FACES!
KRA-KOOOOM!
KRCHOWWW!
YARRRGGH!

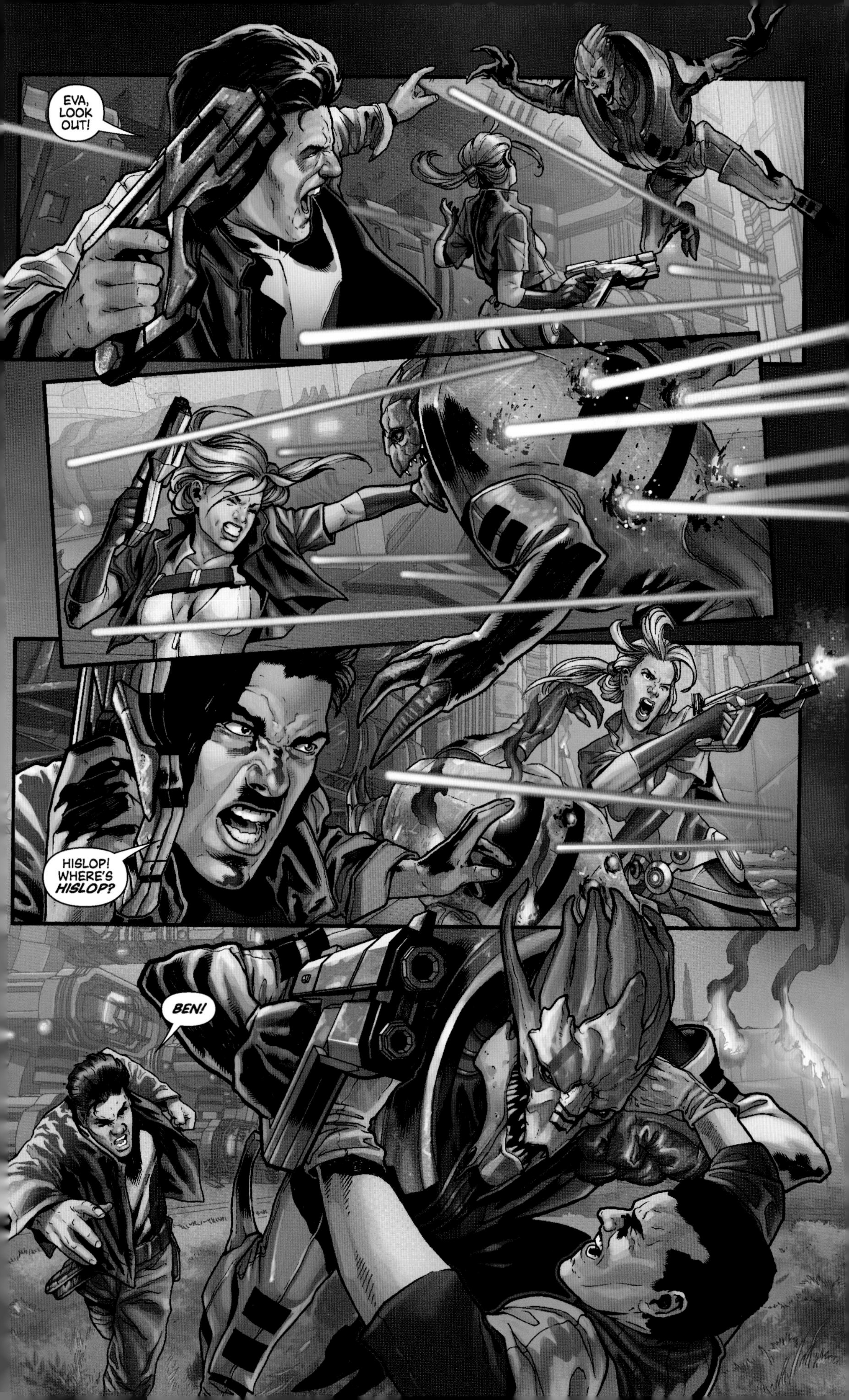
EVA, LOOK OUT!
HISLOP! WHERE'S HISLOP?
BEN!

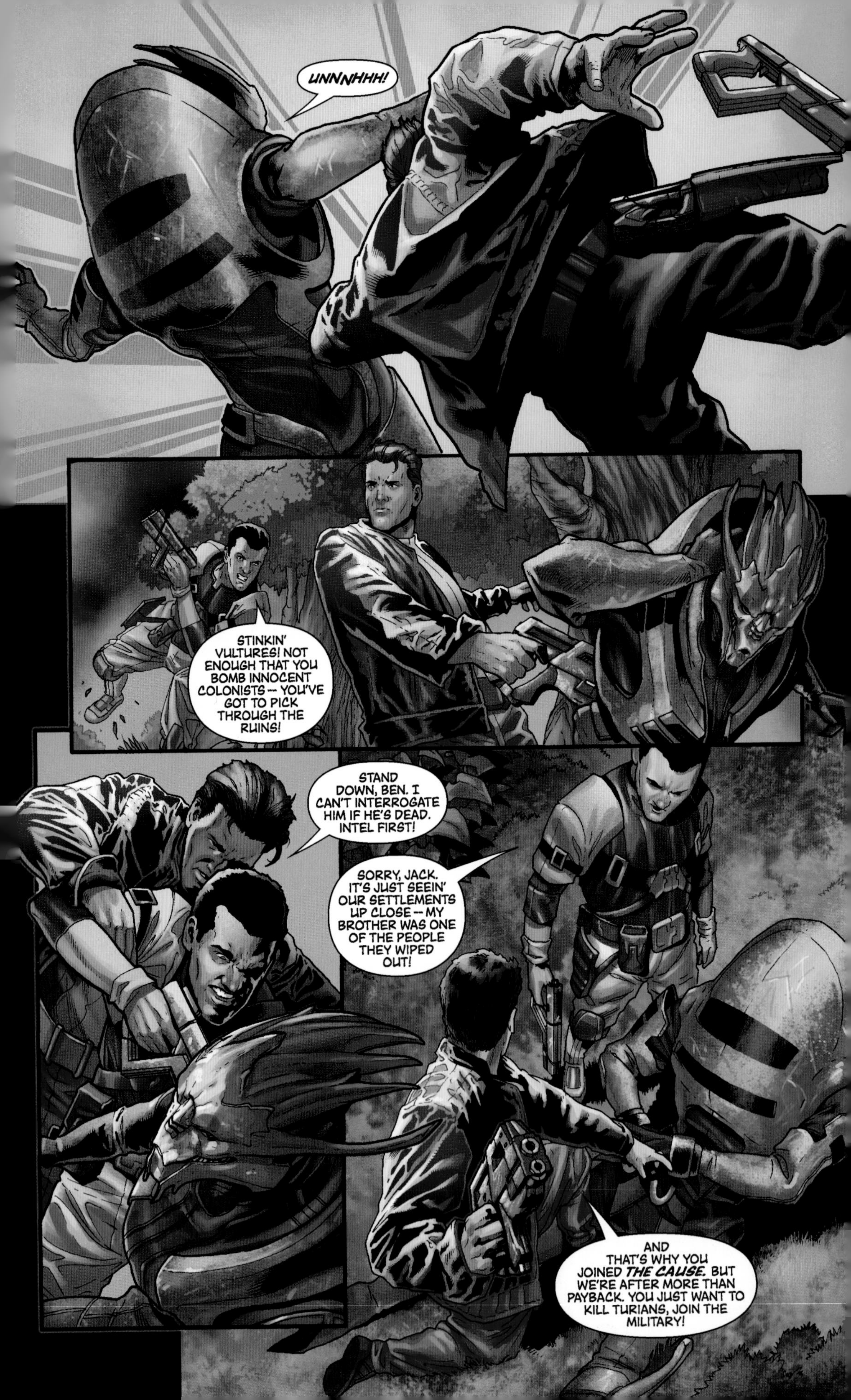
UNNNHHH!
STINKIN' VULTURES! NOT ENOUGH THAT YOU BOMB INNOCENT COLONISTS -- YOU'VE GOT TO PICK THROUGH THE RUINS!
STAND DOWN, BEN. I CAN'T INTERROGATE HIM IF HE'S DEAD. INTEL FIRST!
SORRY, JACK. IT'S JUST SEEIN' OUR SETTLEMENTS UP CLOSE -- MY BROTHER WAS ONE OF THE PEOPLE THEY WIPED OUT!
AND THAT'S WHY YOU JOINED THE CAUSE. BUT WE'RE AFTER MORE THAN PAYBACK. YOU JUST WANT TO KILL TURIANS, JOIN THE MILITARY!

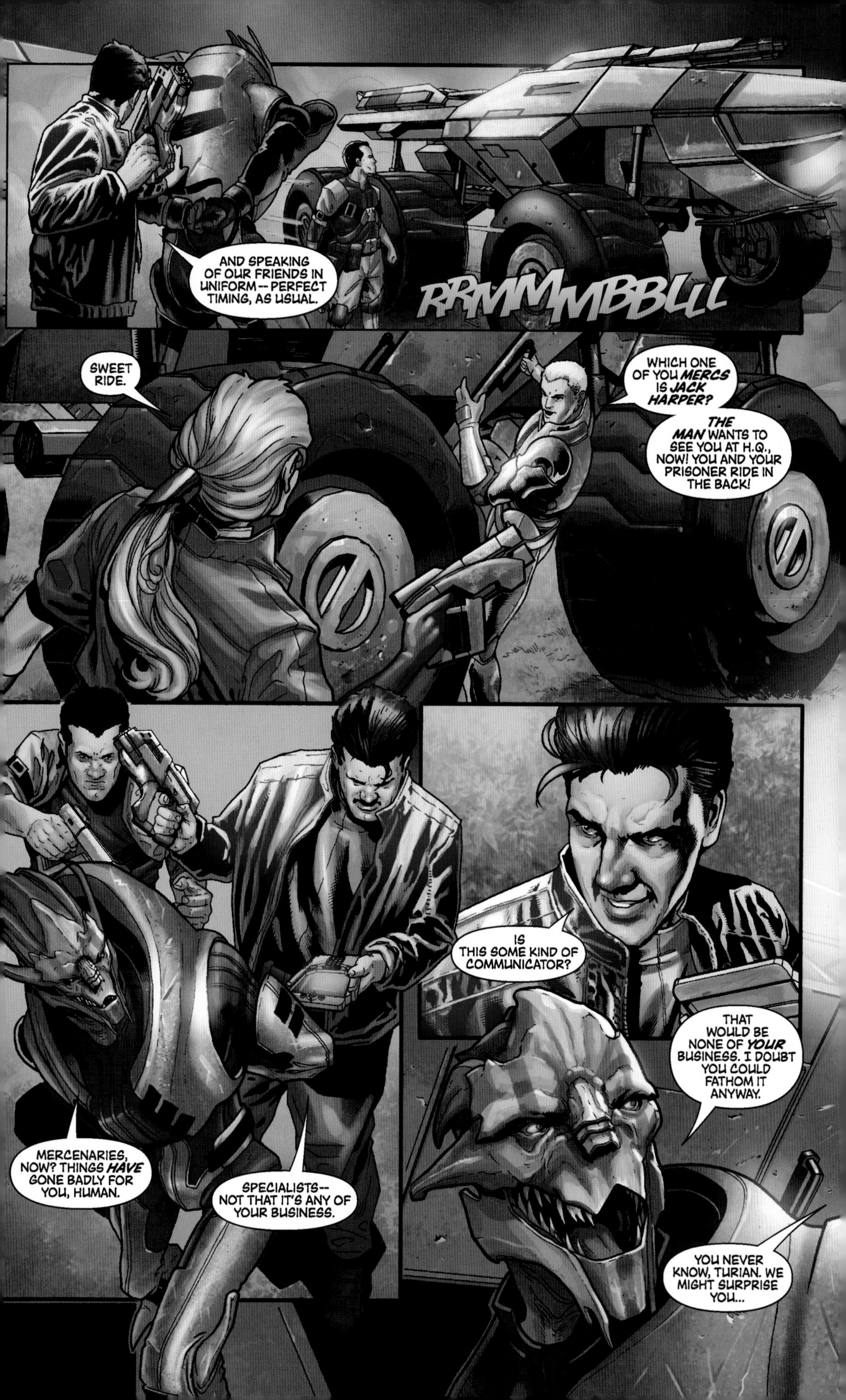

AND SPEAKING OF OUR FRIENDS IN UNIFORM -- PERFECT TIMING, AS USUAL.
RRMMMBBLL
SWEET RIDE.
WHICH ONE OF YOU *MERCS* IS *JACK HARPER?*
THE MAN WANTS TO SEE YOU AT H.Q., NOW! YOU AND YOUR PRISONER RIDE IN THE BACK!
MERCENARIES, NOW? THINGS *HAVE* GONE BADLY FOR YOU, HUMAN.
SPECIALISTS-- NOT THAT IT'S ANY OF YOUR BUSINESS.
IS THIS SOME KIND OF COMMUNICATOR?
THAT WOULD BE NONE OF *YOUR* BUSINESS. I DOUBT YOU COULD FATHOM IT ANYWAY.
YOU NEVER KNOW, TURIAN. WE MIGHT SURPRISE YOU...

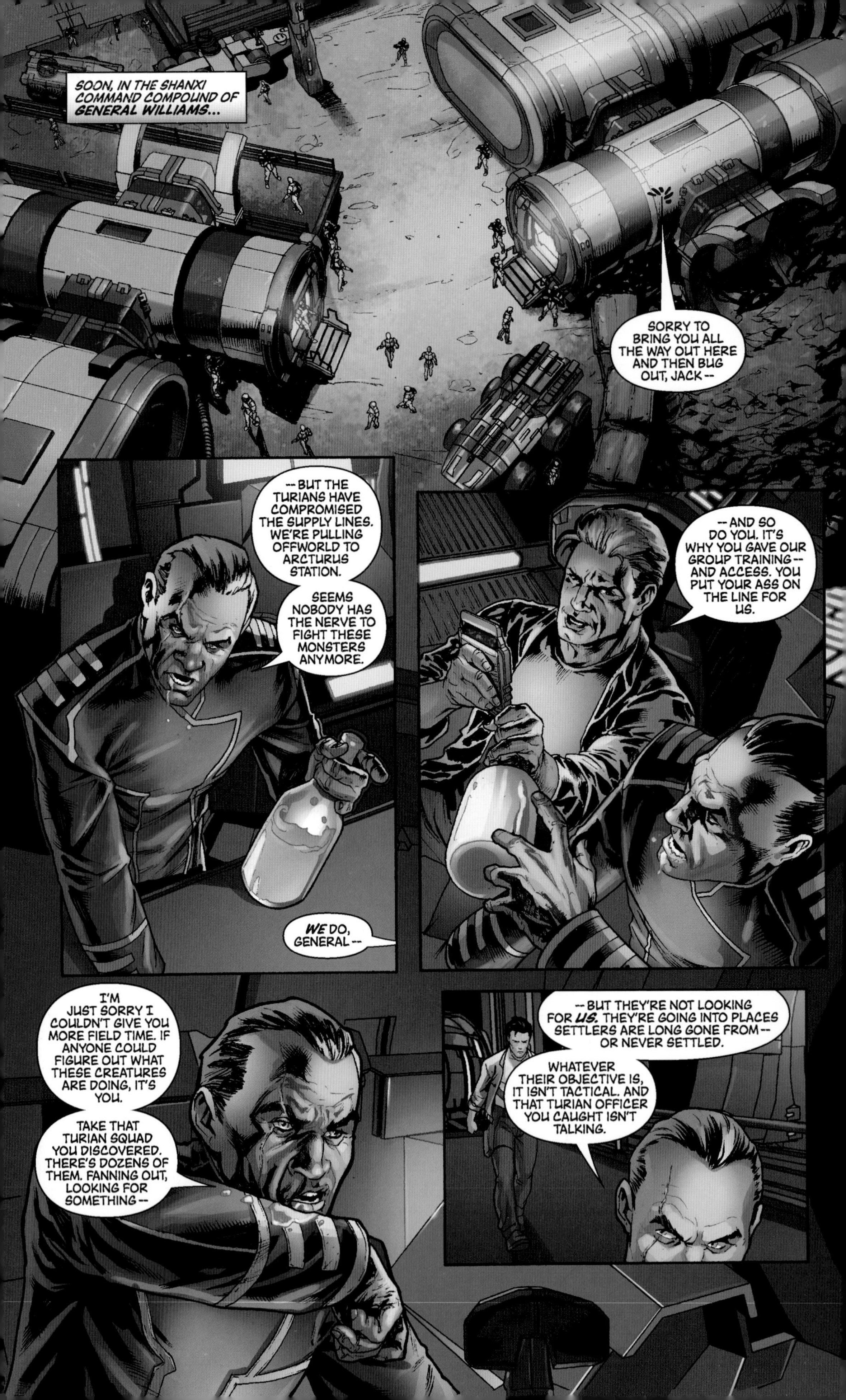
SOON, IN THE SHANXI COMMAND COMPOUND OF GENERAL WILLIAMS...
SORRY TO BRING YOU ALL THE WAY OUT HERE AND THEN BUG OUT, JACK --
-- BUT THE TURIANS HAVE COMPROMISED THE SUPPLY LINES. WE'RE PULLING OFFWORLD TO ARCTURUS STATION.
SEEMS NOBODY HAS THE NERVE TO FIGHT THESE MONSTERS ANYMORE.
WE DO, GENERAL --
-- AND SO DO YOU. IT'S WHY YOU GAVE OUR GROUP TRAINING -- AND ACCESS. YOU PUT YOUR ASS ON THE LINE FOR US.
I'M JUST SORRY I COULDN'T GIVE YOU MORE FIELD TIME. IF ANYONE COULD FIGURE OUT WHAT THESE CREATURES ARE DOING, IT'S YOU.
TAKE THAT TURIAN SQUAD YOU DISCOVERED. THERE'S DOZENS OF THEM. FANNING OUT, LOOKING FOR SOMETHING --
-- BUT THEY'RE NOT LOOKING FOR US. THEY'RE GOING INTO PLACES SETTLERS ARE LONG GONE FROM -- OR NEVER SETTLED.
WHATEVER THEIR OBJECTIVE IS, IT ISN'T TACTICAL. AND THAT TURIAN OFFICER YOU CAUGHT ISN'T TALKING.

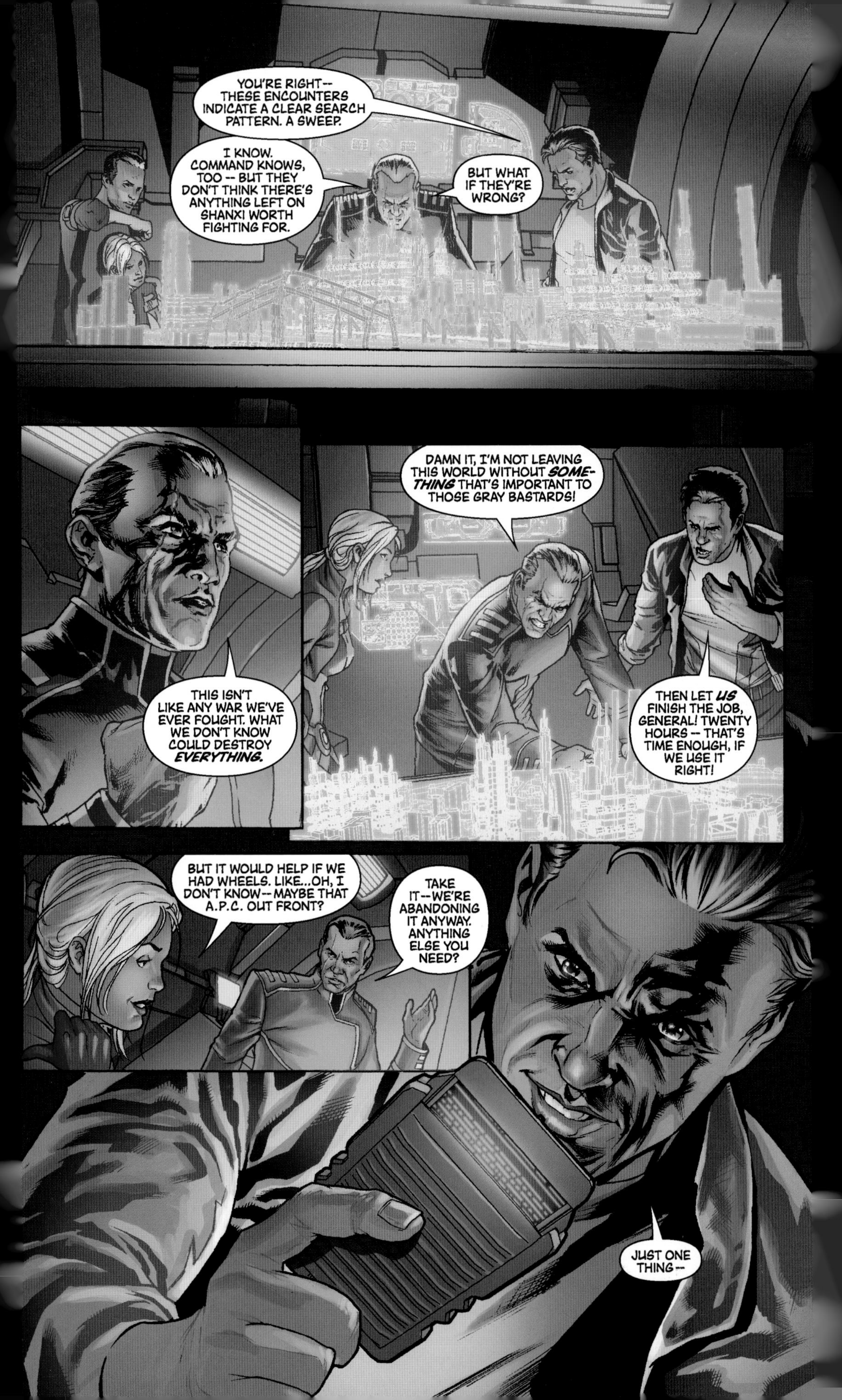

YOU'RE RIGHT-- THESE ENCOUNTERS INDICATE A CLEAR SEARCH PATTERN. A SWEEP.
I KNOW. COMMAND KNOWS, TOO -- BUT THEY DON'T THINK THERE'S ANYTHING LEFT ON SHANXI WORTH FIGHTING FOR.
BUT WHAT IF THEY'RE WRONG?
THIS ISN'T LIKE ANY WAR WE'VE EVER FOUGHT. WHAT WE DON'T KNOW COULD DESTROY EVERYTHING.
DAMN IT, I'M NOT LEAVING THIS WORLD WITHOUT SOME-THING THAT'S IMPORTANT TO THOSE GRAY BASTARDS!
THEN LET US FINISH THE JOB, GENERAL! TWENTY HOURS -- THAT'S TIME ENOUGH, IF WE USE IT RIGHT!
BUT IT WOULD HELP IF WE HAD WHEELS. LIKE...OH, I DON'T KNOW--MAYBE THAT A.P.C. OUT FRONT?
TAKE IT--WE'RE ABANDONING IT ANYWAY. ANYTHING ELSE YOU NEED?
JUST ONE THING--

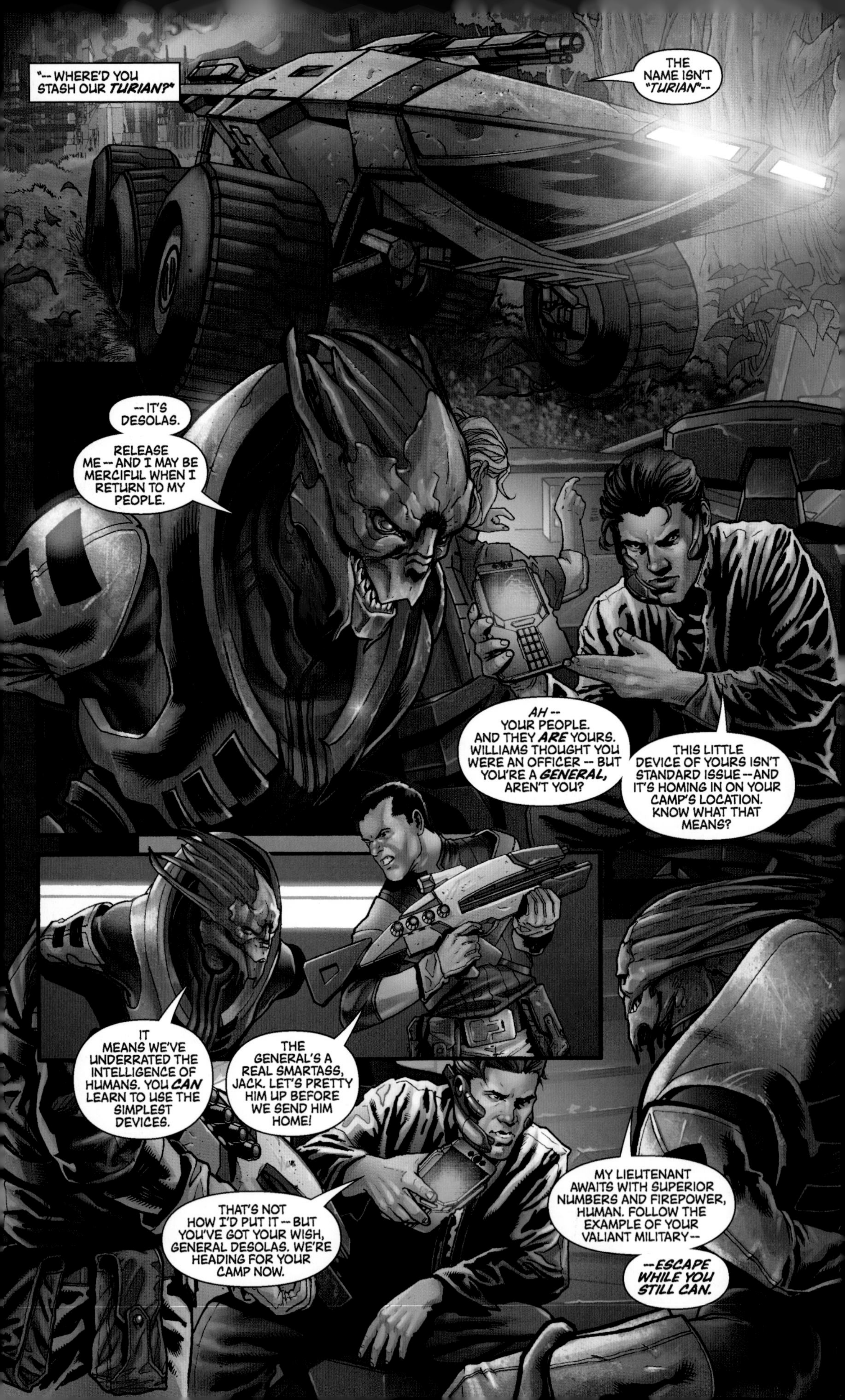
"-- WHERE'D YOU STASH OUR *TURIAN?*"
THE NAME ISN'T *"TURIAN"*--
-- IT'S DESOLAS.
RELEASE ME -- AND I MAY BE MERCIFUL WHEN I RETURN TO MY PEOPLE.
AH -- YOUR PEOPLE. AND THEY *ARE* YOURS. WILLIAMS THOUGHT YOU WERE AN OFFICER -- BUT YOU'RE A *GENERAL,* AREN'T YOU?
THIS LITTLE DEVICE OF YOURS ISN'T STANDARD ISSUE -- AND IT'S HOMING IN ON YOUR CAMP'S LOCATION. KNOW WHAT THAT MEANS?
IT MEANS WE'VE UNDERRATED THE INTELLIGENCE OF HUMANS. YOU *CAN* LEARN TO USE THE SIMPLEST DEVICES.
THE GENERAL'S A REAL SMARTASS, JACK. LET'S PRETTY HIM UP BEFORE WE SEND HIM HOME!
THAT'S NOT HOW I'D PUT IT -- BUT YOU'VE GOT YOUR WISH, GENERAL DESOLAS. WE'RE HEADING FOR YOUR CAMP NOW.
MY LIEUTENANT AWAITS WITH SUPERIOR NUMBERS AND FIREPOWER, HUMAN. FOLLOW THE EXAMPLE OF YOUR VALIANT MILITARY--
--*ESCAPE WHILE YOU STILL CAN.*

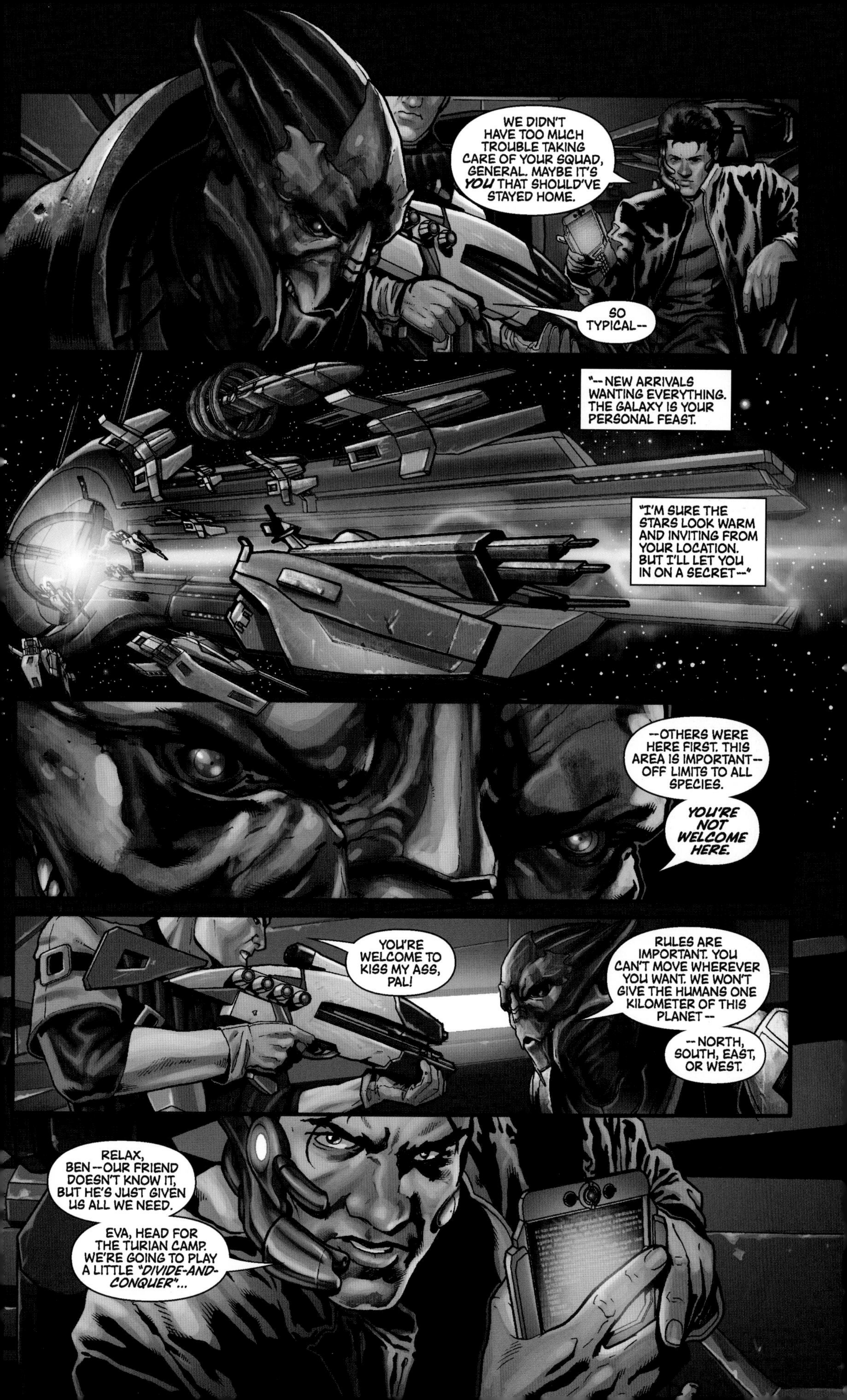
WE DIDN'T HAVE TOO MUCH TROUBLE TAKING CARE OF YOUR SQUAD, GENERAL. MAYBE IT'S *YOU* THAT SHOULD'VE STAYED HOME.
SO TYPICAL--
"--NEW ARRIVALS WANTING EVERYTHING. THE GALAXY IS YOUR PERSONAL FEAST.
"I'M SURE THE STARS LOOK WARM AND INVITING FROM YOUR LOCATION. BUT I'LL LET YOU IN ON A SECRET--"
--OTHERS WERE HERE FIRST. THIS AREA IS IMPORTANT-- OFF LIMITS TO ALL SPECIES.
YOU'RE NOT WELCOME HERE.
YOU'RE WELCOME TO KISS MY ASS, PAL!
RULES ARE IMPORTANT. YOU CAN'T MOVE WHEREVER YOU WANT. WE WON'T GIVE THE HUMANS ONE KILOMETER OF THIS PLANET--
--NORTH, SOUTH, EAST, OR WEST.
RELAX, BEN--OUR FRIEND DOESN'T KNOW IT, BUT HE'S JUST GIVEN US ALL WE NEED.
EVA, HEAD FOR THE TURIAN CAMP. WE'RE GOING TO PLAY A LITTLE *"DIVIDE-AND-CONQUER"*...

WE'VE FOUND IT, LIEUTENANT ABRUDAS! FIVE KILOMETERS WEST, IN A NETWORK OF CAVERNS!
THE RESEARCHERS MUST HAVE TAKEN THE *RELIC* TO A SAFE PLACE AFTER THE CRASH!
THEY'LL HAVE A LOT OF EXPLAINING TO DO. THEY COULD'VE REPAIRED THEIR TRANSMITTER EASILY --AND SAVED US A LOT OF SEARCHING!
BUT AT LEAST WE GOT TO IT BEFORE THE HUMANS.
LET ME RECALL THE COMMANDER FROM HIS --
LIEUTENANT! THIS...IS DESOLAS!

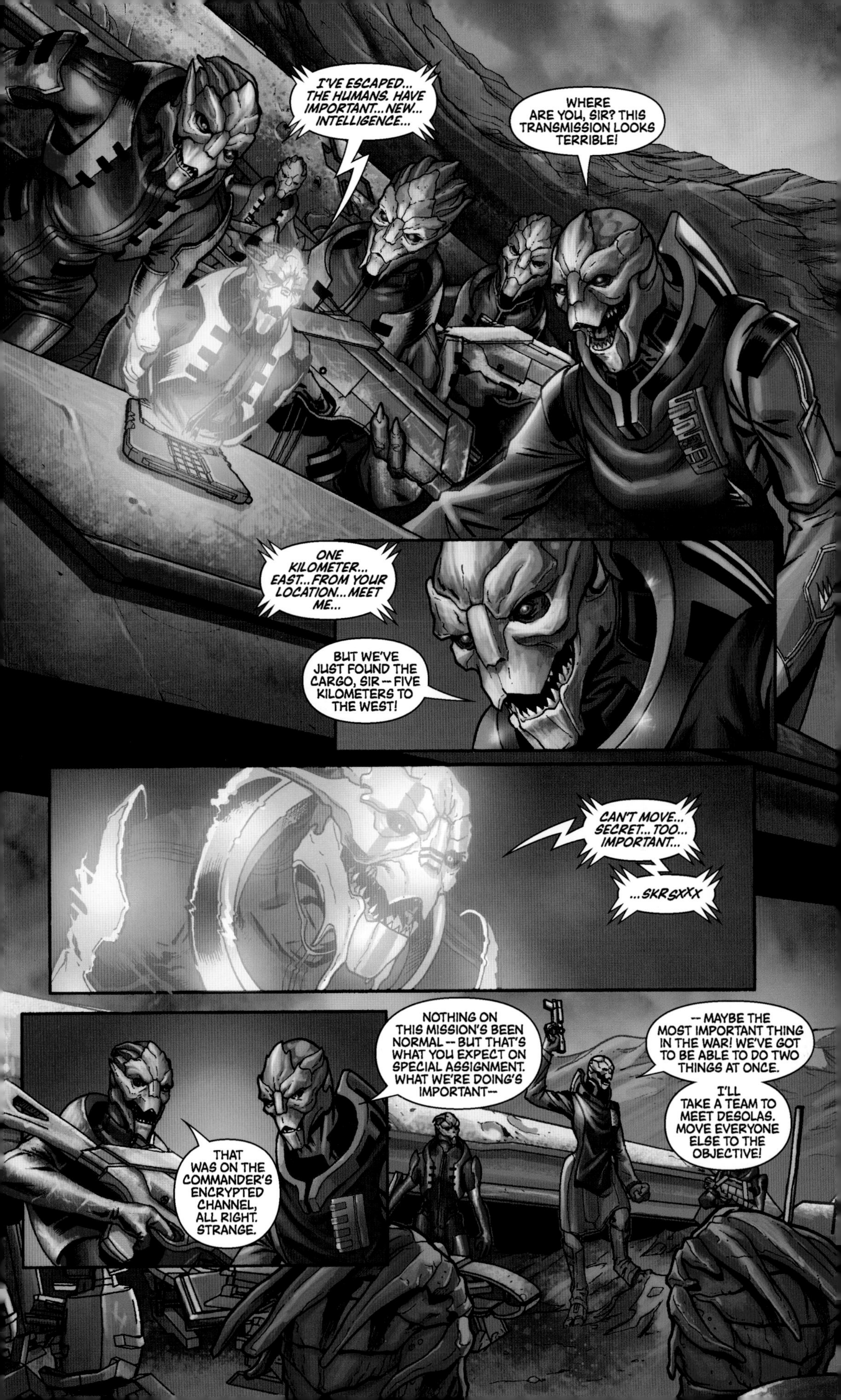
I'VE ESCAPED... THE HUMANS. HAVE IMPORTANT...NEW... INTELLIGENCE...
WHERE ARE YOU, SIR? THIS TRANSMISSION LOOKS TERRIBLE!
ONE KILOMETER... EAST...FROM YOUR LOCATION...MEET ME...
BUT WE'VE JUST FOUND THE CARGO, SIR -- FIVE KILOMETERS TO THE WEST!
CAN'T MOVE... SECRET...TOO... IMPORTANT...
...SKRSXXX
THAT WAS ON THE COMMANDER'S ENCRYPTED CHANNEL, ALL RIGHT. STRANGE.
NOTHING ON THIS MISSION'S BEEN NORMAL -- BUT THAT'S WHAT YOU EXPECT ON SPECIAL ASSIGNMENT. WHAT WE'RE DOING'S IMPORTANT--
-- MAYBE THE MOST IMPORTANT THING IN THE WAR! WE'VE GOT TO BE ABLE TO DO TWO THINGS AT ONCE.
I'LL TAKE A TEAM TO MEET DESOLAS. MOVE EVERYONE ELSE TO THE OBJECTIVE!

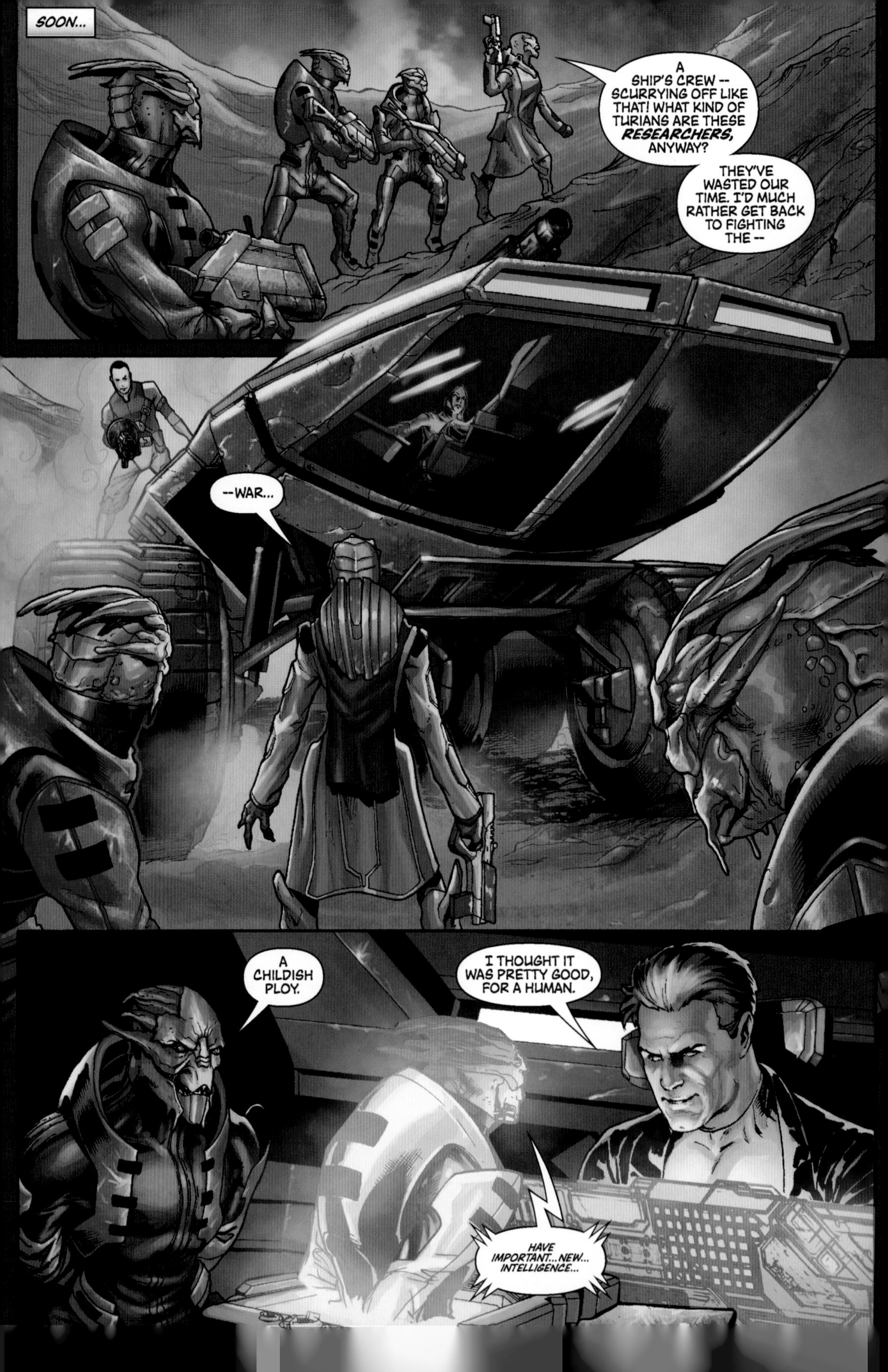
SOON...
A SHIP'S CREW -- SCURRYING OFF LIKE THAT! WHAT KIND OF TURIANS ARE THESE RESEARCHERS, ANYWAY?
THEY'VE WASTED OUR TIME. I'D MUCH RATHER GET BACK TO FIGHTING THE --
--WAR...
A CHILDISH PLOY.
I THOUGHT IT WAS PRETTY GOOD, FOR A HUMAN.
HAVE IMPORTANT...NEW... INTELLIGENCE...

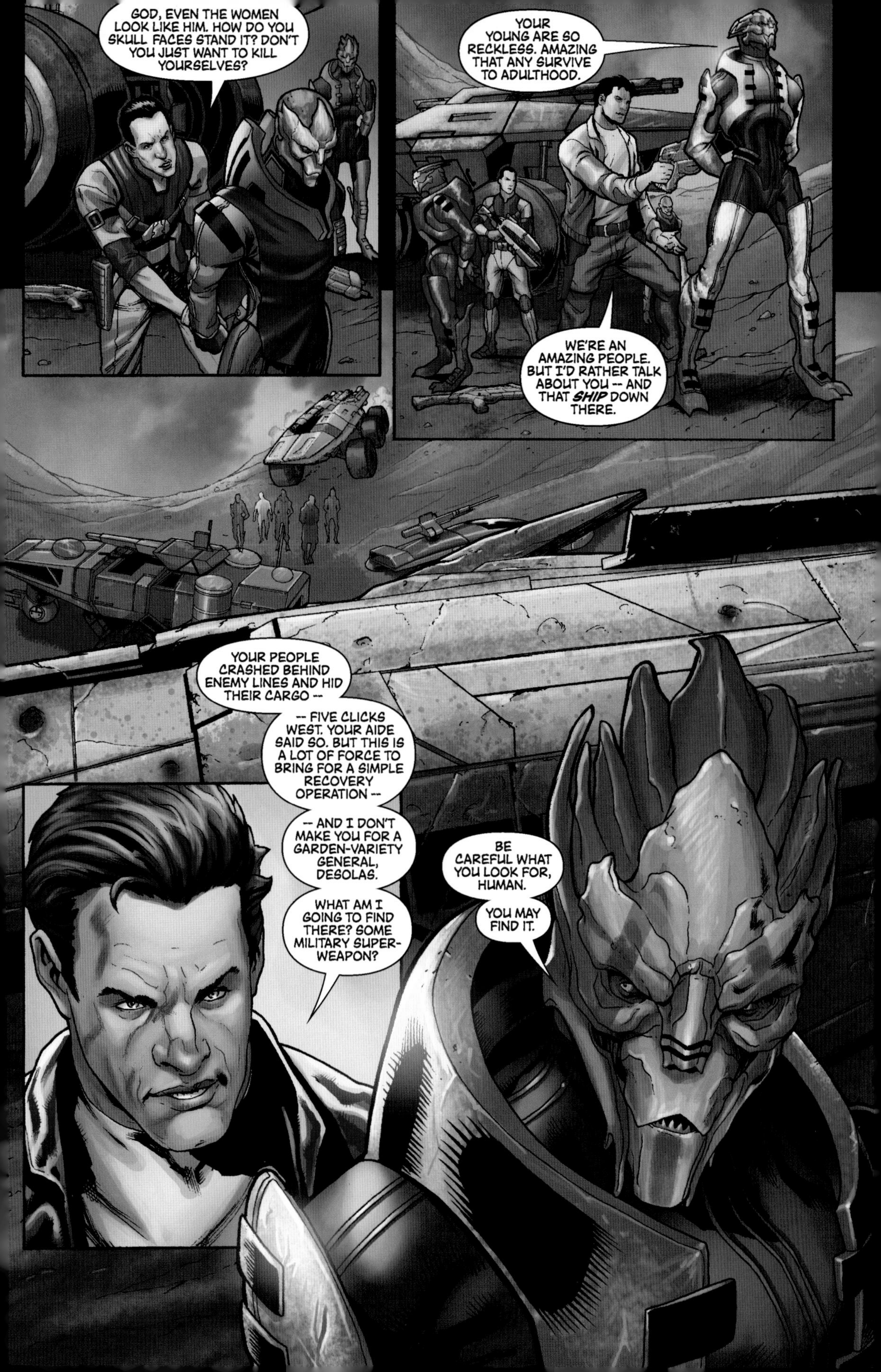
GOD, EVEN THE WOMEN LOOK LIKE HIM. HOW DO YOU SKULL FACES STAND IT? DON'T YOU JUST WANT TO KILL YOURSELVES?
YOUR YOUNG ARE SO RECKLESS. AMAZING THAT ANY SURVIVE TO ADULTHOOD.
WE'RE AN AMAZING PEOPLE. BUT I'D RATHER TALK ABOUT YOU -- AND THAT SHIP DOWN THERE.
YOUR PEOPLE CRASHED BEHIND ENEMY LINES AND HID THEIR CARGO --
-- FIVE CLICKS WEST. YOUR AIDE SAID SO. BUT THIS IS A LOT OF FORCE TO BRING FOR A SIMPLE RECOVERY OPERATION --
-- AND I DON'T MAKE YOU FOR A GARDEN-VARIETY GENERAL, DESOLAS.
WHAT AM I GOING TO FIND THERE? SOME MILITARY SUPER-WEAPON?
BE CAREFUL WHAT YOU LOOK FOR, HUMAN.
YOU MAY FIND IT.

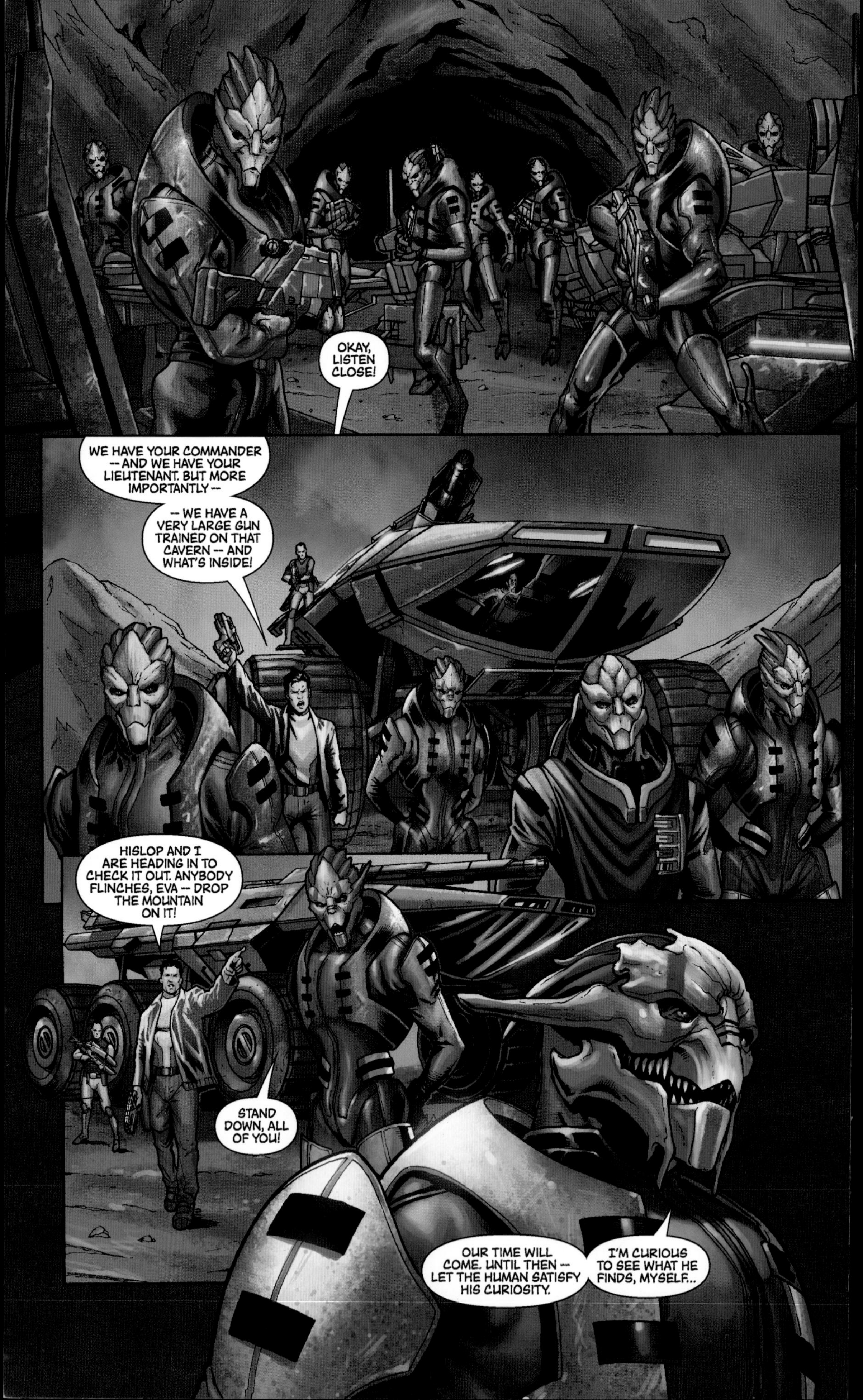
OKAY, LISTEN CLOSE!
WE HAVE YOUR COMMANDER -- AND WE HAVE YOUR LIEUTENANT. BUT MORE IMPORTANTLY --
-- WE HAVE A VERY LARGE GUN TRAINED ON THAT CAVERN -- AND WHAT'S INSIDE!
HISLOP AND I ARE HEADING IN TO CHECK IT OUT. ANYBODY FLINCHES, EVA -- DROP THE MOUNTAIN ON IT!
STAND DOWN, ALL OF YOU!
OUR TIME WILL COME. UNTIL THEN -- LET THE HUMAN SATISFY HIS CURIOSITY.
I'M CURIOUS TO SEE WHAT HE FINDS, MYSELF...

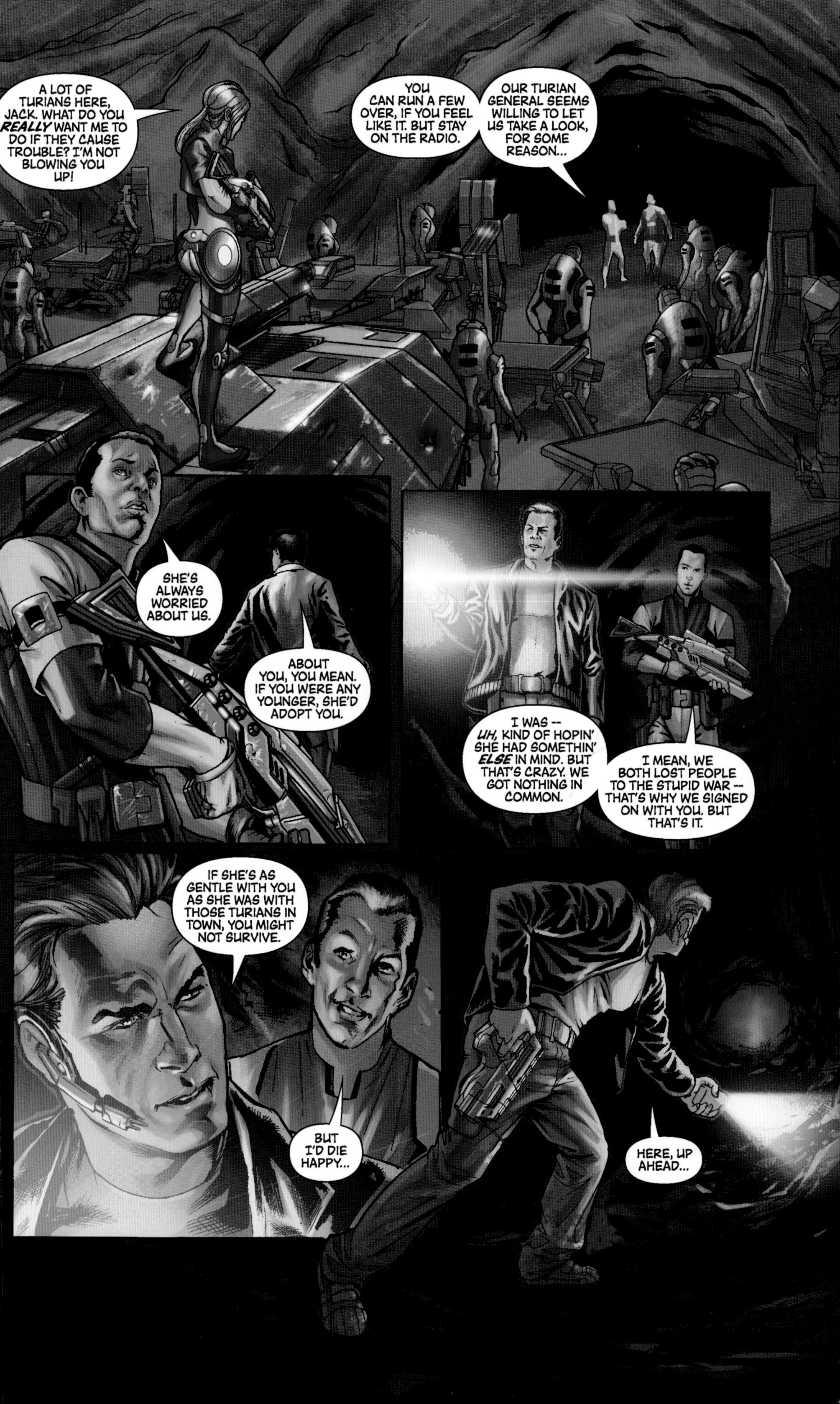

A LOT OF TURIANS HERE, JACK. WHAT DO YOU *REALLY* WANT ME TO DO IF THEY CAUSE TROUBLE? I'M NOT BLOWING YOU UP!
YOU CAN RUN A FEW OVER, IF YOU FEEL LIKE IT. BUT STAY ON THE RADIO.
OUR TURIAN GENERAL SEEMS WILLING TO LET US TAKE A LOOK, FOR SOME REASON...
SHE'S ALWAYS WORRIED ABOUT US.
ABOUT YOU, YOU MEAN. IF YOU WERE ANY YOUNGER, SHE'D ADOPT YOU.
I WAS -- *UH,* KIND OF HOPIN' SHE HAD SOMETHIN' *ELSE* IN MIND. BUT THAT'S CRAZY. WE GOT NOTHING IN COMMON.
I MEAN, WE BOTH LOST PEOPLE TO THE STUPID WAR -- THAT'S WHY WE SIGNED ON WITH YOU. BUT THAT'S IT.
IF SHE'S AS GENTLE WITH YOU AS SHE WAS WITH THOSE TURIANS IN TOWN, YOU MIGHT NOT SURVIVE.
BUT I'D DIE HAPPY...
HERE, UP AHEAD...

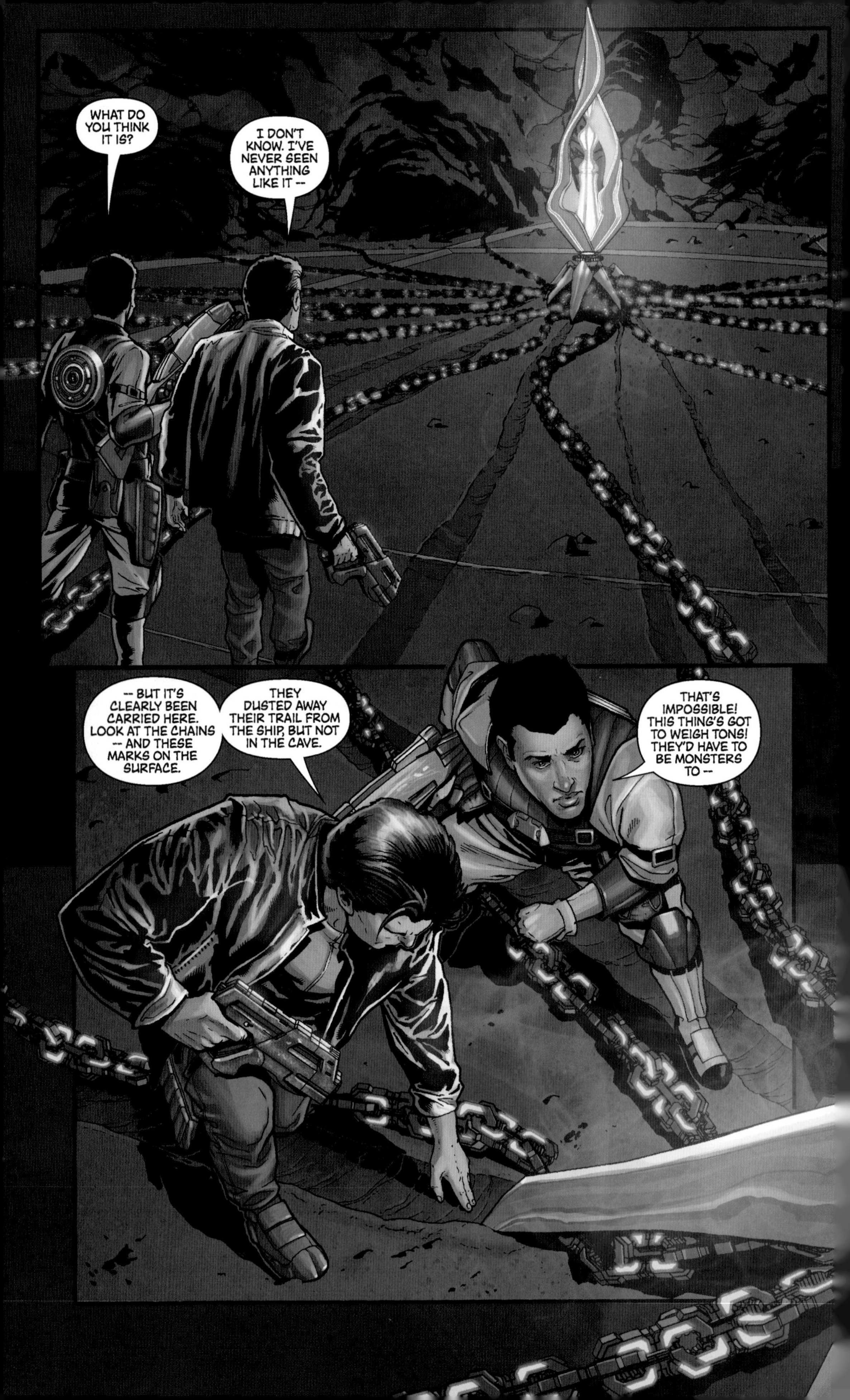
WHAT DO YOU THINK IT IS?
I DON'T KNOW. I'VE NEVER SEEN ANYTHING LIKE IT --
-- BUT IT'S CLEARLY BEEN CARRIED HERE. LOOK AT THE CHAINS -- AND THESE MARKS ON THE SURFACE.
THEY DUSTED AWAY THEIR TRAIL FROM THE SHIP, BUT NOT IN THE CAVE.
THAT'S IMPOSSIBLE! THIS THING'S GOT TO WEIGH TONS! THEY'D HAVE TO BE MONSTERS TO --

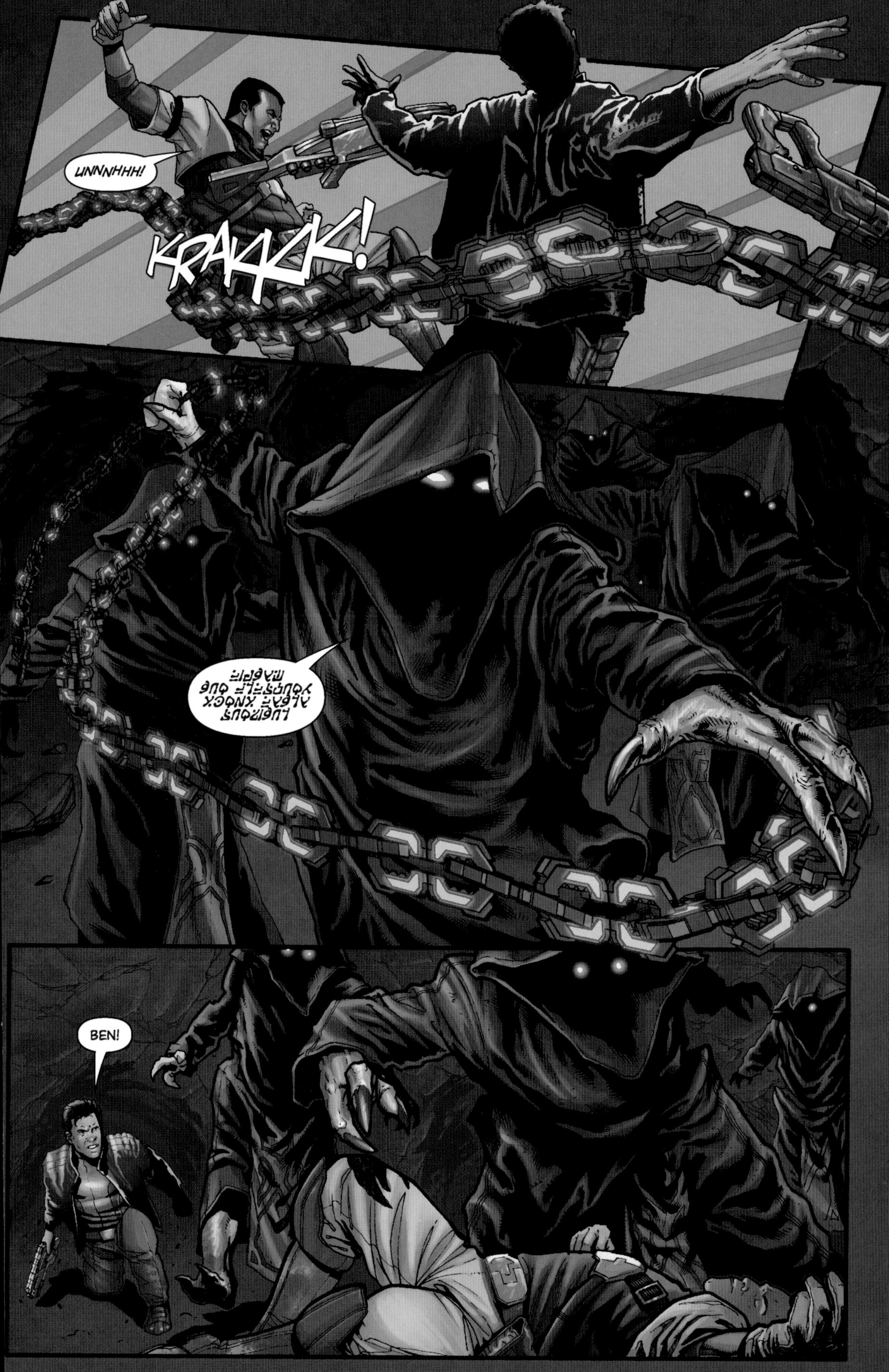
UNNNHHH!
KRAKAK!
BEN!

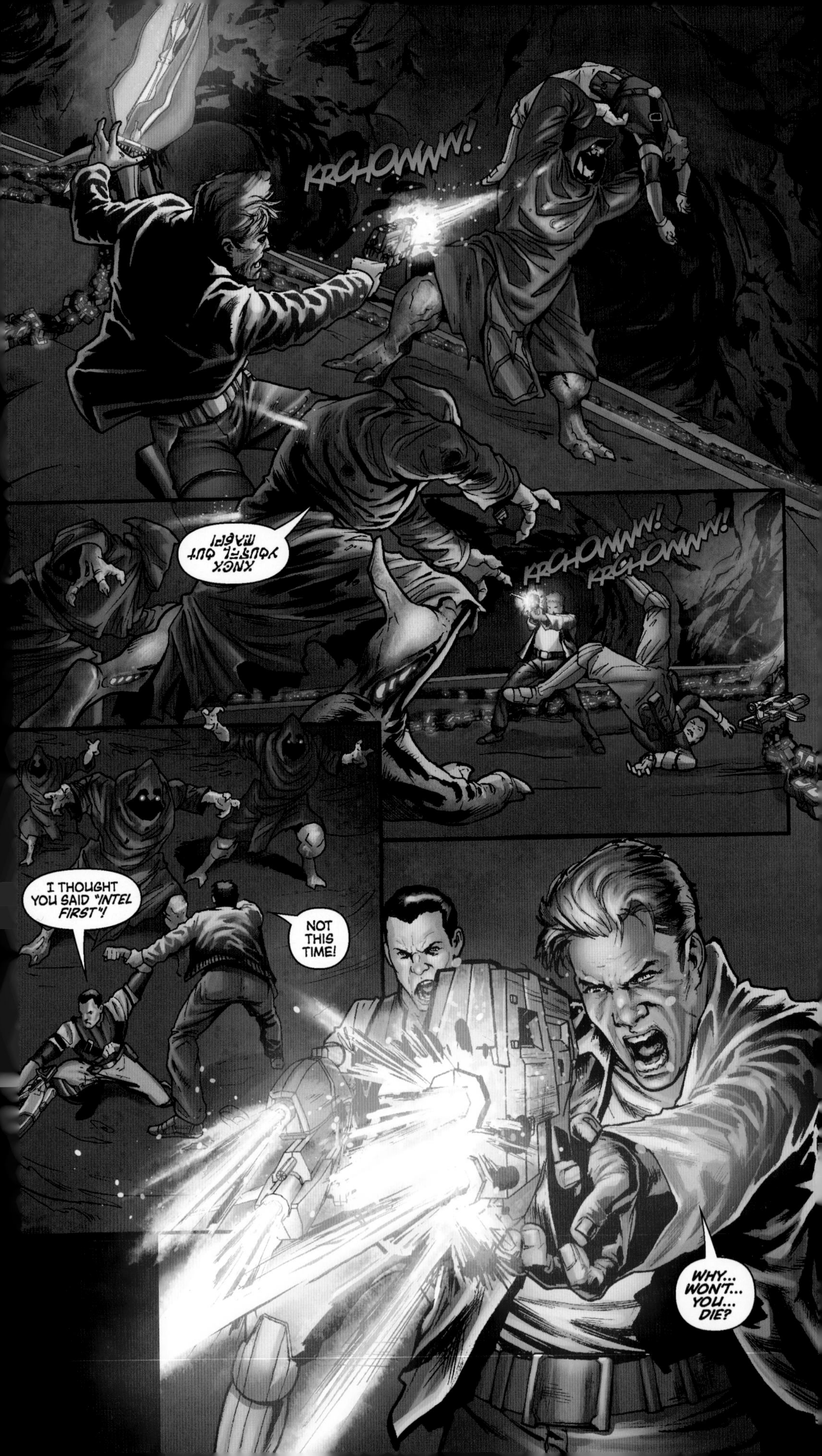
KRCHOWWW!
KRCHOWWW!
KRCHOWWW!
I THOUGHT YOU SAID "INTEL FIRST"!
NOT THIS TIME!
WHY... WON'T... YOU... DIE?

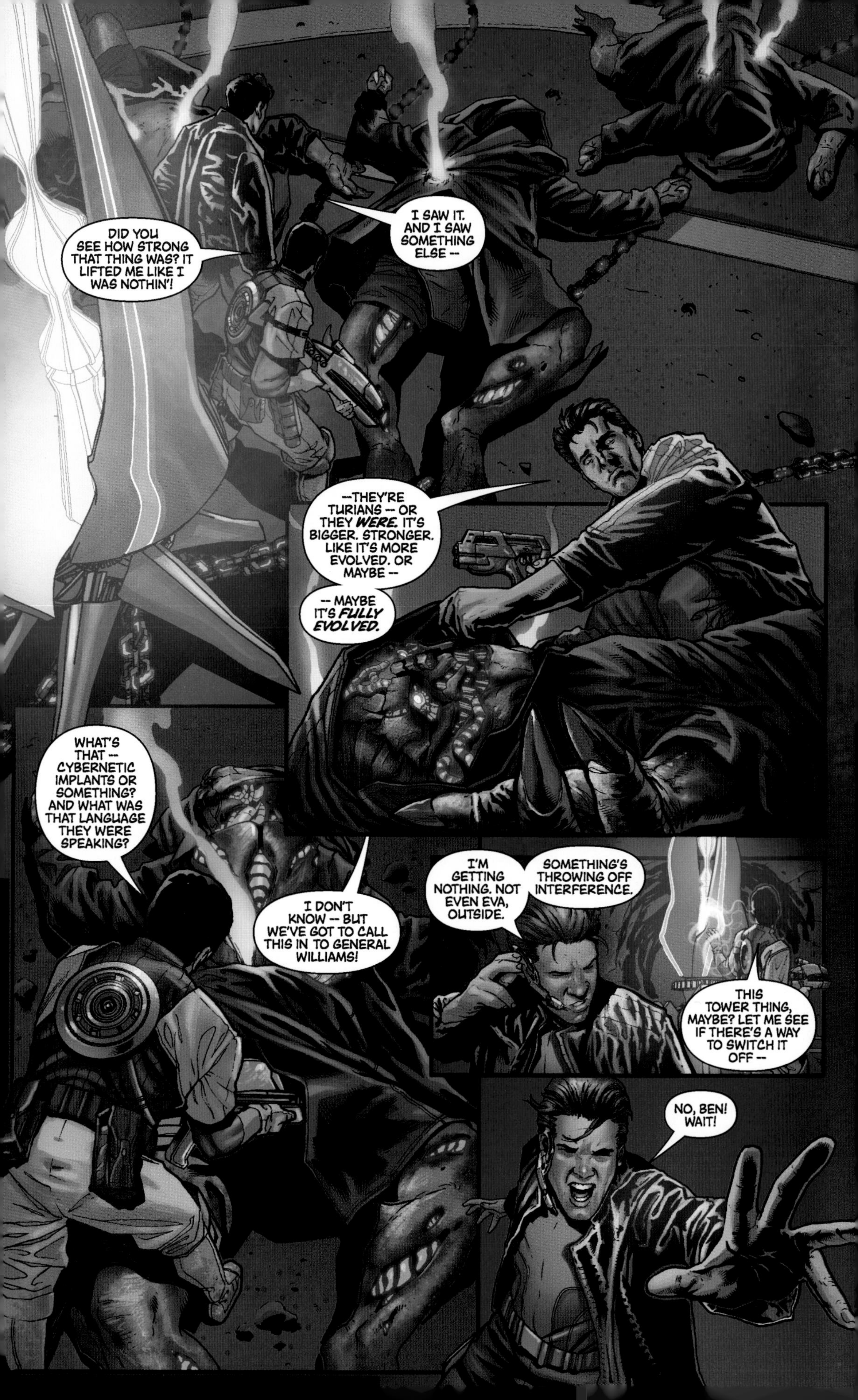
DID YOU SEE HOW STRONG THAT THING WAS? IT LIFTED ME LIKE I WAS NOTHIN'!
I SAW IT. AND I SAW SOMETHING ELSE --
--THEY'RE TURIANS -- OR THEY *WERE.* IT'S BIGGER. STRONGER. LIKE IT'S MORE EVOLVED. OR MAYBE --
-- MAYBE IT'S ***FULLY EVOLVED.***
WHAT'S THAT -- CYBERNETIC IMPLANTS OR SOMETHING? AND WHAT WAS THAT LANGUAGE THEY WERE SPEAKING?
I DON'T KNOW -- BUT WE'VE GOT TO CALL THIS IN TO GENERAL WILLIAMS!
I'M GETTING NOTHING. NOT EVEN EVA, OUTSIDE.
SOMETHING'S THROWING OFF INTERFERENCE.
THIS TOWER THING, MAYBE? LET ME SEE IF THERE'S A WAY TO SWITCH IT OFF --
NO, BEN! WAIT!

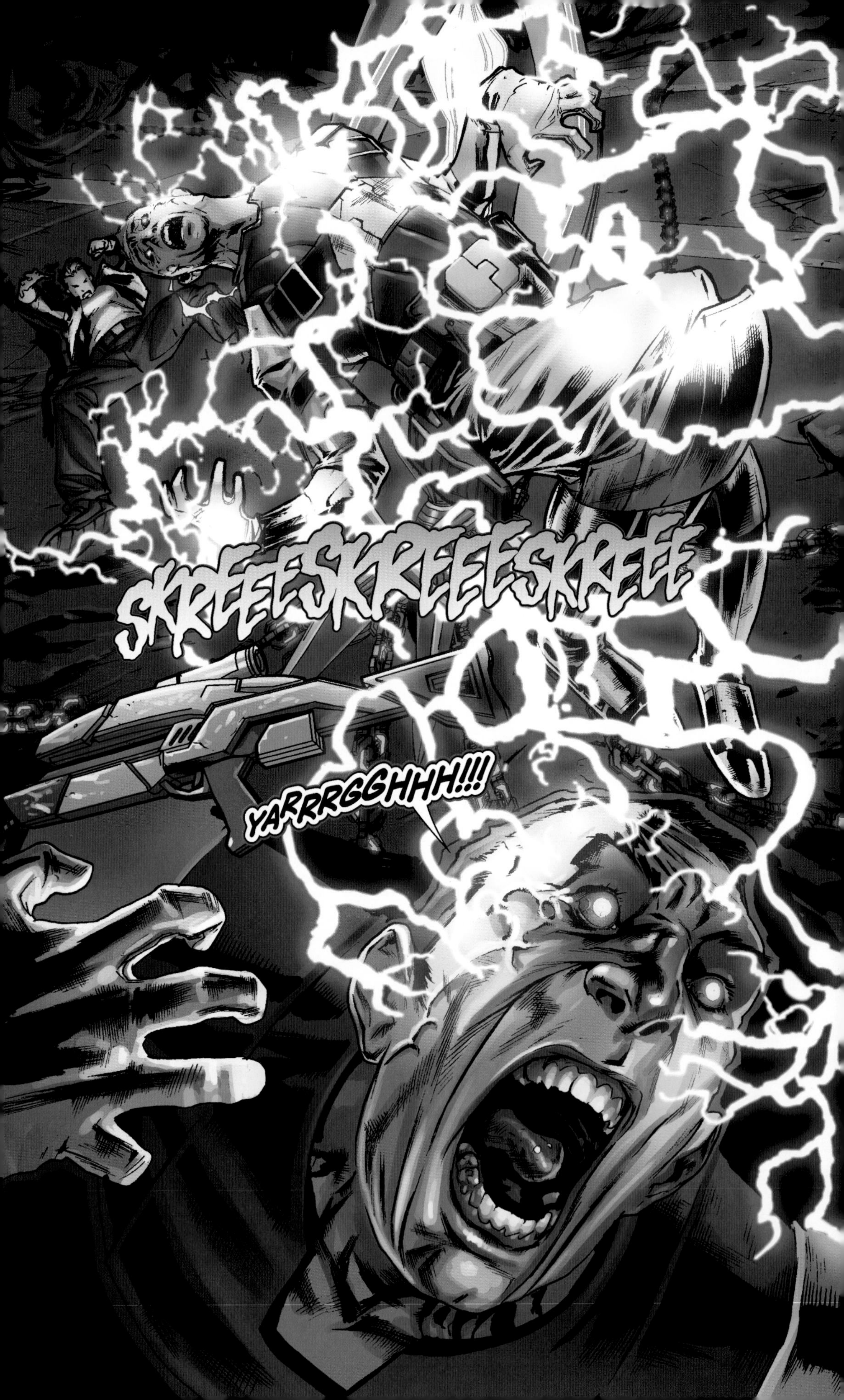
SKREEESKREEESKREEE
YARRRGGHHH!!!

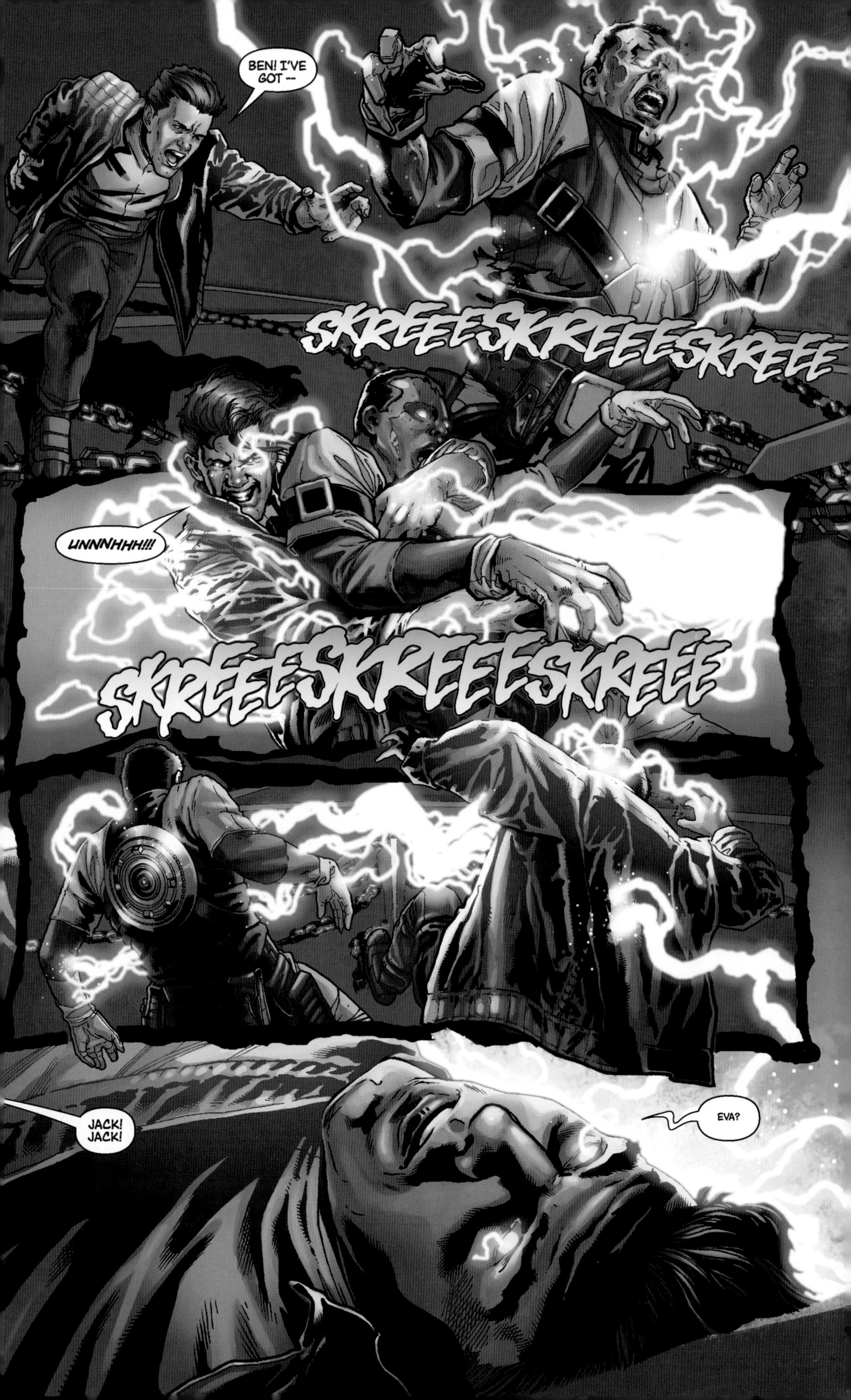

BEN! I'VE GOT ---
SKREEESKREEESKREEE
UNNNHHH!!!
SKREEESKREEESKREEE
JACK! JACK!
EVA?

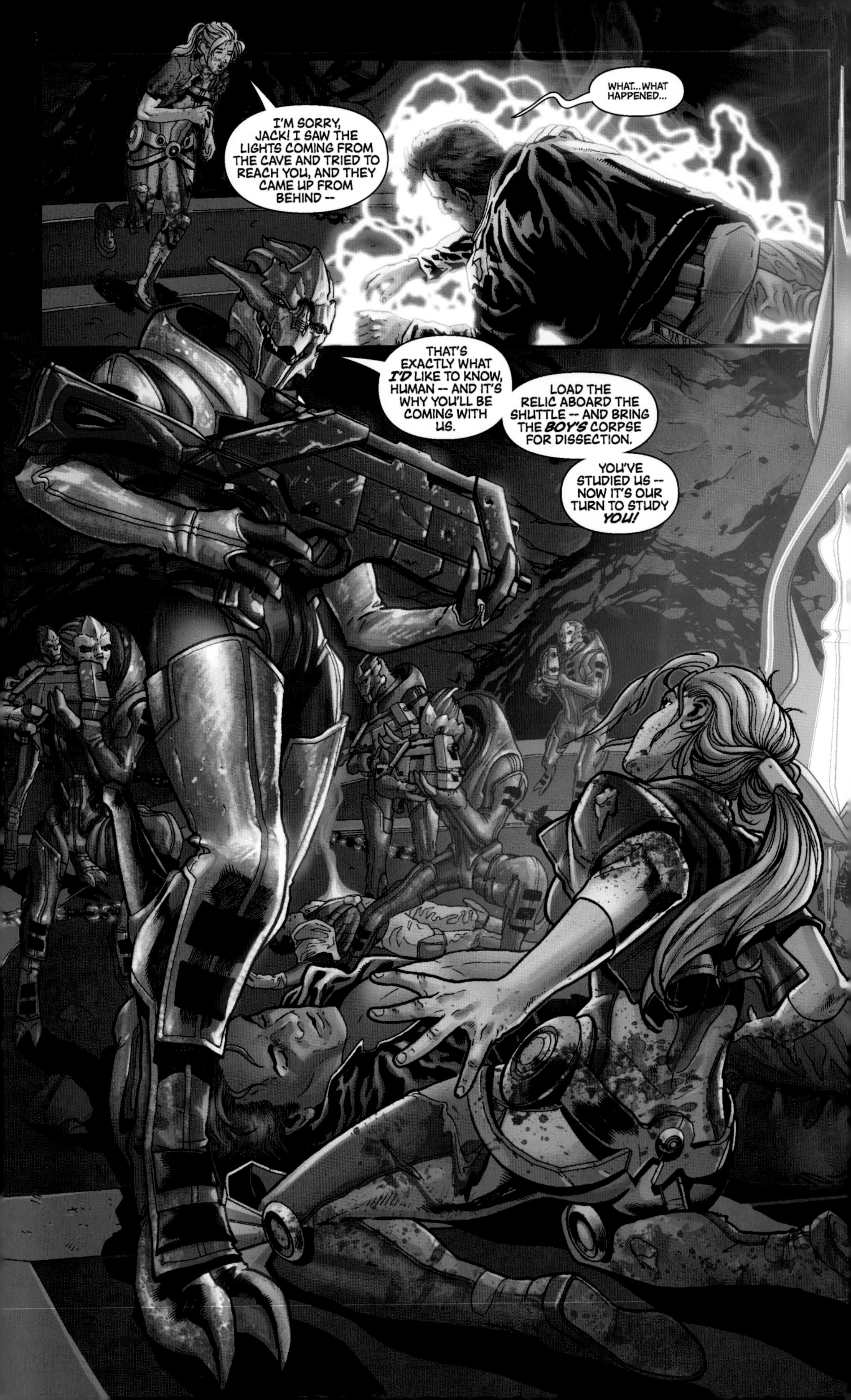
I'M SORRY, JACK! I SAW THE LIGHTS COMING FROM THE CAVE AND TRIED TO REACH YOU, AND THEY CAME UP FROM BEHIND --
WHAT... WHAT HAPPENED...
THAT'S EXACTLY WHAT I'D LIKE TO KNOW, HUMAN -- AND IT'S WHY YOU'LL BE COMING WITH US.
LOAD THE RELIC ABOARD THE SHUTTLE -- AND BRING THE BOY'S CORPSE FOR DISSECTION.
YOU'VE STUDIED US -- NOW IT'S OUR TURN TO STUDY YOU!

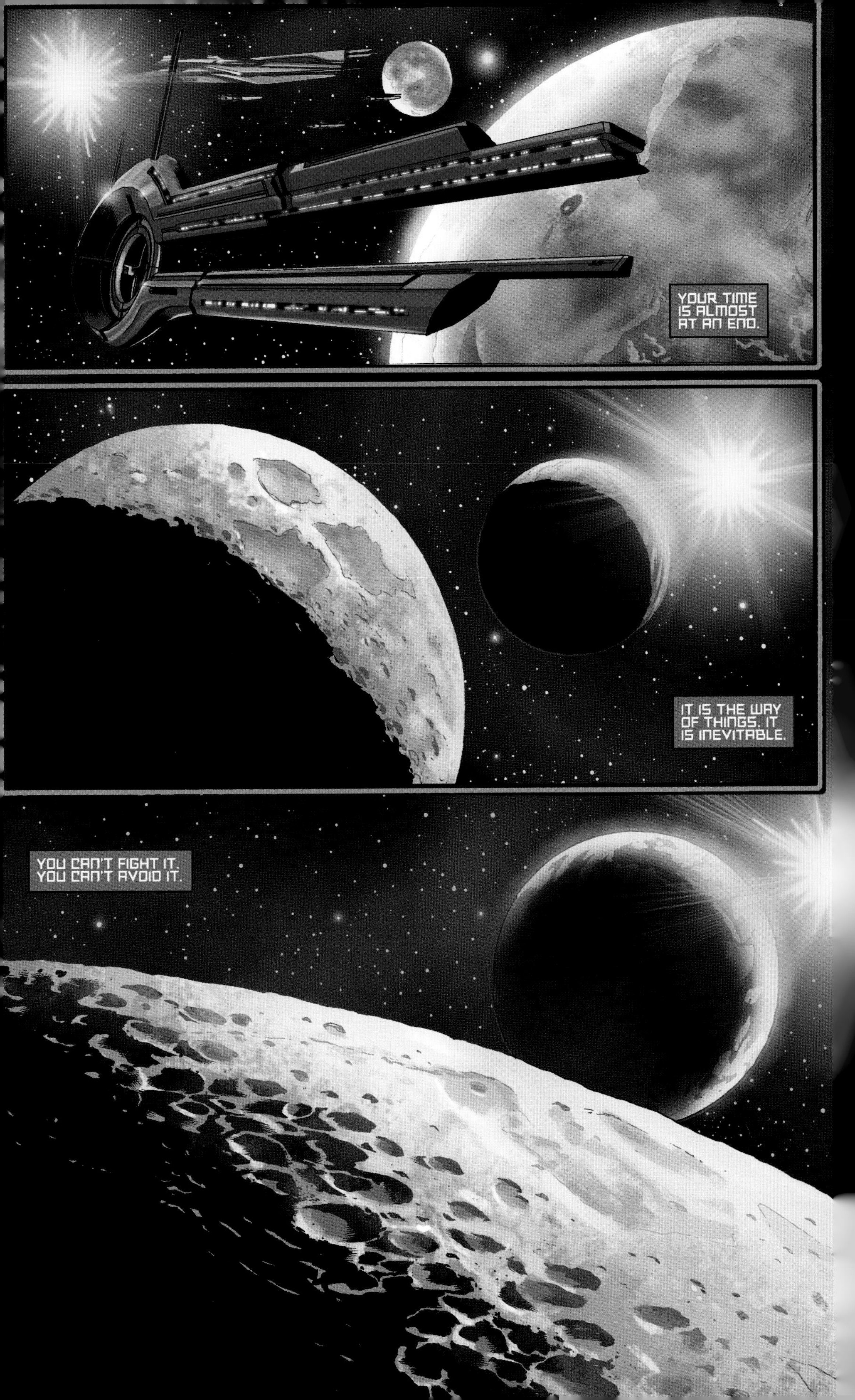
YOUR TIME IS ALMOST AT AN END.
IT IS THE WAY OF THINGS. IT IS INEVITABLE.
YOU CAN'T FIGHT IT. YOU CAN'T AVOID IT.

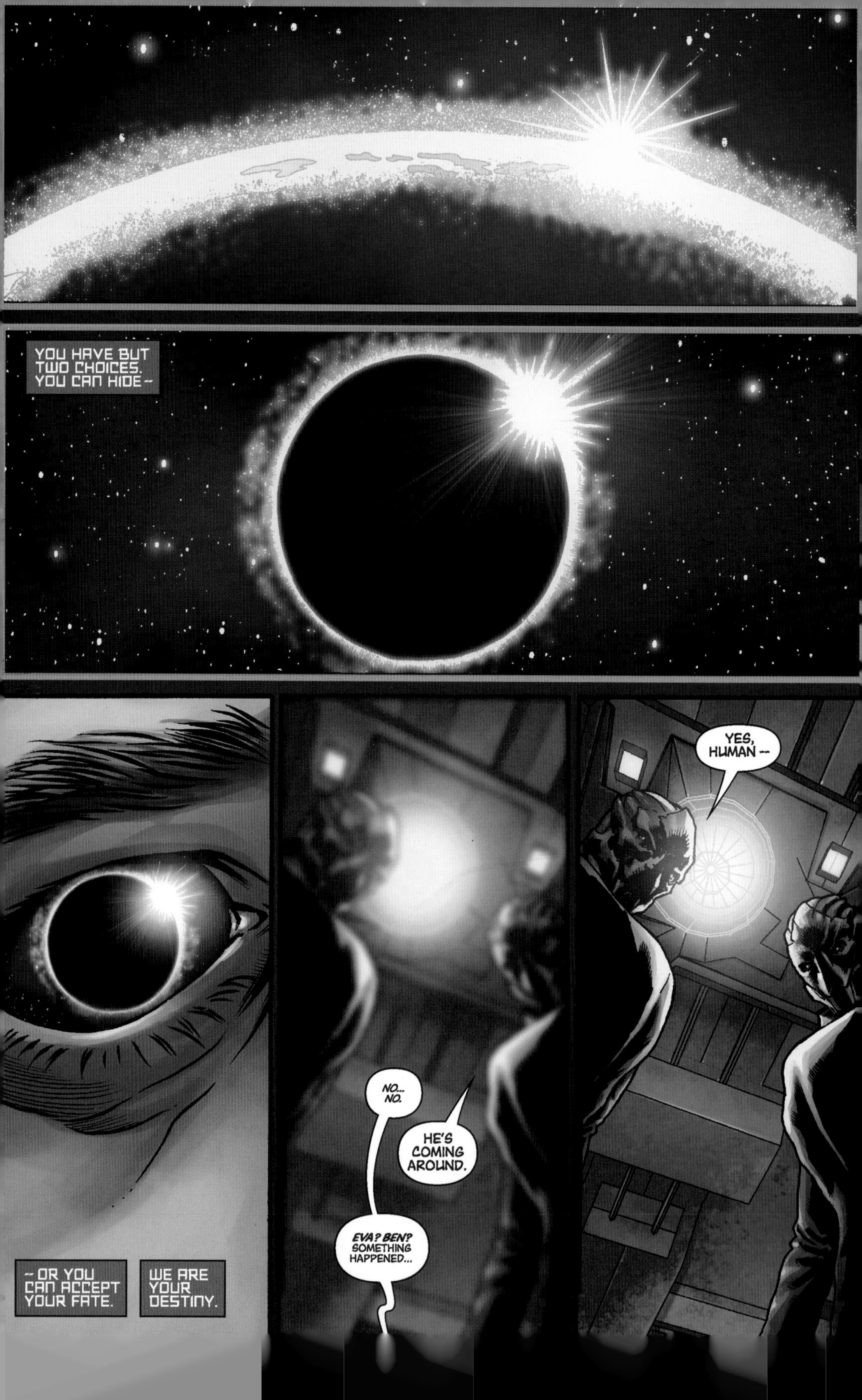
YOU HAVE BUT TWO CHOICES. YOU CAN HIDE--
--OR YOU CAN ACCEPT YOUR FATE.
WE ARE YOUR DESTINY.
NO... NO.
HE'S COMING AROUND.
EVA? BEN? SOMETHING HAPPENED...
YES, HUMAN --

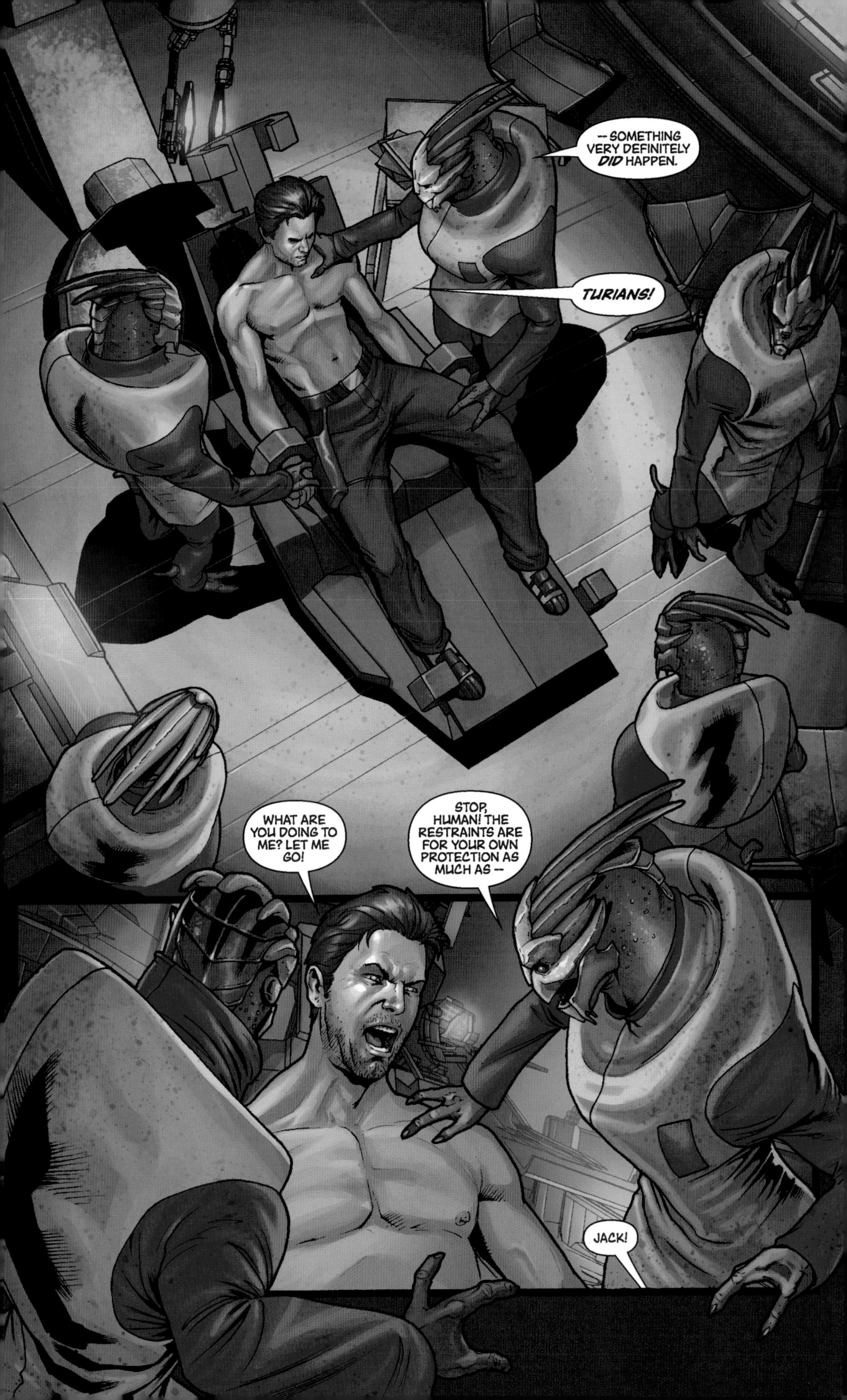
-- SOMETHING VERY DEFINITELY *DID* HAPPEN.
TURIANS!
WHAT ARE YOU DOING TO ME? LET ME GO!
STOP, HUMAN! THE RESTRAINTS ARE FOR YOUR OWN PROTECTION AS MUCH AS --
JACK!

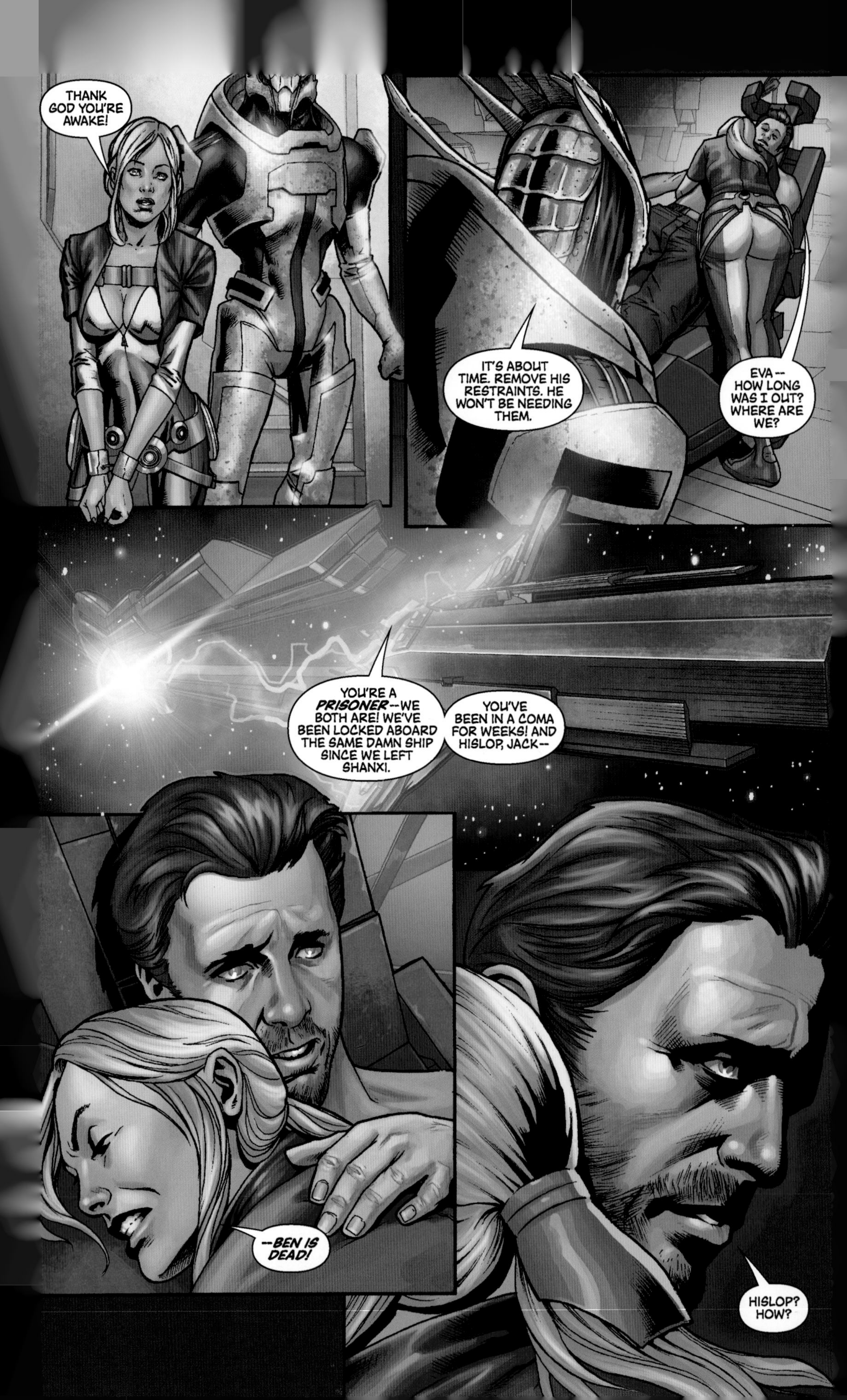
THANK GOD YOU'RE AWAKE!
IT'S ABOUT TIME. REMOVE HIS RESTRAINTS. HE WON'T BE NEEDING THEM.
EVA -- HOW LONG WAS I OUT? WHERE ARE WE?
YOU'RE A PRISONER--WE BOTH ARE! WE'VE BEEN LOCKED ABOARD THE SAME DAMN SHIP SINCE WE LEFT SHANXI.
YOU'VE BEEN IN A COMA FOR WEEKS! AND HISLOP, JACK--
--BEN IS DEAD!
HISLOP? HOW?

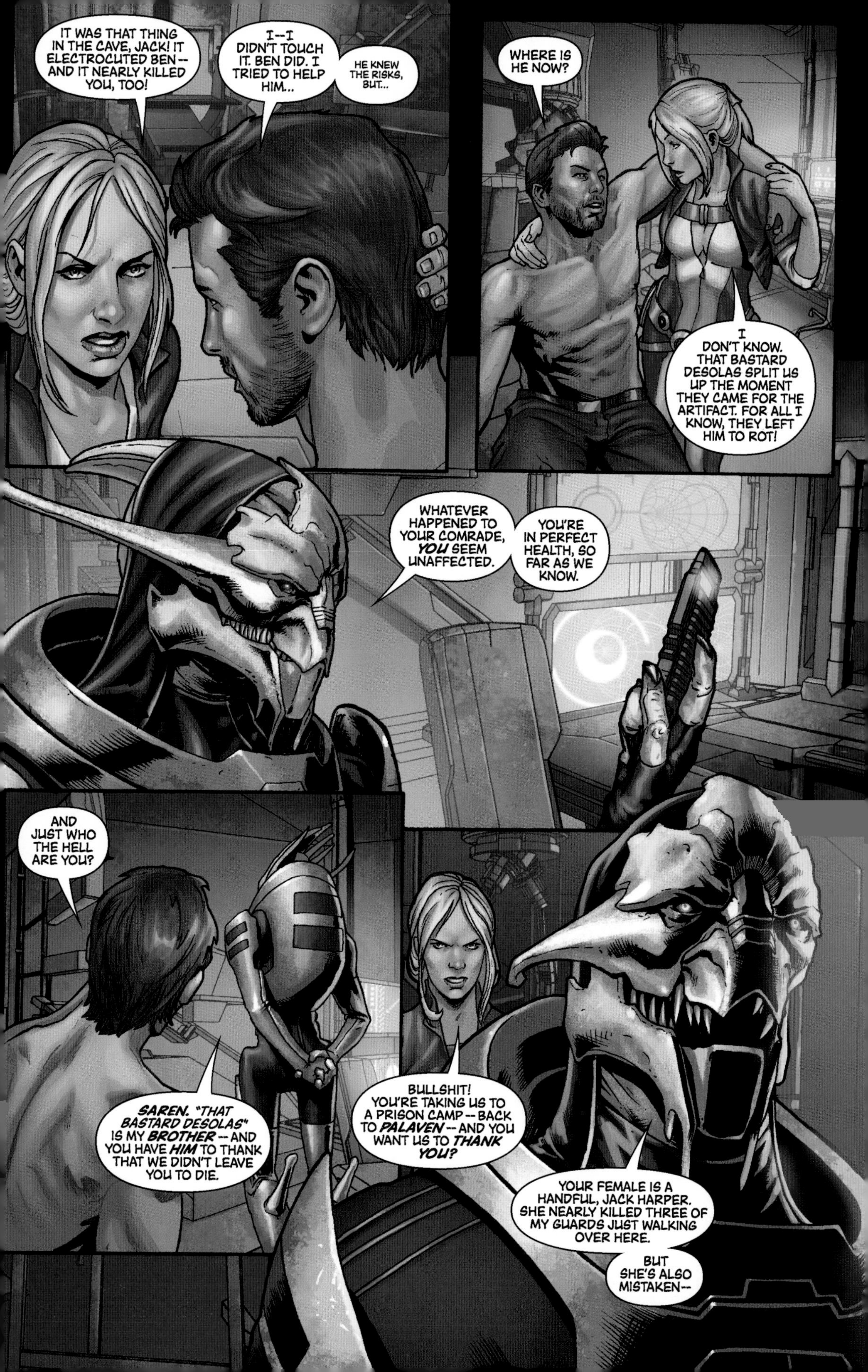
IT WAS THAT THING IN THE CAVE, JACK! IT ELECTROCUTED BEN -- AND IT NEARLY KILLED YOU, TOO!
I--I DIDN'T TOUCH IT. BEN DID. I TRIED TO HELP HIM...
HE KNEW THE RISKS, BUT...
WHERE IS HE NOW?
I DON'T KNOW. THAT BASTARD DESOLAS SPLIT US UP THE MOMENT THEY CAME FOR THE ARTIFACT. FOR ALL I KNOW, THEY LEFT HIM TO ROT!
WHATEVER HAPPENED TO YOUR COMRADE, *YOU* SEEM UNAFFECTED.
YOU'RE IN PERFECT HEALTH, SO FAR AS WE KNOW.
AND JUST WHO THE HELL ARE YOU?
SAREN. "THAT BASTARD DESOLAS" IS MY *BROTHER* -- AND YOU HAVE *HIM* TO THANK THAT WE DIDN'T LEAVE YOU TO DIE.
BULLSHIT! YOU'RE TAKING US TO A PRISON CAMP -- BACK TO *PALAVEN* -- AND YOU WANT US TO *THANK YOU?*
YOUR FEMALE IS A HANDFUL, JACK HARPER. SHE NEARLY KILLED THREE OF MY GUARDS JUST WALKING OVER HERE.
BUT SHE'S ALSO MISTAKEN--

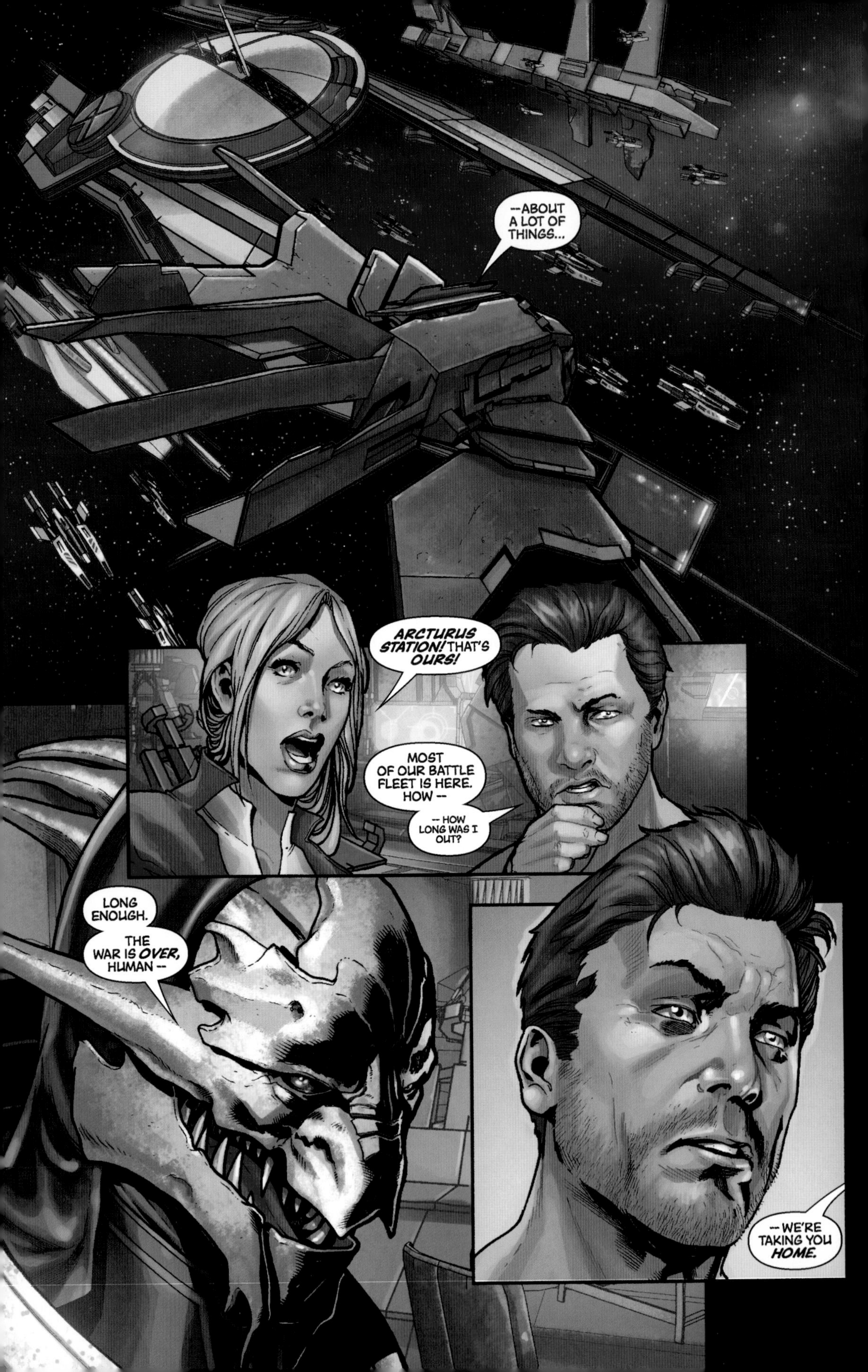
--ABOUT A LOT OF THINGS...
ARCTURUS STATION! THAT'S OURS!
MOST OF OUR BATTLE FLEET IS HERE. HOW --
-- HOW LONG WAS I OUT?
LONG ENOUGH.
THE WAR IS OVER, HUMAN --
-- WE'RE TAKING YOU HOME.

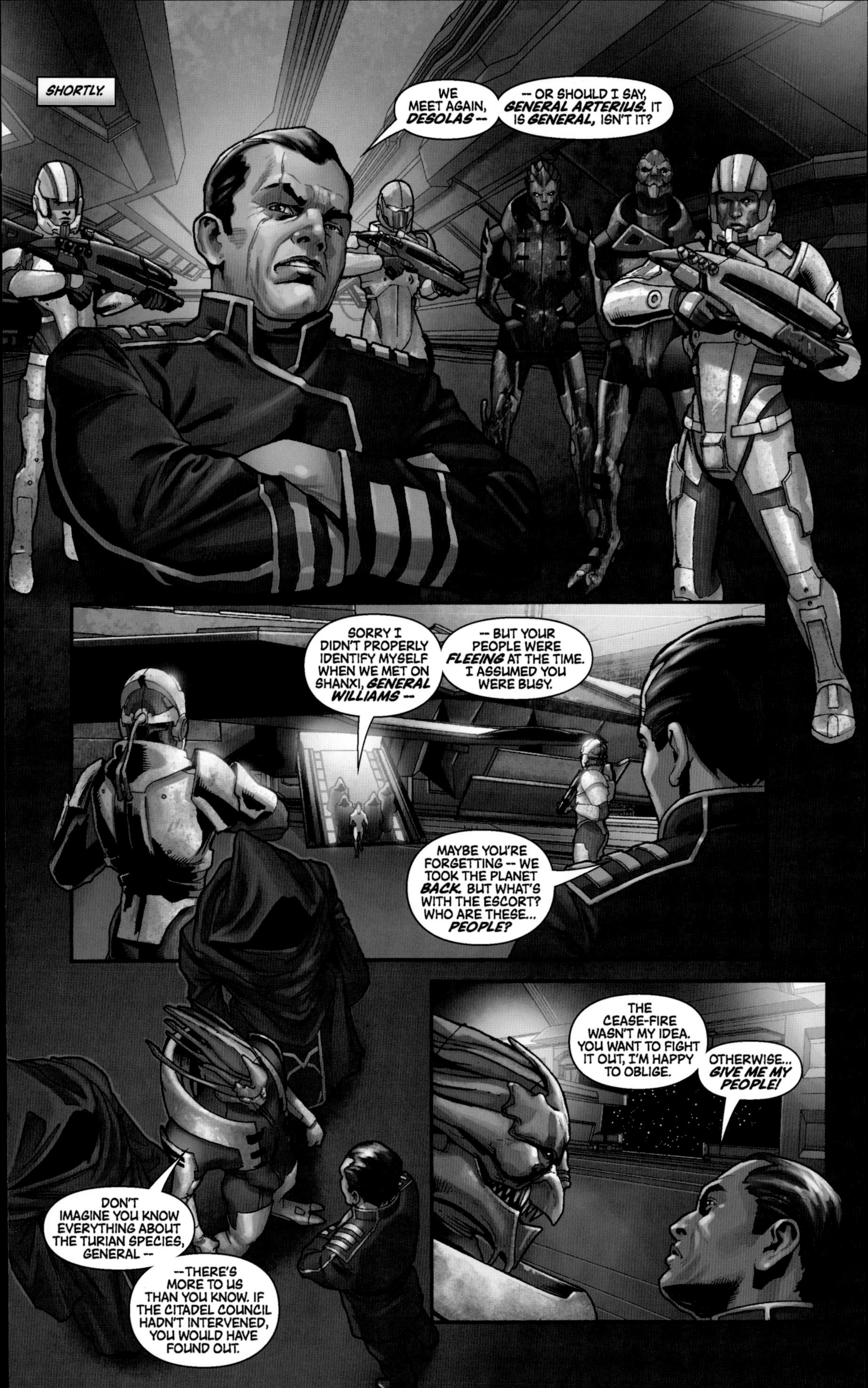
SHORTLY.
WE MEET AGAIN, DESOLAS --
-- OR SHOULD I SAY, GENERAL ARTERIUS. IT IS GENERAL, ISN'T IT?
SORRY I DIDN'T PROPERLY IDENTIFY MYSELF WHEN WE MET ON SHANXI, GENERAL WILLIAMS --
-- BUT YOUR PEOPLE WERE FLEEING AT THE TIME. I ASSUMED YOU WERE BUSY.
MAYBE YOU'RE FORGETTING -- WE TOOK THE PLANET BACK. BUT WHAT'S WITH THE ESCORT? WHO ARE THESE... PEOPLE?
DON'T IMAGINE YOU KNOW EVERYTHING ABOUT THE TURIAN SPECIES, GENERAL --
--THERE'S MORE TO US THAN YOU KNOW. IF THE CITADEL COUNCIL HADN'T INTERVENED, YOU WOULD HAVE FOUND OUT.
THE CEASE-FIRE WASN'T MY IDEA. YOU WANT TO FIGHT IT OUT, I'M HAPPY TO OBLIGE.
OTHERWISE... GIVE ME MY PEOPLE!

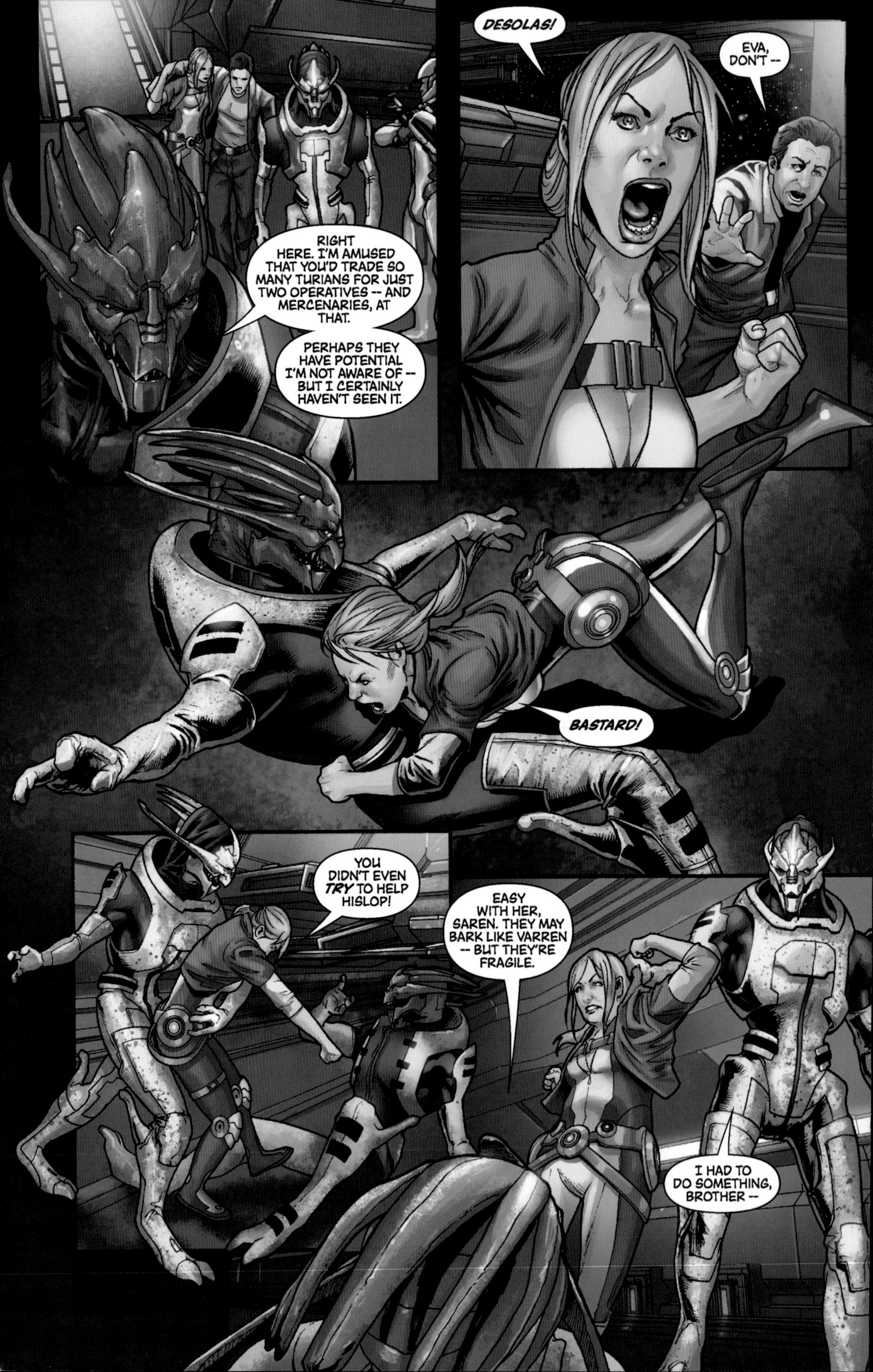
RIGHT HERE. I'M AMUSED THAT YOU'D TRADE SO MANY TURIANS FOR JUST TWO OPERATIVES -- AND MERCENARIES, AT THAT.
PERHAPS THEY HAVE POTENTIAL I'M NOT AWARE OF -- BUT I CERTAINLY HAVEN'T SEEN IT.
DESOLAS!
EVA, DON'T --
BASTARD!
YOU DIDN'T EVEN TRY TO HELP HISLOP!
EASY WITH HER, SAREN. THEY MAY BARK LIKE VARREN -- BUT THEY'RE FRAGILE.
I HAD TO DO SOMETHING, BROTHER --

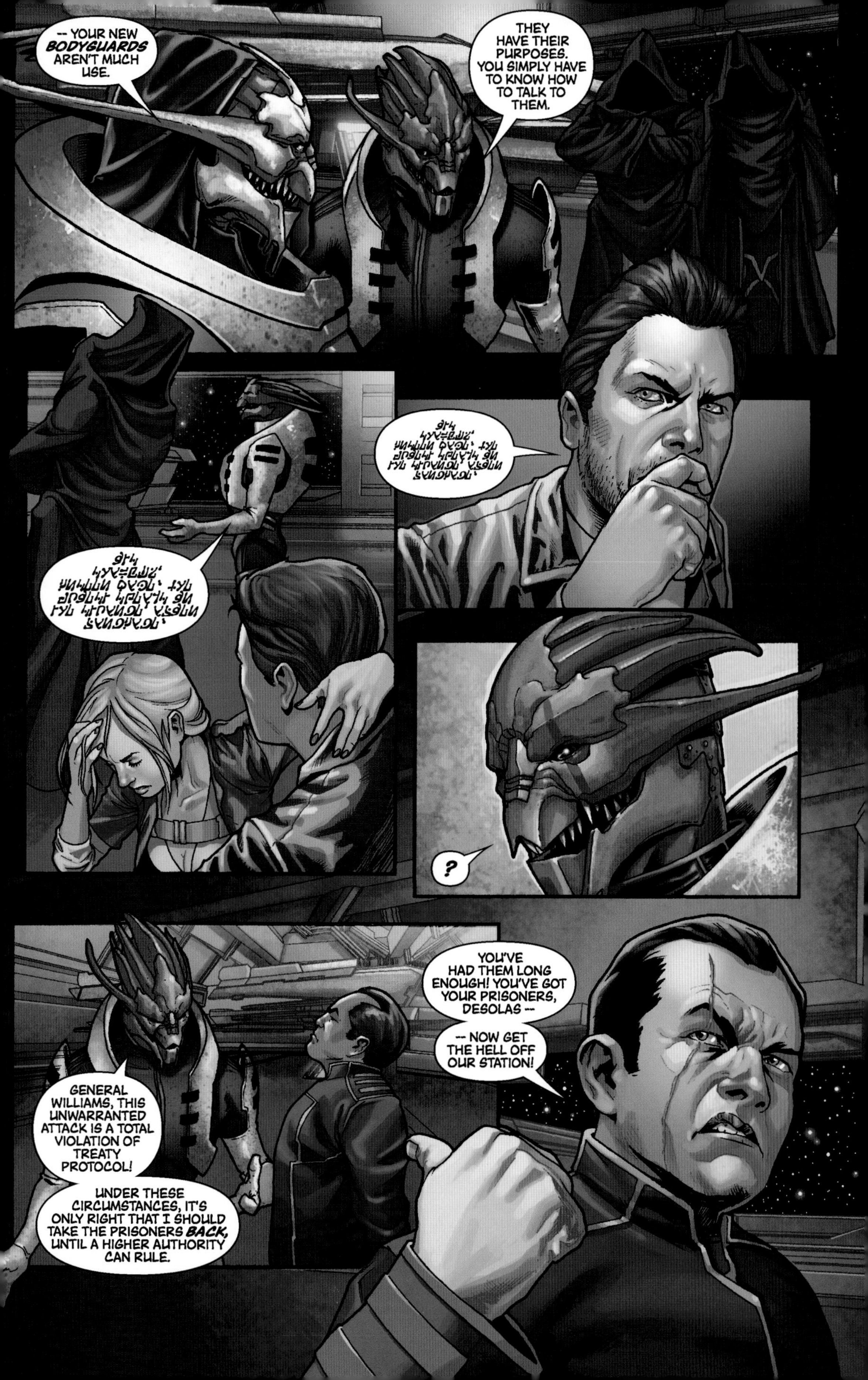
-- YOUR NEW BODYGUARDS AREN'T MUCH USE.
THEY HAVE THEIR PURPOSES. YOU SIMPLY HAVE TO KNOW HOW TO TALK TO THEM.
?
YOU'VE HAD THEM LONG ENOUGH! YOU'VE GOT YOUR PRISONERS, DESOLAS --
-- NOW GET THE HELL OFF OUR STATION!
GENERAL WILLIAMS, THIS UNWARRANTED ATTACK IS A TOTAL VIOLATION OF TREATY PROTOCOL!
UNDER THESE CIRCUMSTANCES, IT'S ONLY RIGHT THAT I SHOULD TAKE THE PRISONERS BACK, UNTIL A HIGHER AUTHORITY CAN RULE.

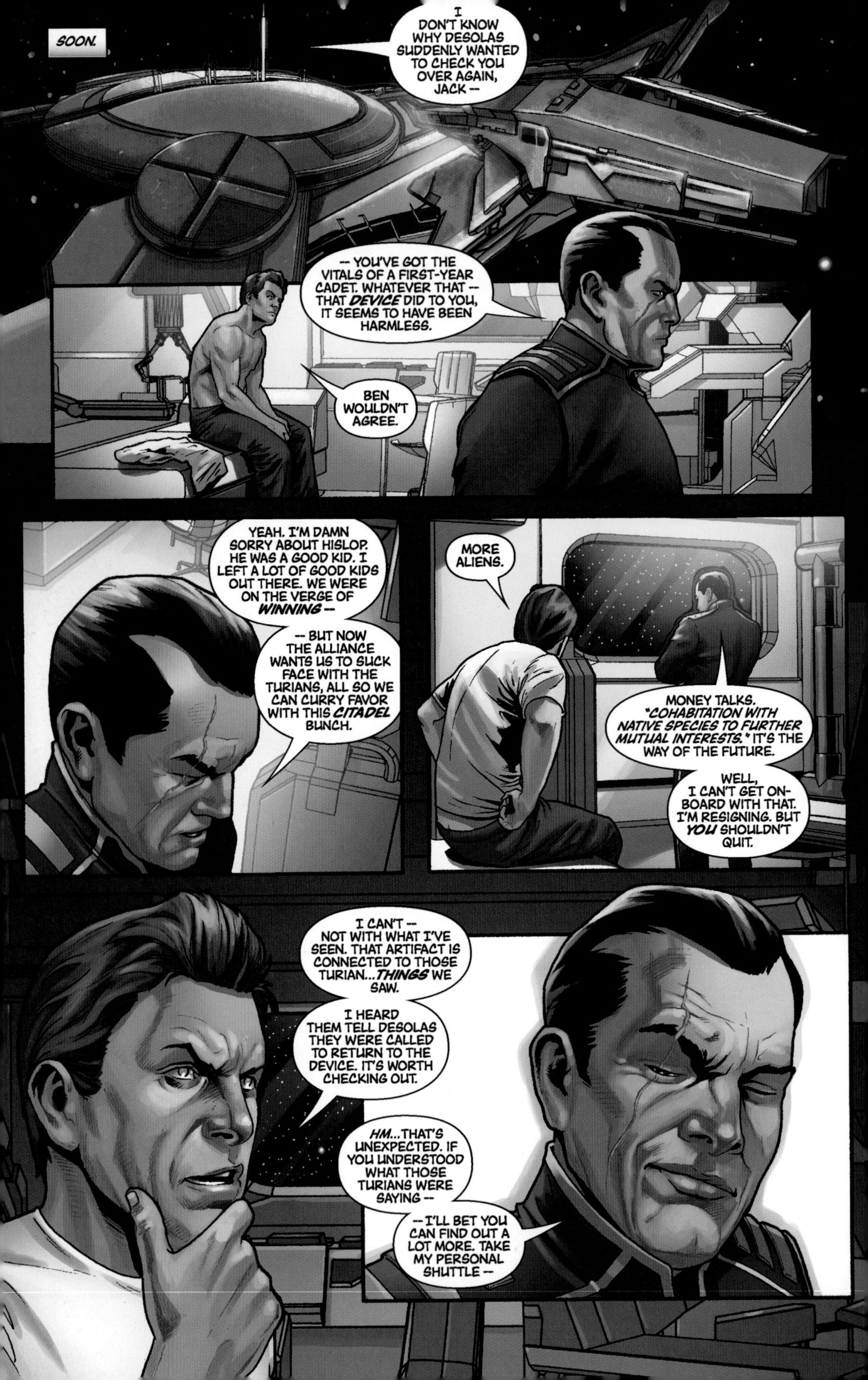
SOON.
I DON'T KNOW WHY DESOLAS SUDDENLY WANTED TO CHECK YOU OVER AGAIN, JACK --
-- YOU'VE GOT THE VITALS OF A FIRST-YEAR CADET. WHATEVER THAT -- THAT *DEVICE* DID TO YOU, IT SEEMS TO HAVE BEEN HARMLESS.
BEN WOULDN'T AGREE.
YEAH. I'M DAMN SORRY ABOUT HISLOP. HE WAS A GOOD KID. I LEFT A LOT OF GOOD KIDS OUT THERE. WE WERE ON THE VERGE OF *WINNING* --
-- BUT NOW THE ALLIANCE WANTS US TO SUCK FACE WITH THE TURIANS, ALL SO WE CAN CURRY FAVOR WITH THIS *CITADEL* BUNCH.
MORE ALIENS.
MONEY TALKS. *"COHABITATION WITH NATIVE SPECIES TO FURTHER MUTUAL INTERESTS."* IT'S THE WAY OF THE FUTURE.
WELL, I CAN'T GET ON-BOARD WITH THAT. I'M RESIGNING. BUT *YOU* SHOULDN'T QUIT.
I CAN'T -- NOT WITH WHAT I'VE SEEN. THAT ARTIFACT IS CONNECTED TO THOSE TURIAN... *THINGS* WE SAW.
I HEARD THEM TELL DESOLAS THEY WERE CALLED TO RETURN TO THE DEVICE. IT'S WORTH CHECKING OUT.
HM... THAT'S UNEXPECTED. IF YOU UNDERSTOOD WHAT THOSE TURIANS WERE SAYING --
-- I'LL BET YOU CAN FIND OUT A LOT MORE. TAKE MY PERSONAL SHUTTLE --

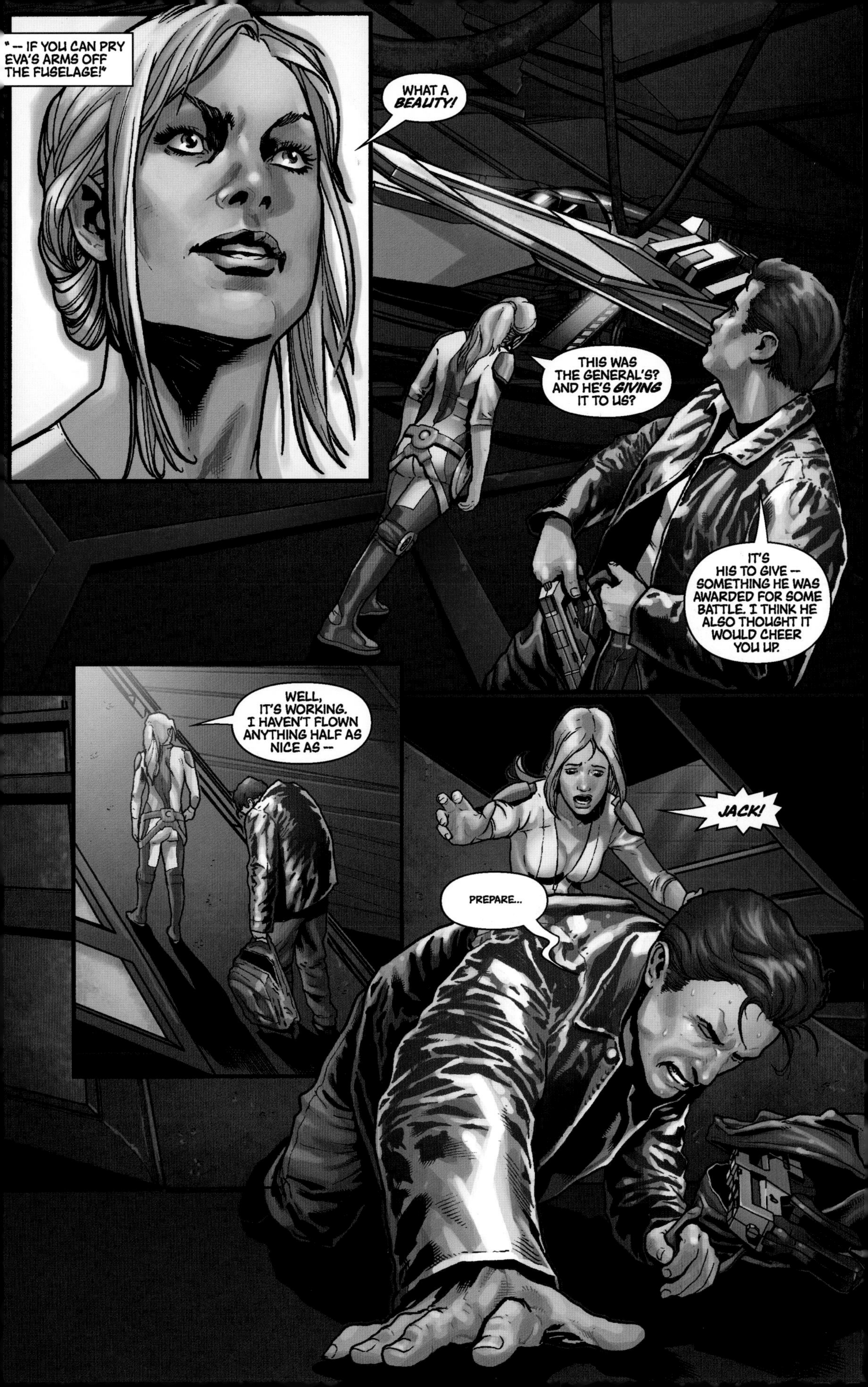
"-- IF YOU CAN PRY EVA'S ARMS OFF THE FUSELAGE!"
WHAT A *BEAUTY!*
THIS WAS THE GENERAL'S? AND HE'S *GIVING* IT TO US?
IT'S HIS TO GIVE -- SOMETHING HE WAS AWARDED FOR SOME BATTLE. I THINK HE ALSO THOUGHT IT WOULD CHEER YOU UP.
WELL, IT'S WORKING. I HAVEN'T FLOWN ANYTHING HALF AS NICE AS --
JACK!
PREPARE...

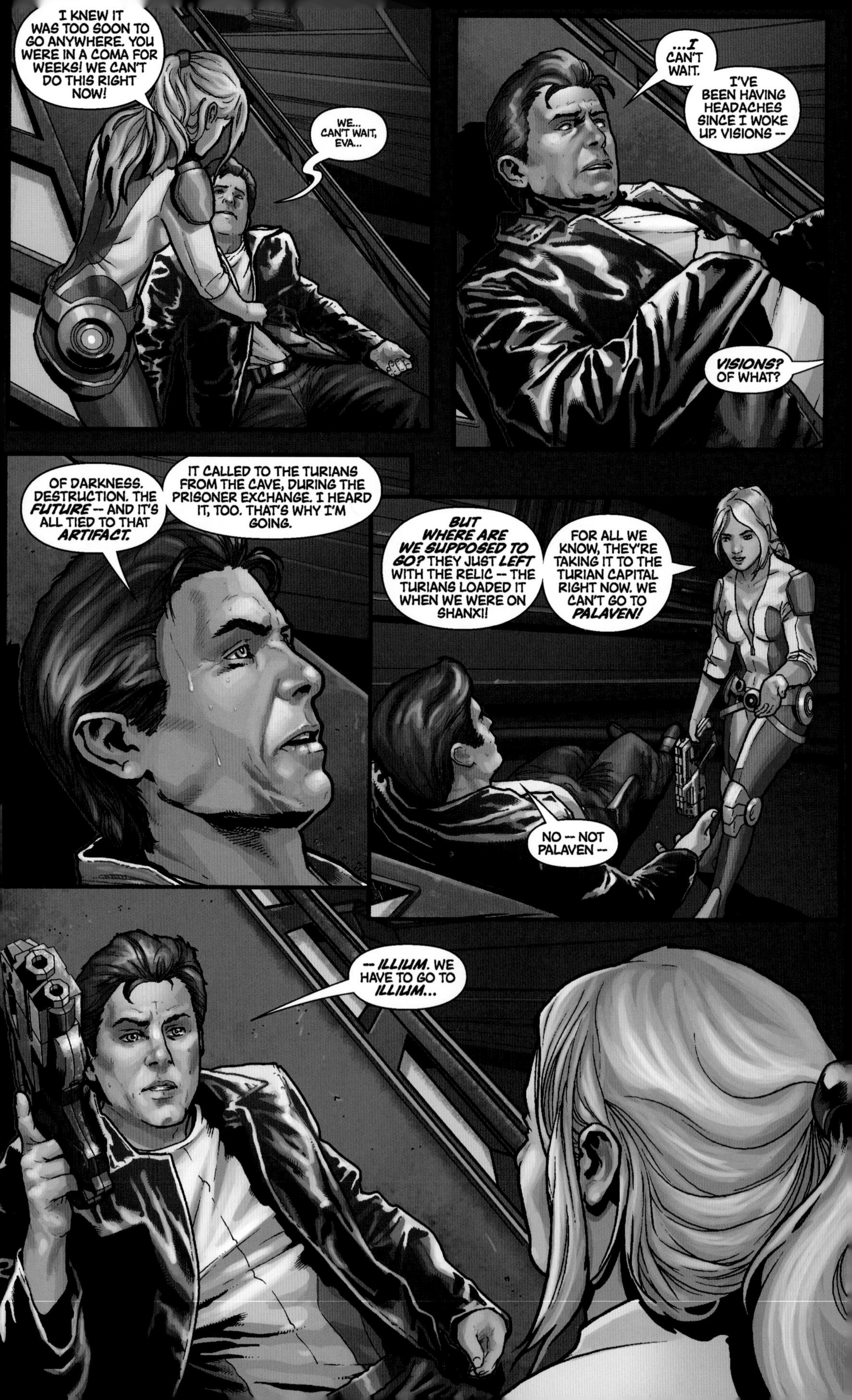
I KNEW IT WAS TOO SOON TO GO ANYWHERE. YOU WERE IN A COMA FOR WEEKS! WE CAN'T DO THIS RIGHT NOW!
WE... CAN'T WAIT, EVA...
...*I* CAN'T WAIT.
I'VE BEEN HAVING HEADACHES SINCE I WOKE UP. VISIONS --
VISIONS? OF WHAT?
OF DARKNESS. DESTRUCTION. THE *FUTURE* -- AND IT'S ALL TIED TO THAT *ARTIFACT.*
IT CALLED TO THE TURIANS FROM THE CAVE, DURING THE PRISONER EXCHANGE. I HEARD IT, TOO. THAT'S WHY I'M GOING.
BUT WHERE ARE WE SUPPOSED TO GO? THEY JUST *LEFT* WITH THE RELIC -- THE TURIANS LOADED IT WHEN WE WERE ON SHANXI!
FOR ALL WE KNOW, THEY'RE TAKING IT TO THE TURIAN CAPITAL RIGHT NOW. WE CAN'T GO TO *PALAVEN!*
NO -- NOT PALAVEN --
-- *ILLIUM*. WE HAVE TO GO TO *ILLIUM...*

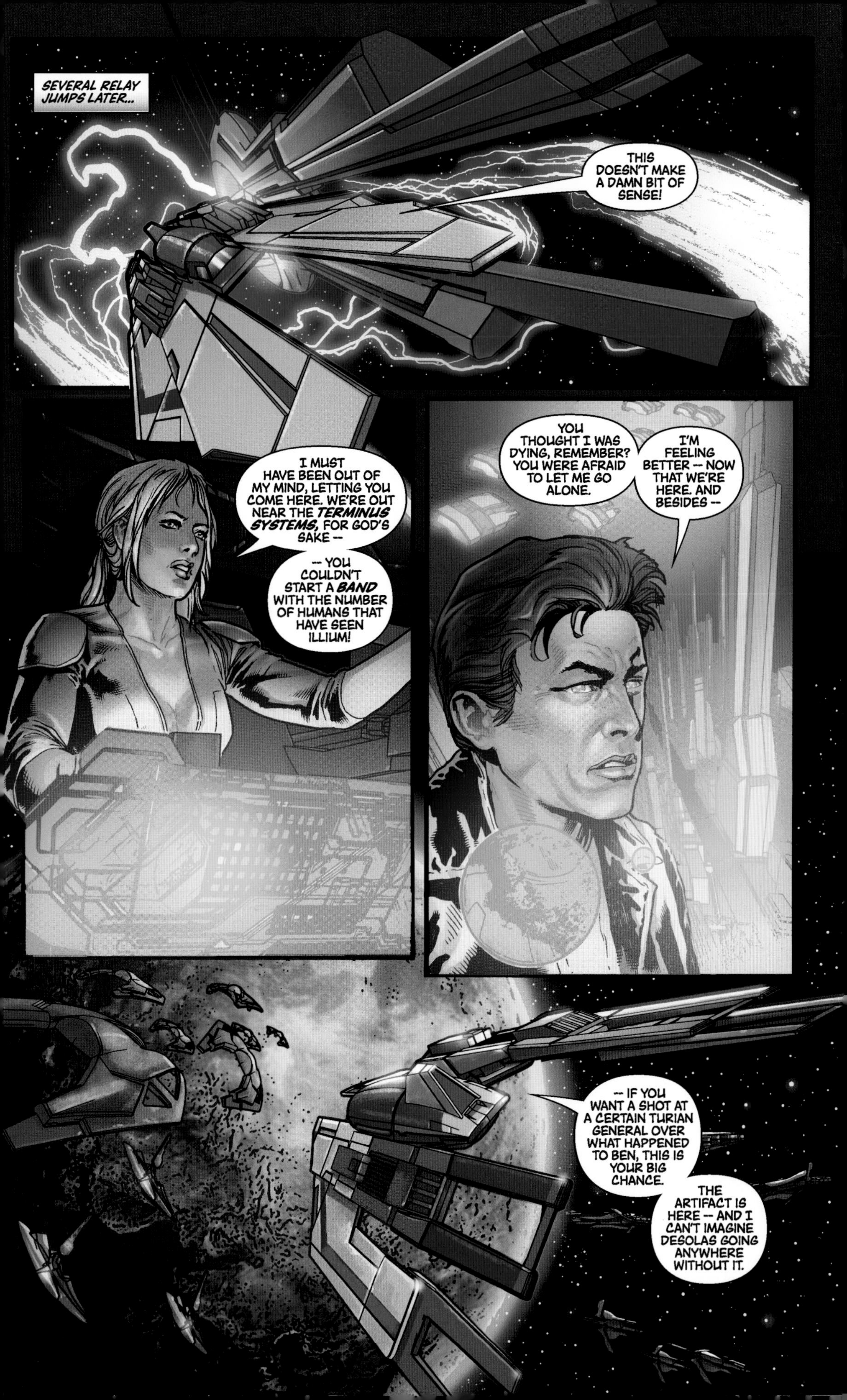
SEVERAL RELAY JUMPS LATER...
THIS DOESN'T MAKE A DAMN BIT OF SENSE!
I MUST HAVE BEEN OUT OF MY MIND, LETTING YOU COME HERE. WE'RE OUT NEAR THE *TERMINUS SYSTEMS,* FOR GOD'S SAKE --
-- YOU COULDN'T START A *BAND* WITH THE NUMBER OF HUMANS THAT HAVE SEEN ILLIUM!
YOU THOUGHT I WAS DYING, REMEMBER? YOU WERE AFRAID TO LET ME GO ALONE.
I'M FEELING BETTER -- NOW THAT WE'RE HERE. AND BESIDES --
-- IF YOU WANT A SHOT AT A CERTAIN TURIAN GENERAL OVER WHAT HAPPENED TO BEN, THIS IS YOUR BIG CHANCE.
THE ARTIFACT IS HERE -- AND I CAN'T IMAGINE DESOLAS GOING ANYWHERE WITHOUT IT.

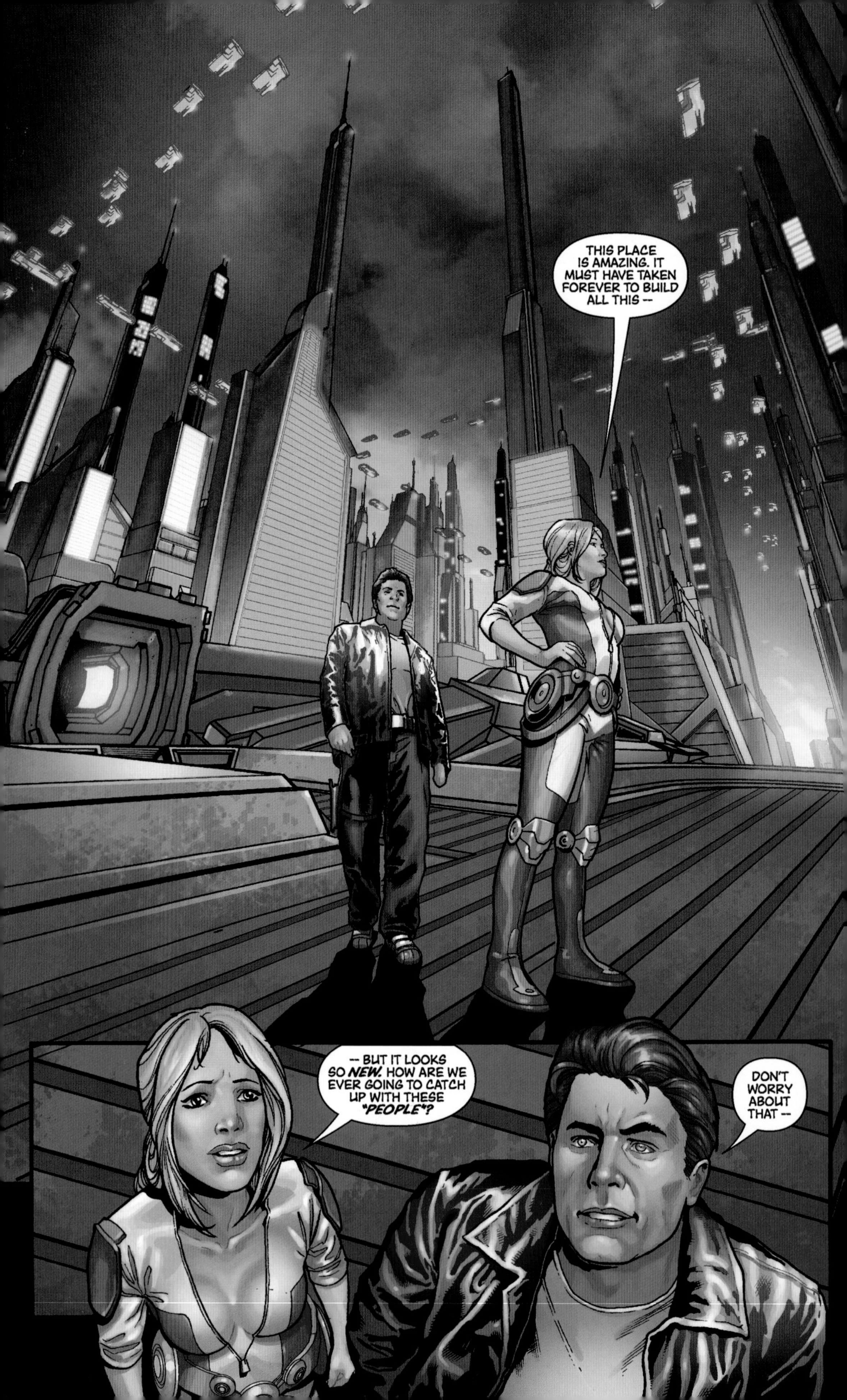
THIS PLACE IS AMAZING. IT MUST HAVE TAKEN FOREVER TO BUILD ALL THIS --
-- BUT IT LOOKS SO *NEW.* HOW ARE WE EVER GOING TO CATCH UP WITH THESE *"PEOPLE"*?
DON'T WORRY ABOUT THAT --

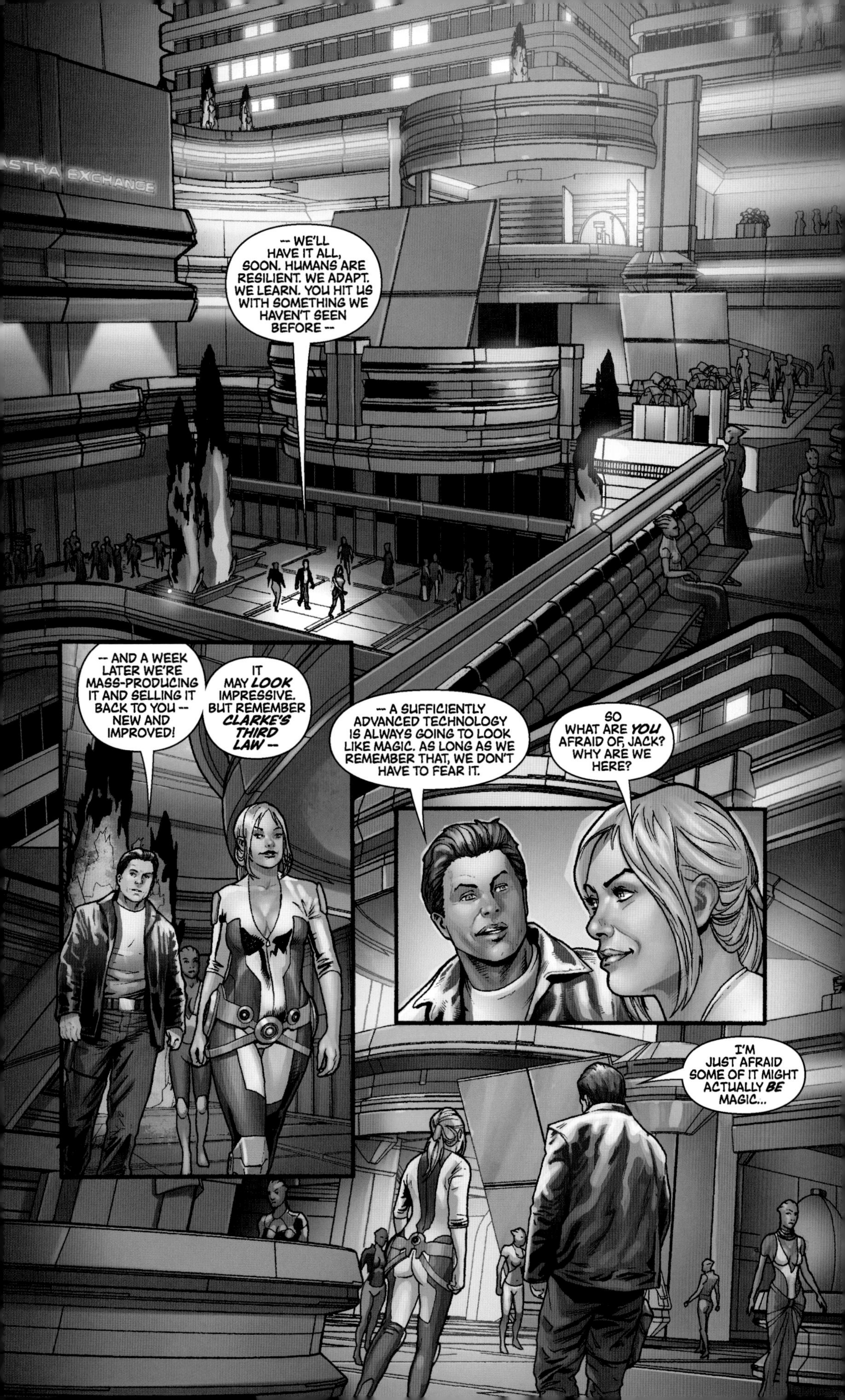
ASTRA EXCHANGE
-- WE'LL HAVE IT ALL, SOON. HUMANS ARE RESILIENT. WE ADAPT. WE LEARN. YOU HIT US WITH SOMETHING WE HAVEN'T SEEN BEFORE --
-- AND A WEEK LATER WE'RE MASS-PRODUCING IT AND SELLING IT BACK TO YOU -- NEW AND IMPROVED!
IT MAY *LOOK* IMPRESSIVE. BUT REMEMBER *CLARKE'S THIRD LAW* --
-- A SUFFICIENTLY ADVANCED TECHNOLOGY IS ALWAYS GOING TO LOOK LIKE MAGIC. AS LONG AS WE REMEMBER THAT, WE DON'T HAVE TO FEAR IT.
SO WHAT ARE *YOU* AFRAID OF, JACK? WHY ARE WE HERE?
I'M JUST AFRAID SOME OF IT MIGHT ACTUALLY *BE* MAGIC...

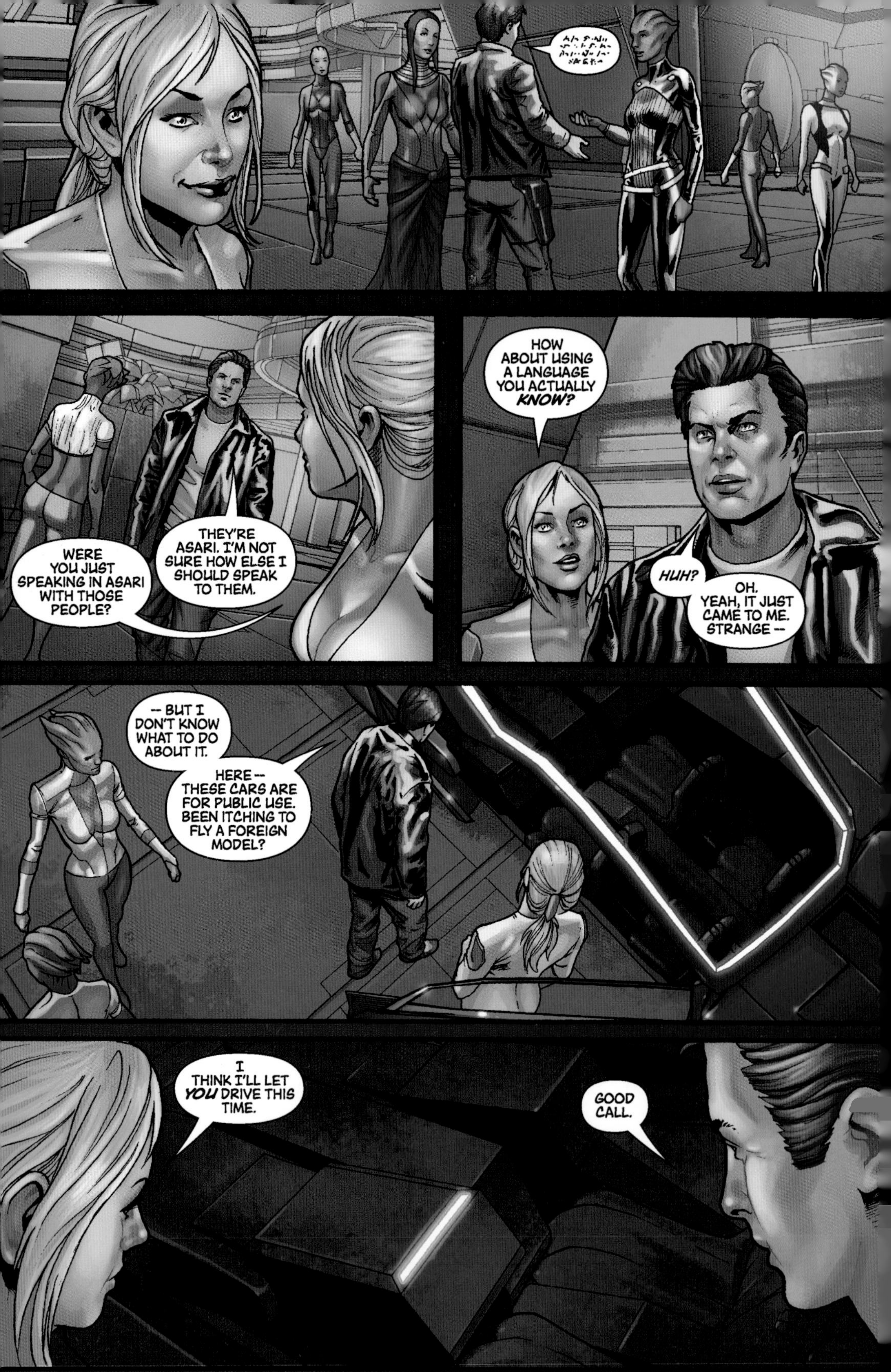
WERE YOU JUST SPEAKING IN ASARI WITH THOSE PEOPLE?
THEY'RE ASARI. I'M NOT SURE HOW ELSE I SHOULD SPEAK TO THEM.
HOW ABOUT USING A LANGUAGE YOU ACTUALLY *KNOW?*
HUH?
OH. YEAH, IT JUST CAME TO ME. STRANGE --
-- BUT I DON'T KNOW WHAT TO DO ABOUT IT.
HERE -- THESE CARS ARE FOR PUBLIC USE. BEEN ITCHING TO FLY A FOREIGN MODEL?
I THINK I'LL LET *YOU* DRIVE THIS TIME.
GOOD CALL.

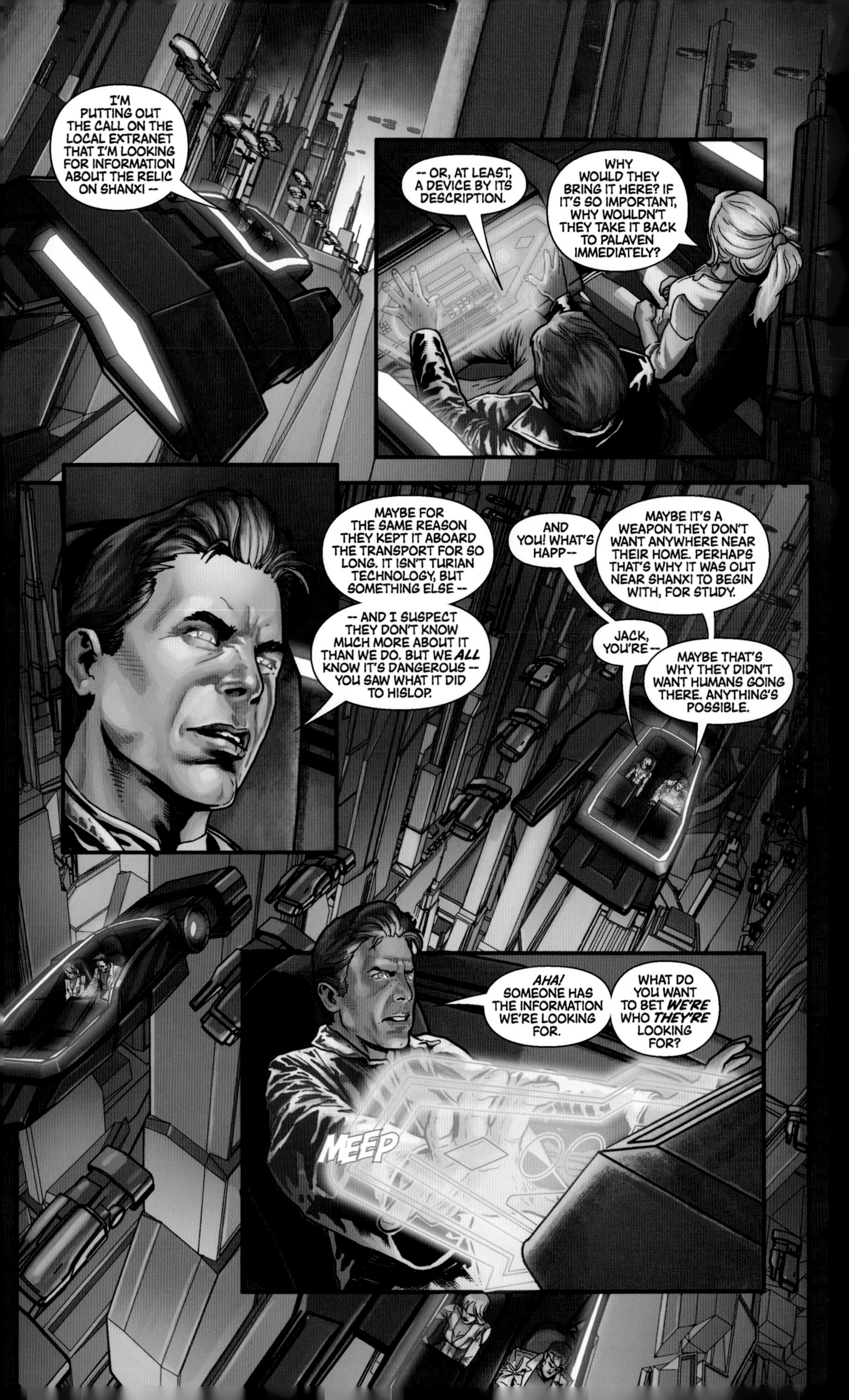
I'M PUTTING OUT THE CALL ON THE LOCAL EXTRANET THAT I'M LOOKING FOR INFORMATION ABOUT THE RELIC ON SHANXI --
-- OR, AT LEAST, A DEVICE BY ITS DESCRIPTION.
WHY WOULD THEY BRING IT HERE? IF IT'S SO IMPORTANT, WHY WOULDN'T THEY TAKE IT BACK TO PALAVEN IMMEDIATELY?
MAYBE FOR THE SAME REASON THEY KEPT IT ABOARD THE TRANSPORT FOR SO LONG. IT ISN'T TURIAN TECHNOLOGY, BUT SOMETHING ELSE --
-- AND I SUSPECT THEY DON'T KNOW MUCH MORE ABOUT IT THAN WE DO. BUT WE ALL KNOW IT'S DANGEROUS -- YOU SAW WHAT IT DID TO HISLOP.
MAYBE IT'S A WEAPON THEY DON'T WANT ANYWHERE NEAR THEIR HOME. PERHAPS THAT'S WHY IT WAS OUT NEAR SHANXI TO BEGIN WITH, FOR STUDY.
AND YOU! WHAT'S HAPP--
JACK, YOU'RE--
MAYBE THAT'S WHY THEY DIDN'T WANT HUMANS GOING THERE. ANYTHING'S POSSIBLE.
AHA! SOMEONE HAS THE INFORMATION WE'RE LOOKING FOR.
WHAT DO YOU WANT TO BET WE'RE WHO THEY'RE LOOKING FOR?
MEEP

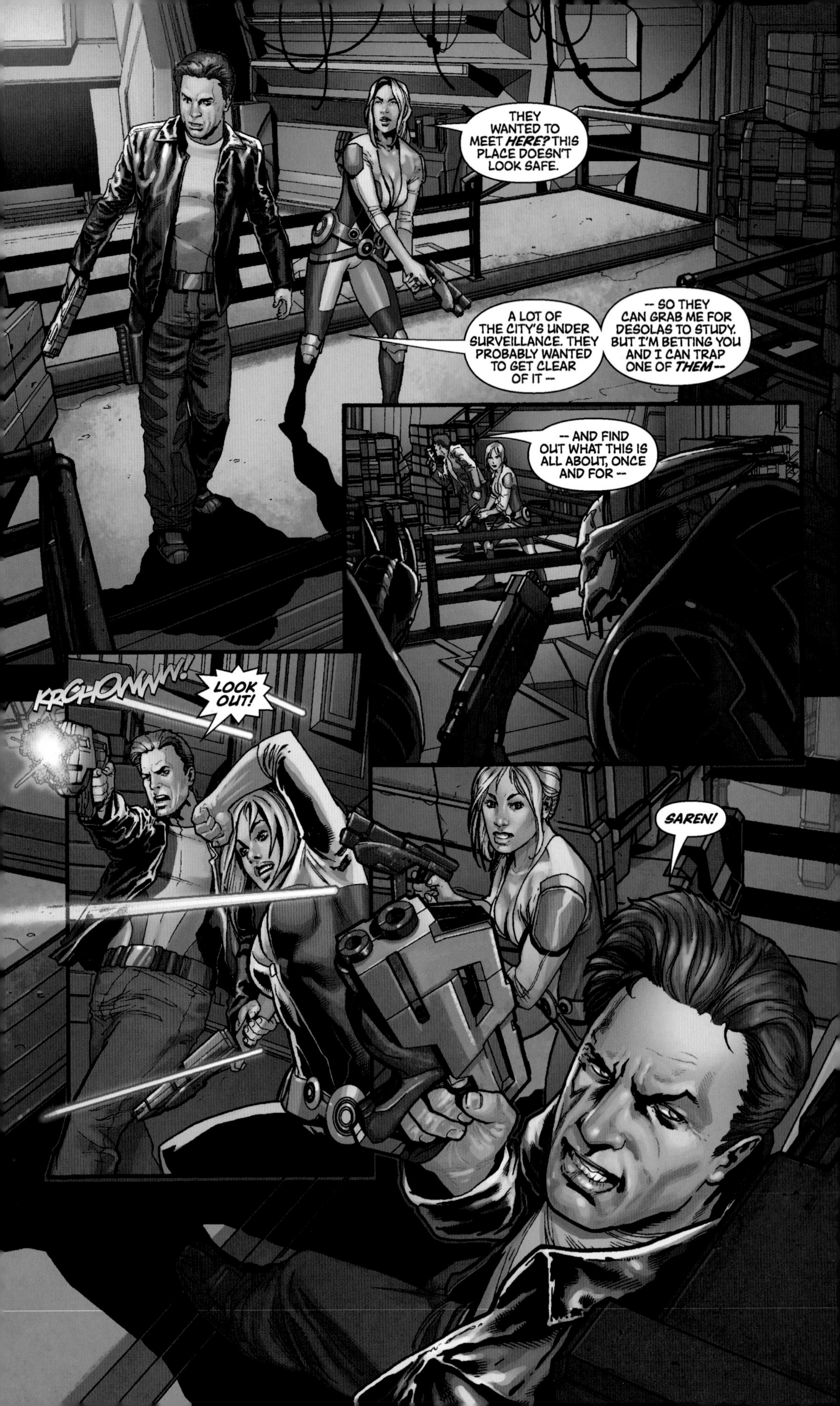
THEY WANTED TO MEET *HERE?* THIS PLACE DOESN'T LOOK SAFE.
A LOT OF THE CITY'S UNDER SURVEILLANCE. THEY PROBABLY WANTED TO GET CLEAR OF IT --
-- SO THEY CAN GRAB ME FOR DESOLAS TO STUDY. BUT I'M BETTING YOU AND I CAN TRAP ONE OF *THEM* --
-- AND FIND OUT WHAT THIS IS ALL ABOUT, ONCE AND FOR --
KRCHOWWW!
LOOK OUT!
SAREN!

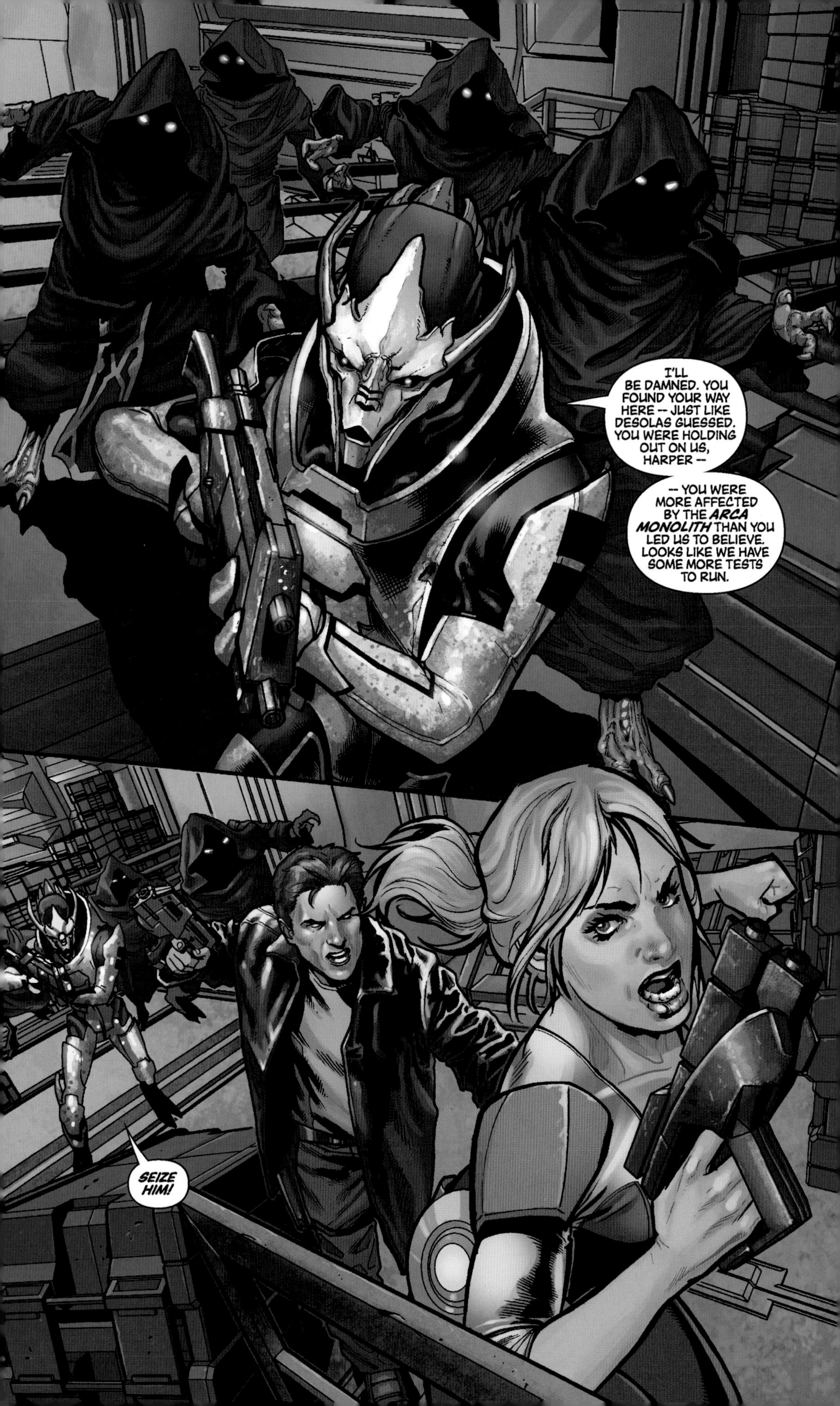
I'LL BE DAMNED. YOU FOUND YOUR WAY HERE -- JUST LIKE DESOLAS GUESSED. YOU WERE HOLDING OUT ON US, HARPER --
-- YOU WERE MORE AFFECTED BY THE ARCA MONOLITH THAN YOU LED US TO BELIEVE. LOOKS LIKE WE HAVE SOME MORE TESTS TO RUN.
SEIZE HIM!

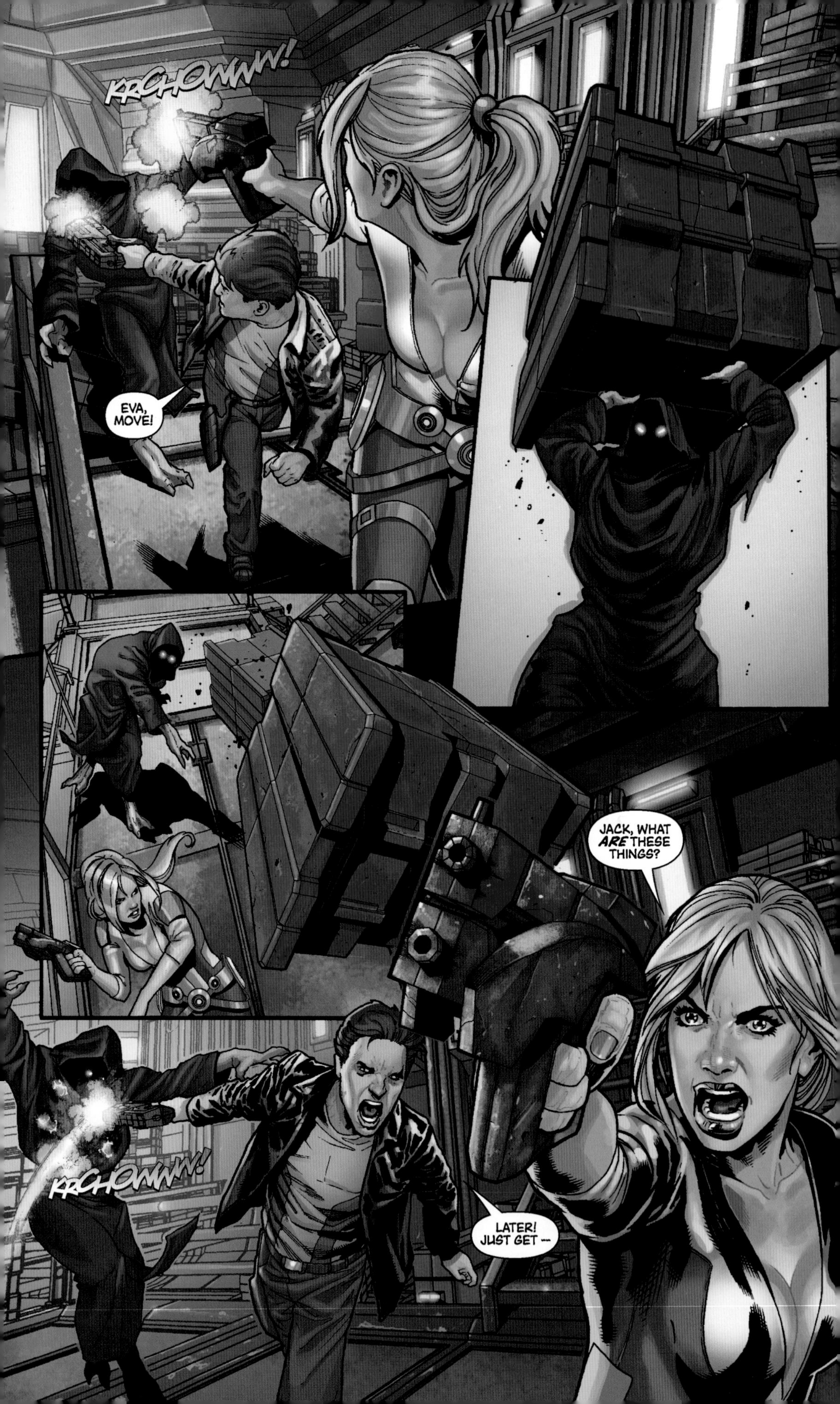
KRCHOWWW!
EVA, MOVE!
JACK, WHAT *ARE* THESE THINGS?
KRCHOWWW!
LATER! JUST GET --

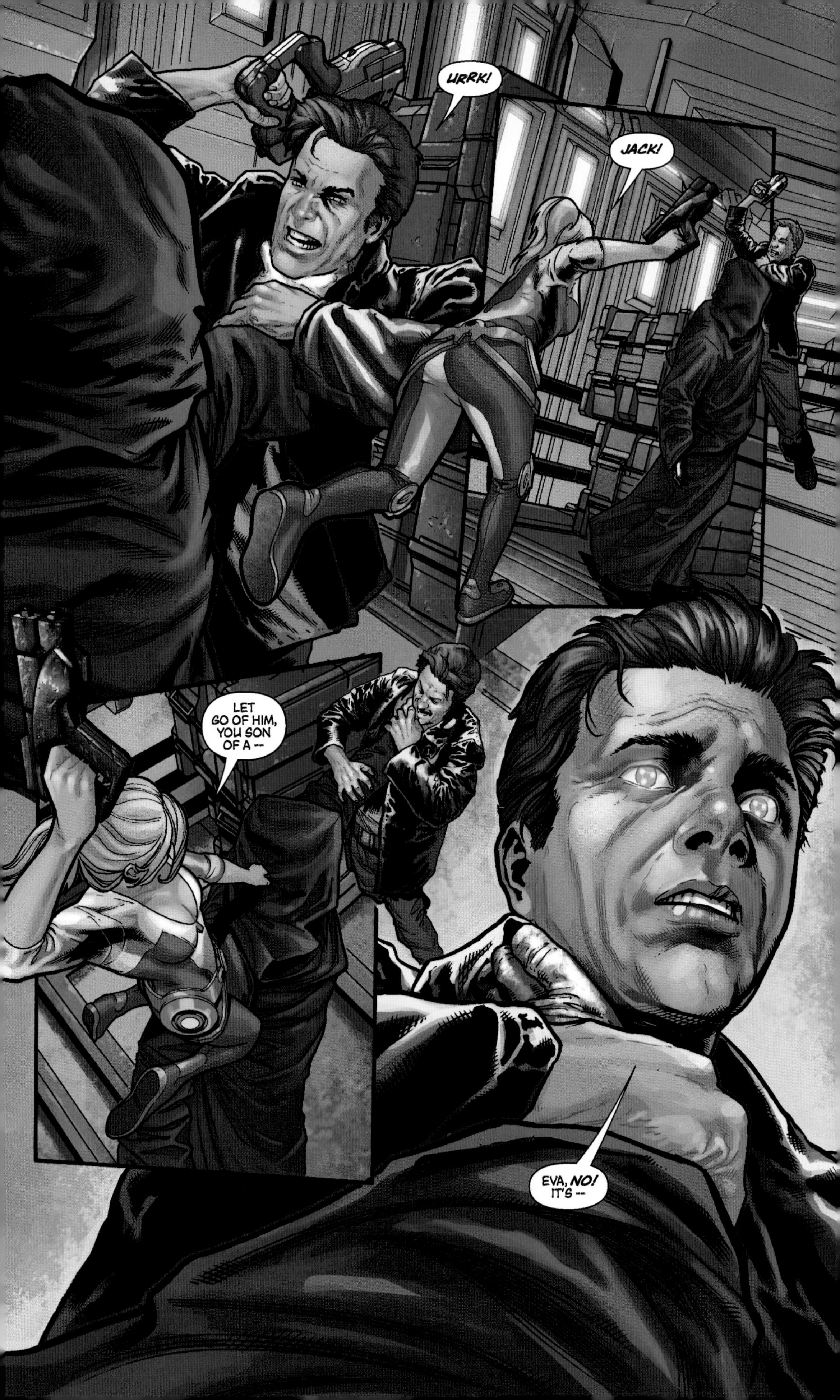
URRK!
JACK!
LET GO OF HIM, YOU SON OF A --
EVA, NO! IT'S --

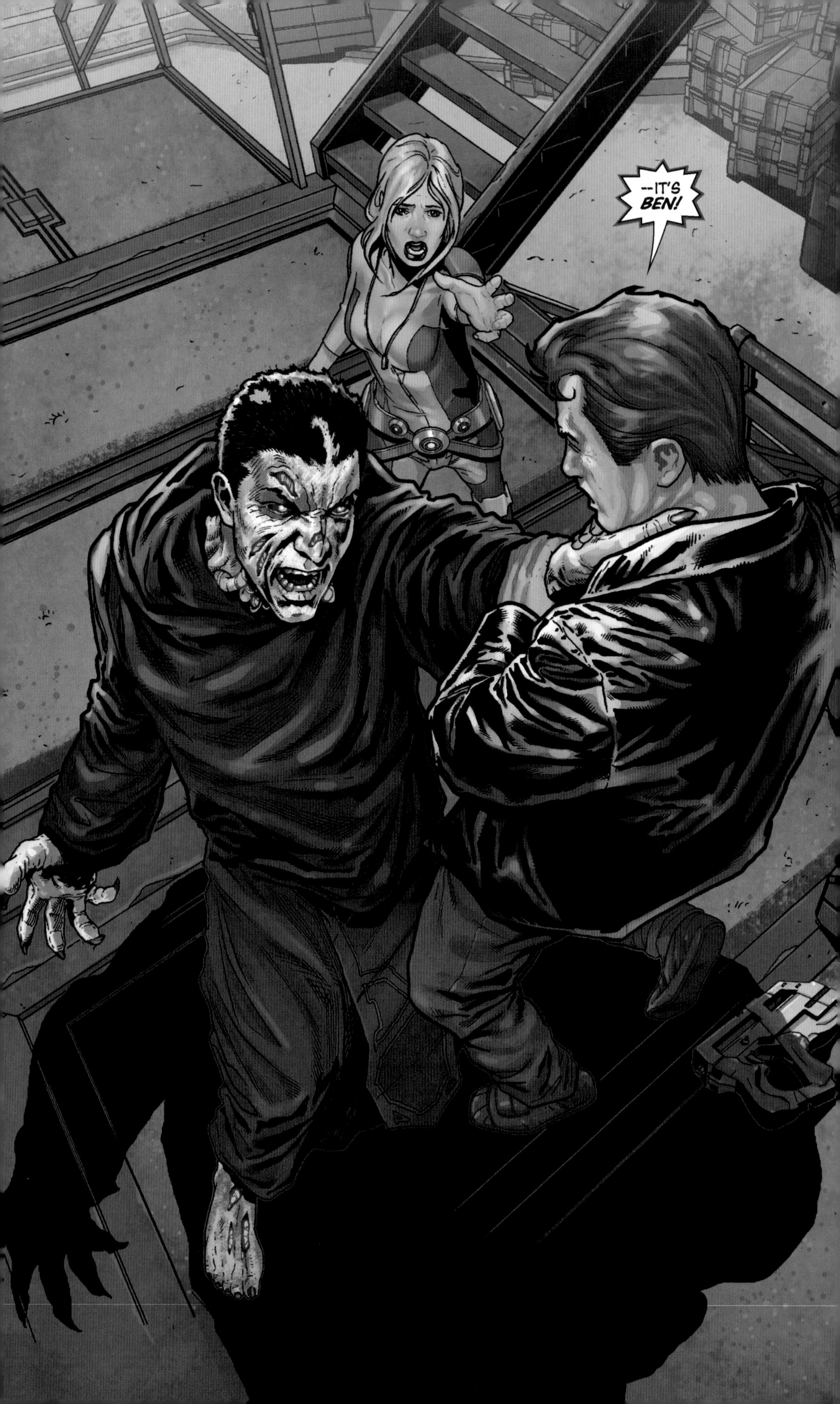
--IT'S BEN!

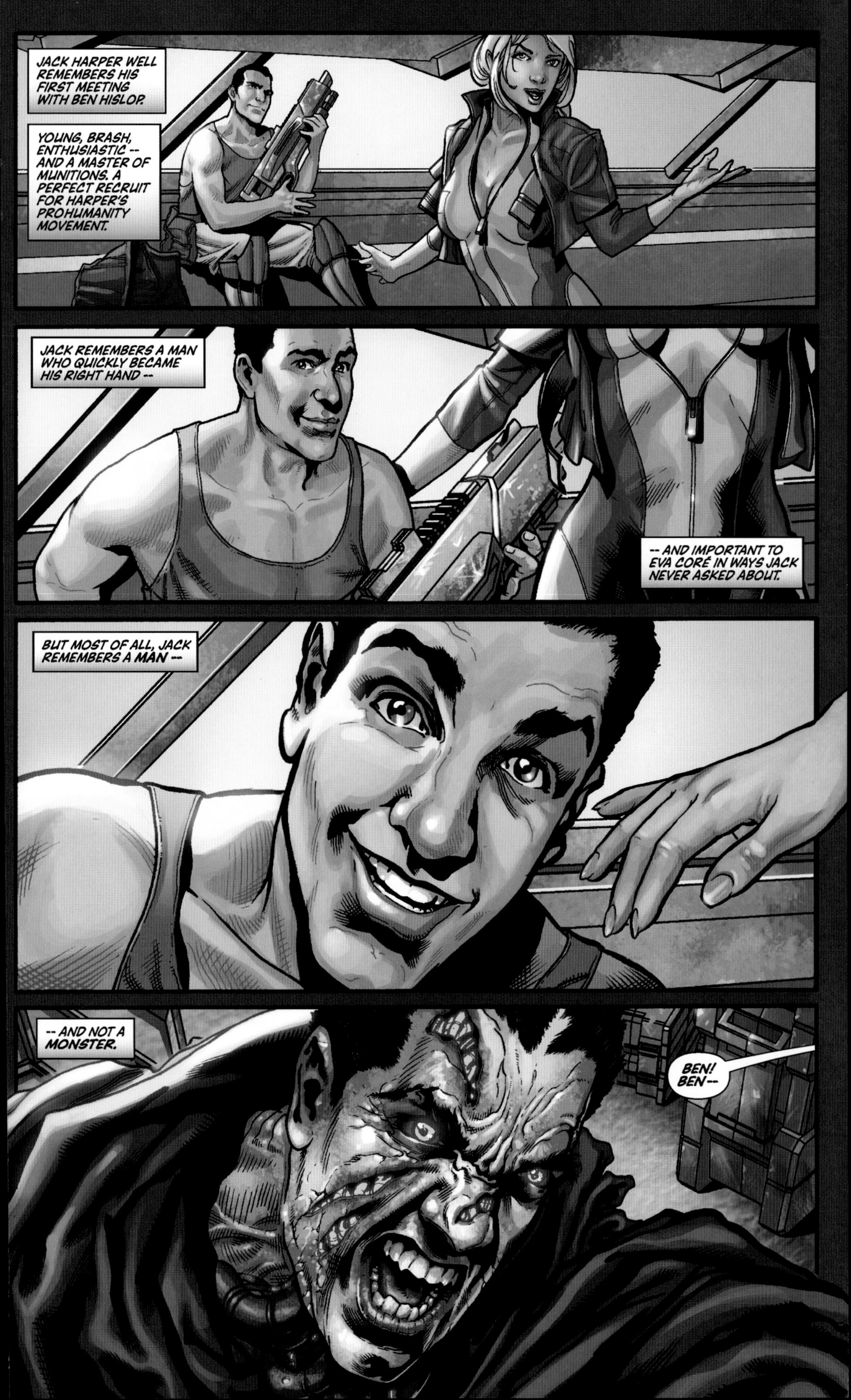
JACK HARPER WELL REMEMBERS HIS FIRST MEETING WITH BEN HISLOP.
YOUNG, BRASH, ENTHUSIASTIC -- AND A MASTER OF MUNITIONS. A PERFECT RECRUIT FOR HARPER'S PROHUMANITY MOVEMENT.
JACK REMEMBERS A MAN WHO QUICKLY BECAME HIS RIGHT HAND --
-- AND IMPORTANT TO EVA CORÉ IN WAYS JACK NEVER ASKED ABOUT.
BUT MOST OF ALL, JACK REMEMBERS A MAN --
-- AND NOT A MONSTER.
BEN! BEN--

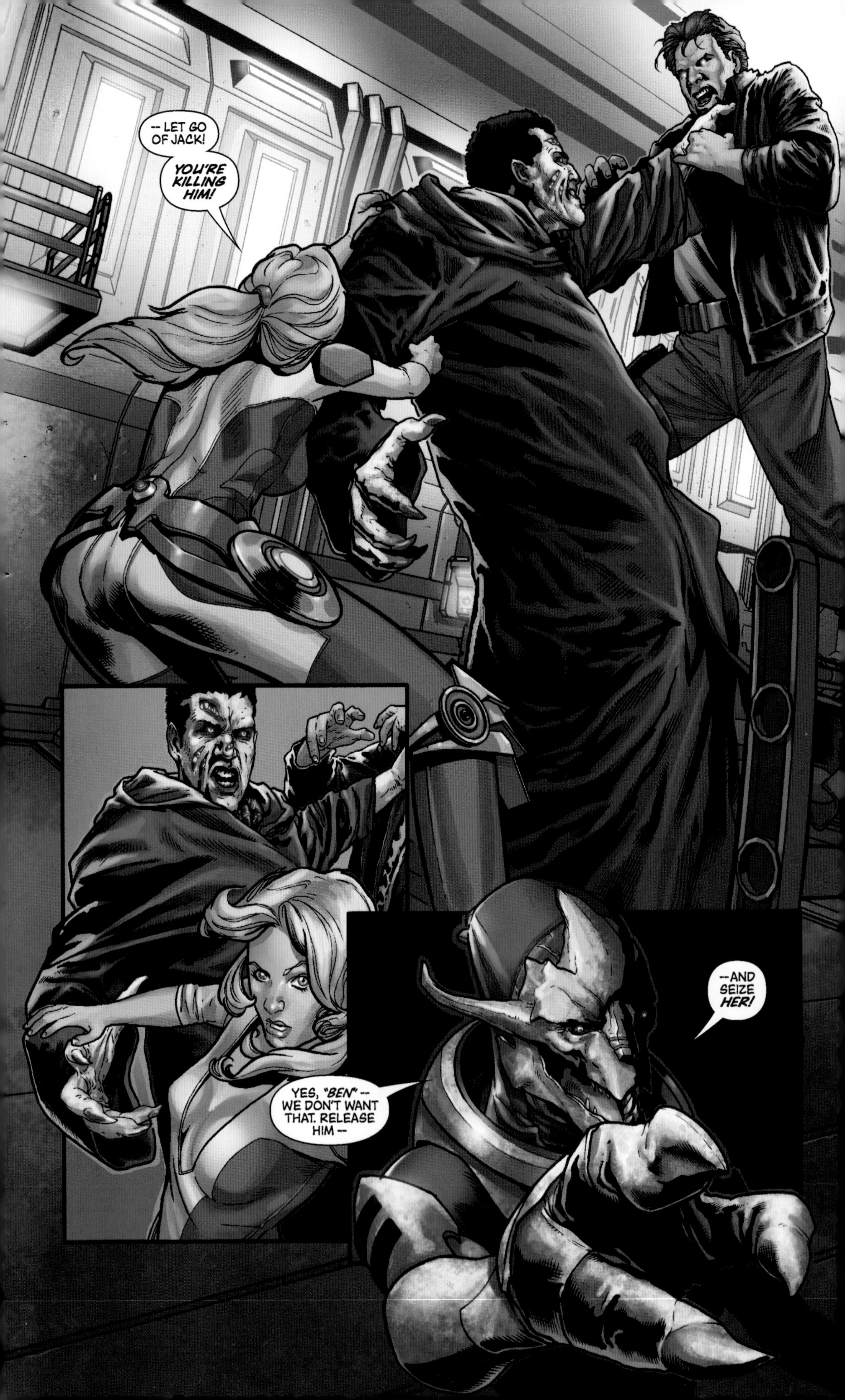
-- LET GO OF JACK!
YOU'RE KILLING HIM!
YES, "BEN" -- WE DON'T WANT THAT. RELEASE HIM --
--AND SEIZE HER!

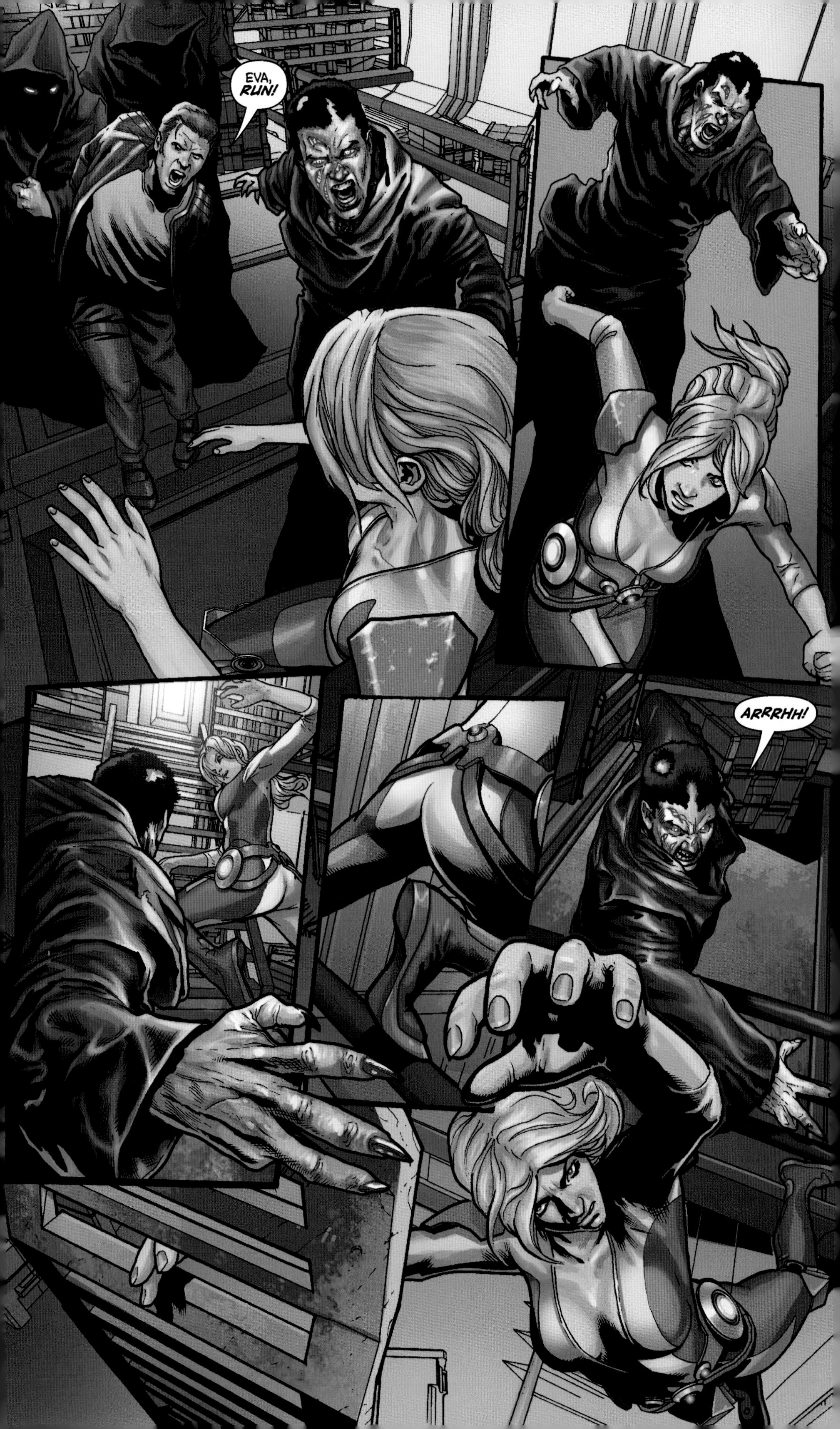
EVA, RUN!
ARRRHH!

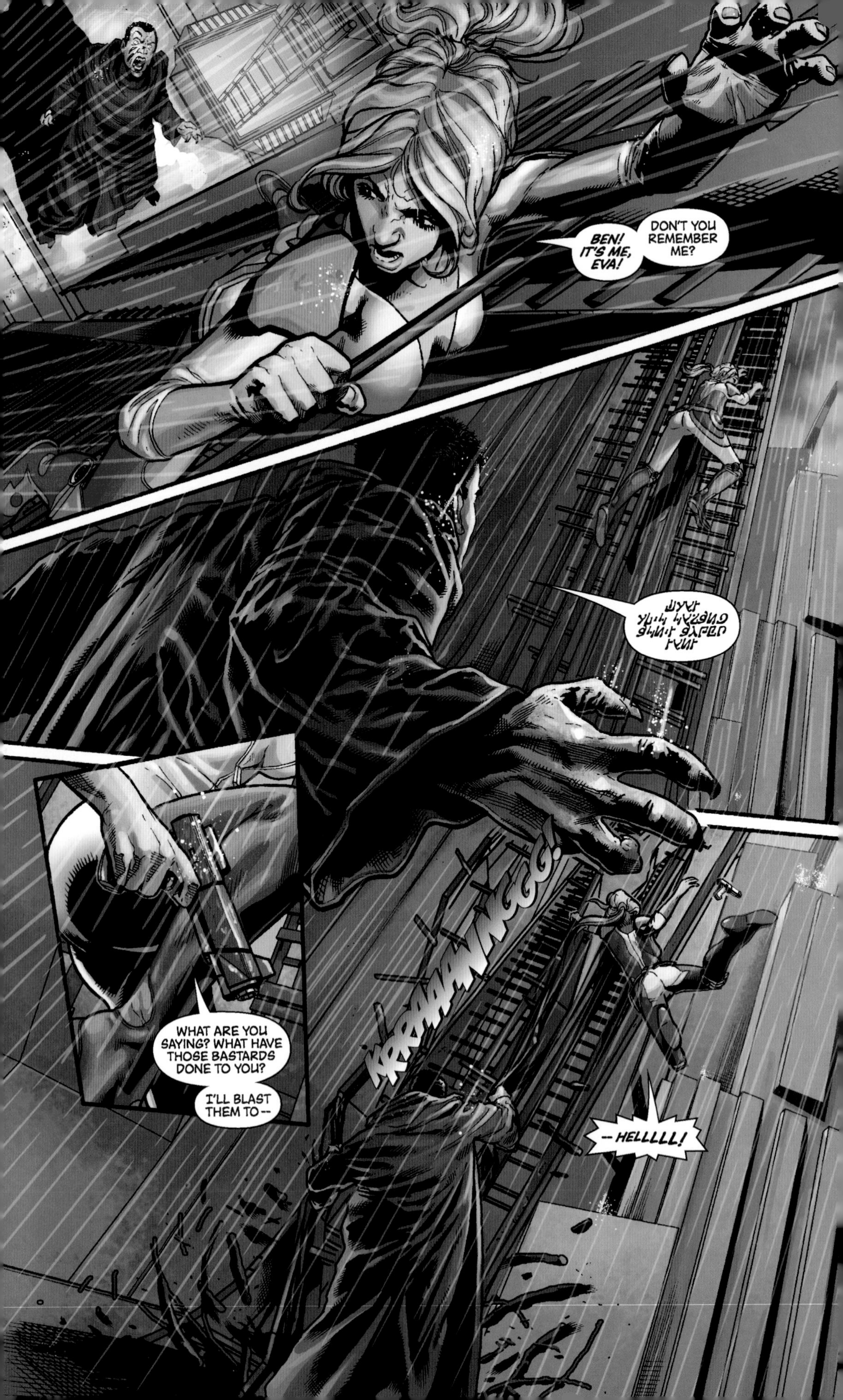
BEN! IT'S ME, EVA!
DON'T YOU REMEMBER ME?
WHAT ARE YOU SAYING? WHAT HAVE THOSE BASTARDS DONE TO YOU?
I'LL BLAST THEM TO --
KRRAAANNGGG!
-- HELLLLL!

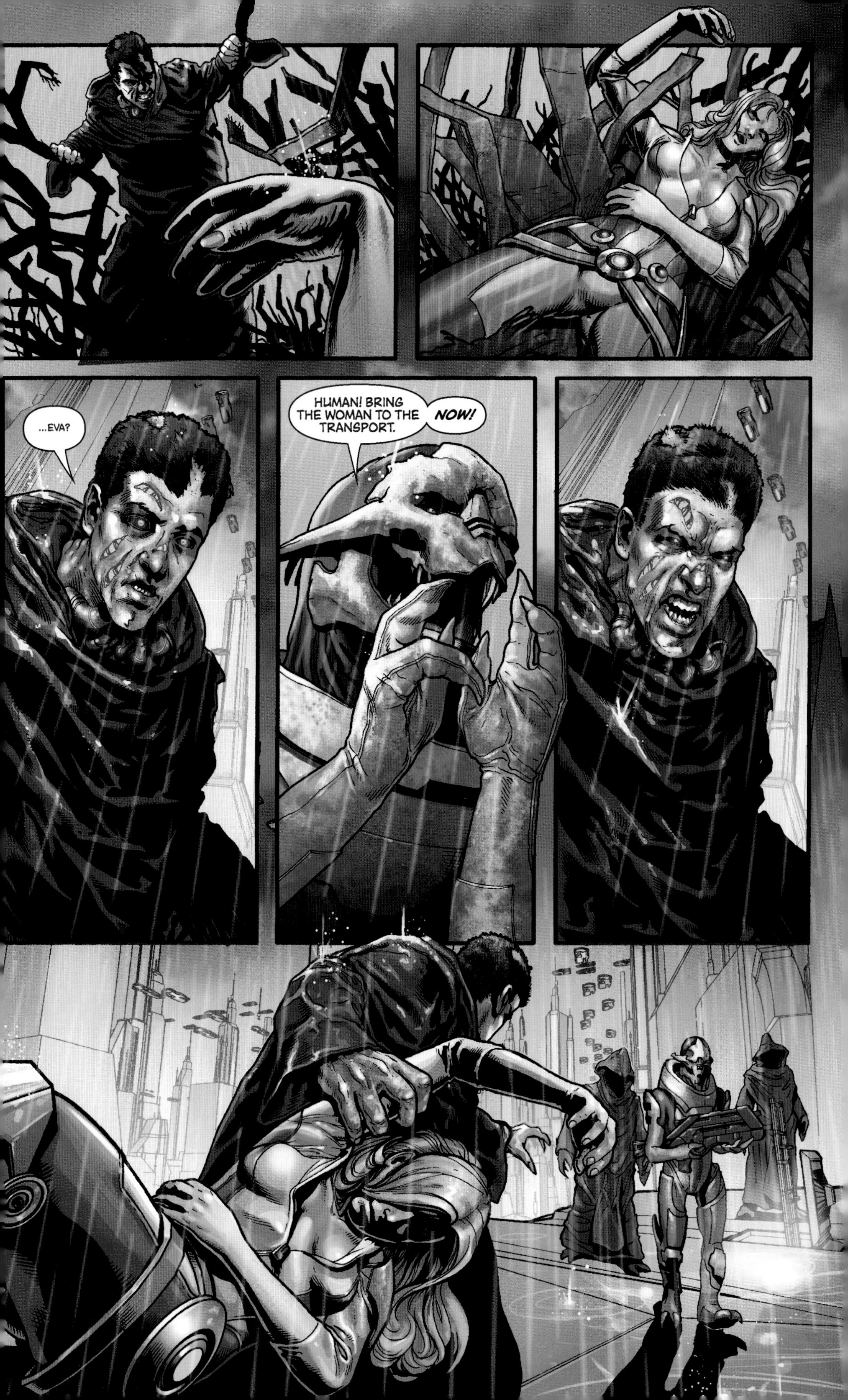

...EVA?
HUMAN! BRING THE WOMAN TO THE TRANSPORT.
NOW!

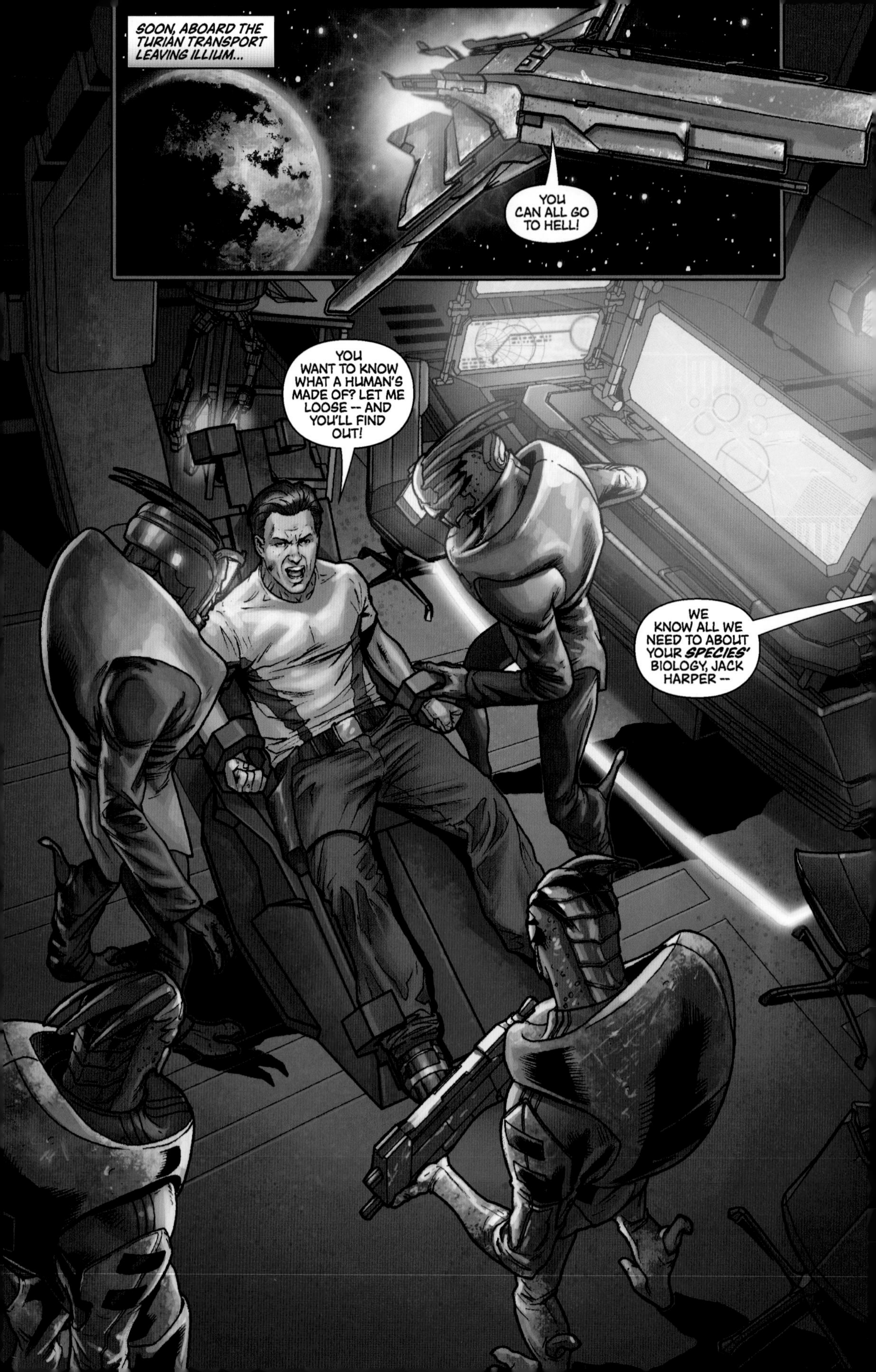
SOON, ABOARD THE TURIAN TRANSPORT LEAVING ILLIUM...
YOU CAN ALL GO TO HELL!
YOU WANT TO KNOW WHAT A HUMAN'S MADE OF? LET ME LOOSE -- AND YOU'LL FIND OUT!
WE KNOW ALL WE NEED TO ABOUT YOUR *SPECIES'* BIOLOGY, JACK HARPER --

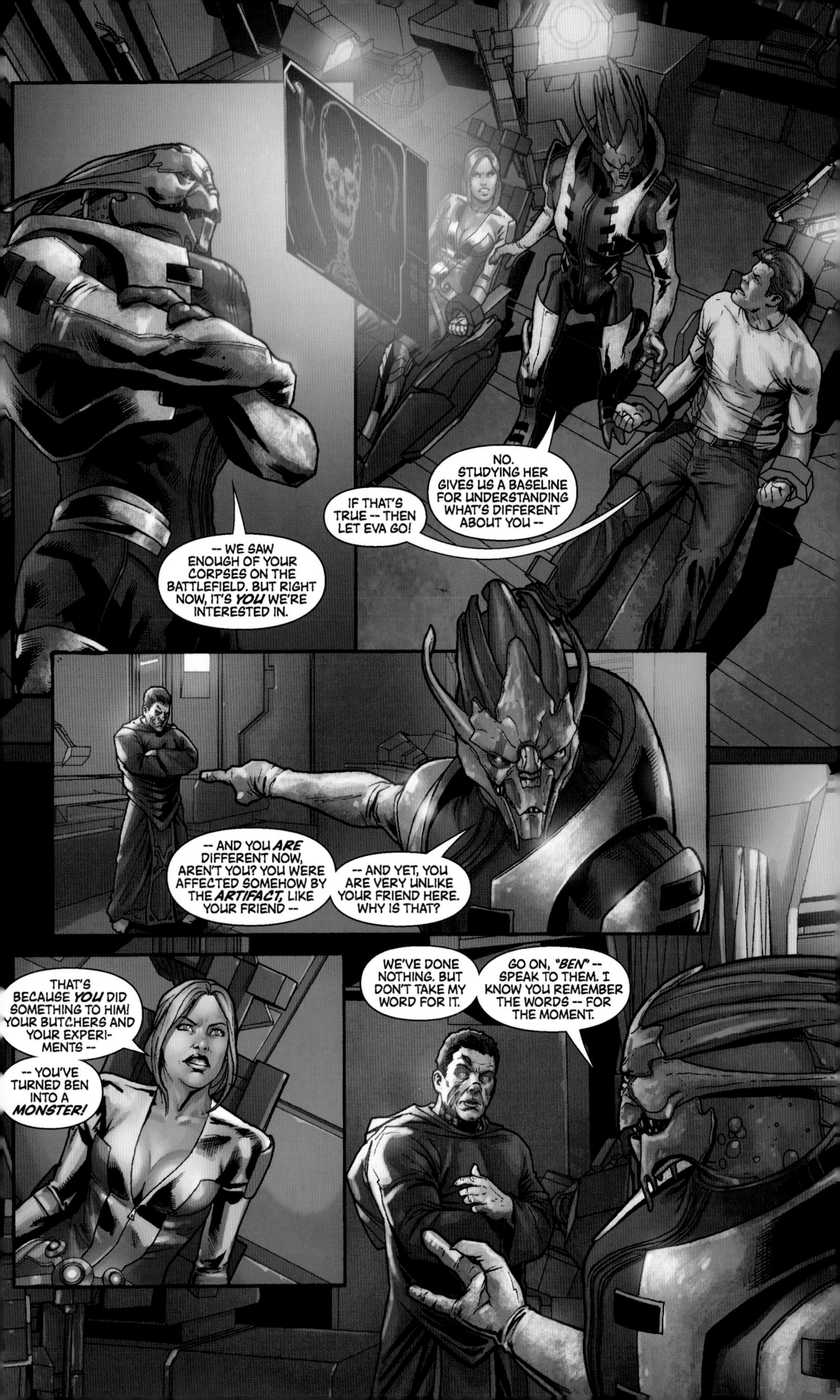
-- WE SAW ENOUGH OF YOUR CORPSES ON THE BATTLEFIELD. BUT RIGHT NOW, IT'S *YOU* WE'RE INTERESTED IN.
IF THAT'S TRUE -- THEN LET EVA GO!
NO. STUDYING HER GIVES US A BASELINE FOR UNDERSTANDING WHAT'S DIFFERENT ABOUT YOU --
-- AND YOU *ARE* DIFFERENT NOW, AREN'T YOU? YOU WERE AFFECTED SOMEHOW BY THE *ARTIFACT,* LIKE YOUR FRIEND --
-- AND YET, YOU ARE VERY UNLIKE YOUR FRIEND HERE. WHY IS THAT?
THAT'S BECAUSE *YOU* DID SOMETHING TO HIM! YOUR BUTCHERS AND YOUR EXPERI-MENTS --
-- YOU'VE TURNED BEN INTO A *MONSTER!*
WE'VE DONE NOTHING. BUT DON'T TAKE MY WORD FOR IT.
GO ON, *"BEN"* -- SPEAK TO THEM. I KNOW YOU REMEMBER THE WORDS -- FOR THE MOMENT.

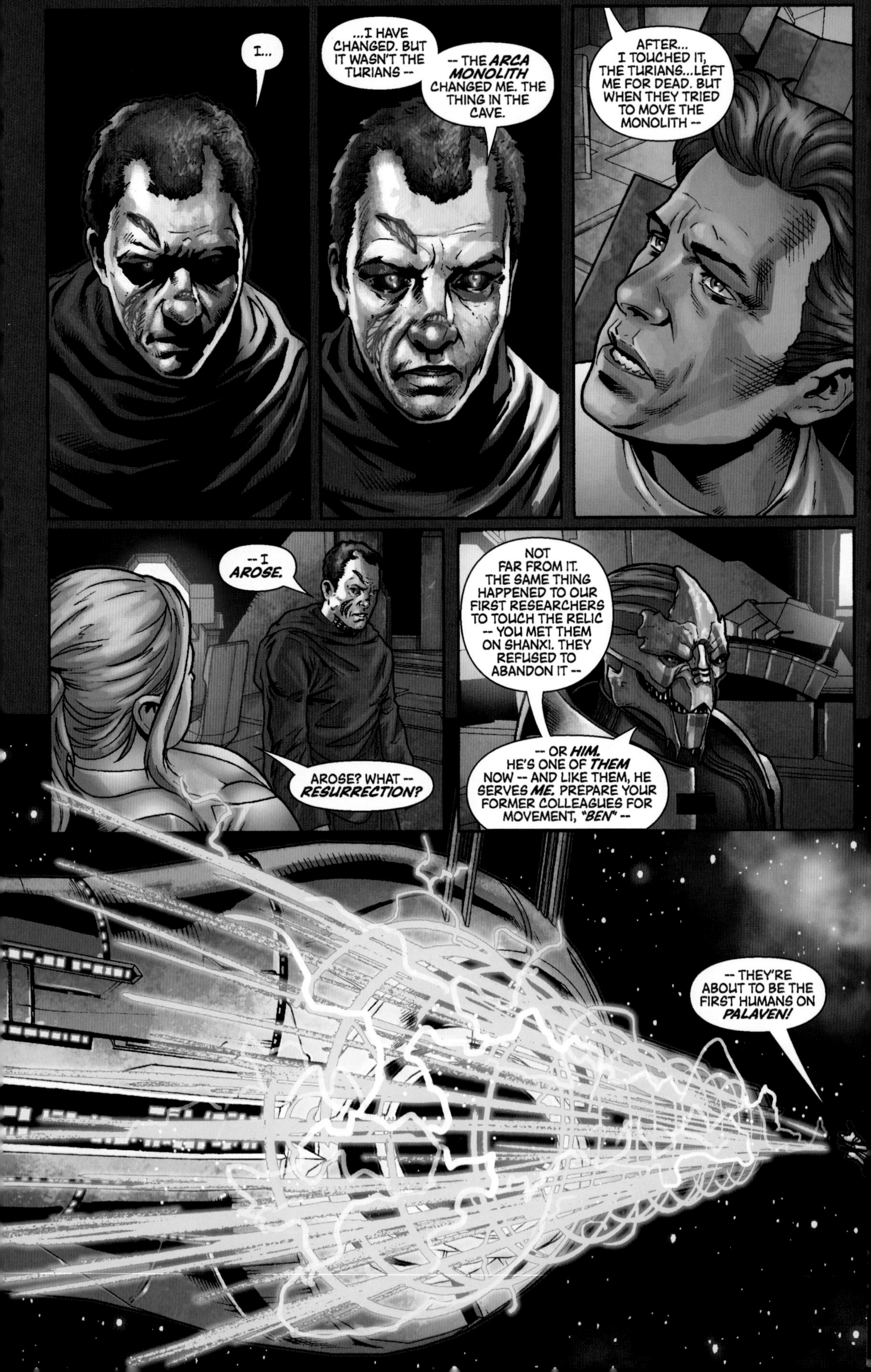
I...
...I HAVE CHANGED. BUT IT WASN'T THE TURIANS --
-- THE ARCA MONOLITH CHANGED ME. THE THING IN THE CAVE.
AFTER... I TOUCHED IT, THE TURIANS...LEFT ME FOR DEAD. BUT WHEN THEY TRIED TO MOVE THE MONOLITH --
-- I AROSE.
AROSE? WHAT -- RESURRECTION?
NOT FAR FROM IT. THE SAME THING HAPPENED TO OUR FIRST RESEARCHERS TO TOUCH THE RELIC -- YOU MET THEM ON SHANXI. THEY REFUSED TO ABANDON IT --
-- OR HIM. HE'S ONE OF THEM NOW -- AND LIKE THEM, HE SERVES ME. PREPARE YOUR FORMER COLLEAGUES FOR MOVEMENT, "BEN" --
-- THEY'RE ABOUT TO BE THE FIRST HUMANS ON PALAVEN!

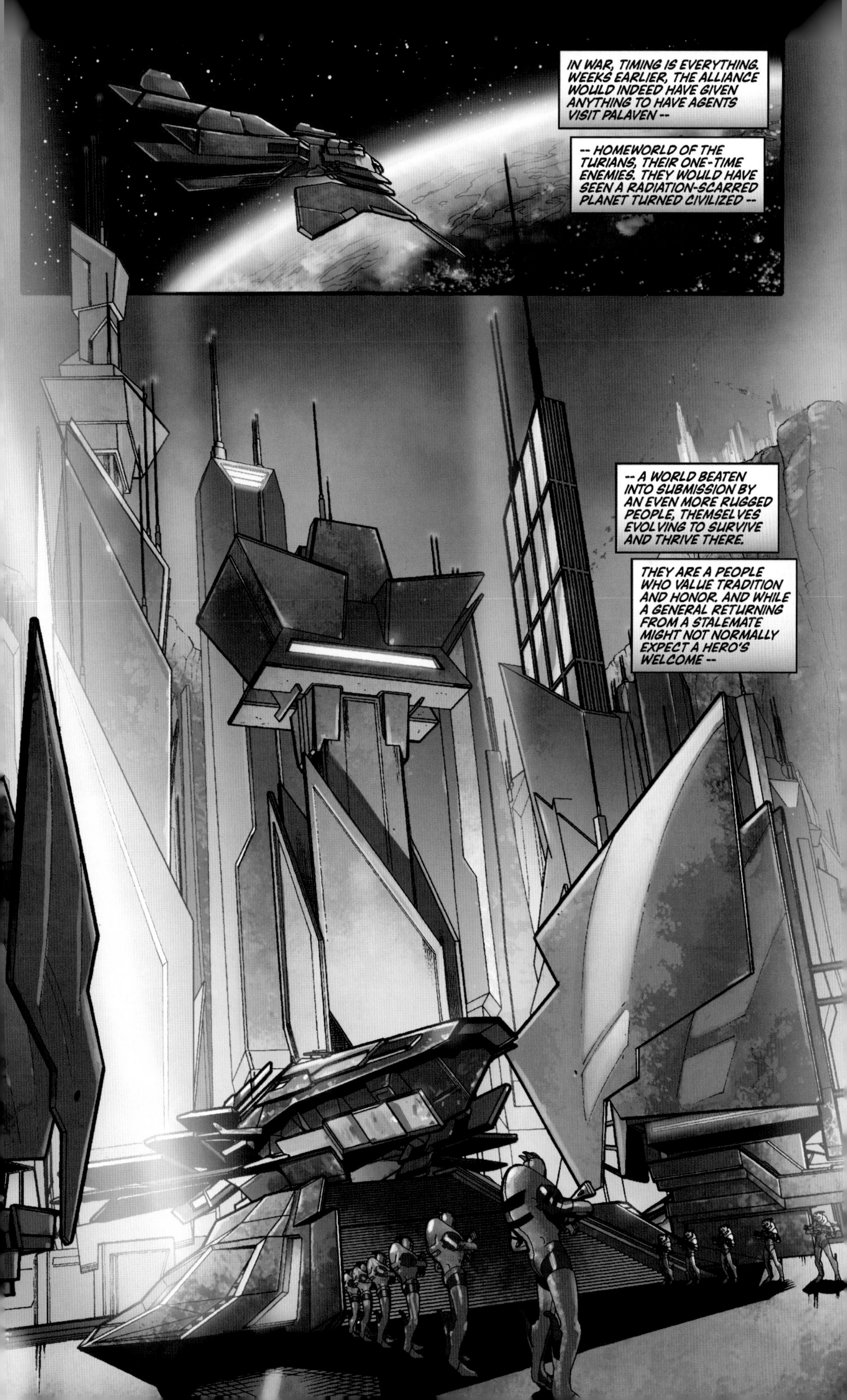
IN WAR, TIMING IS EVERYTHING. WEEKS EARLIER, THE ALLIANCE WOULD INDEED HAVE GIVEN ANYTHING TO HAVE AGENTS VISIT PALAVEN --
-- HOMEWORLD OF THE TURIANS, THEIR ONE-TIME ENEMIES. THEY WOULD HAVE SEEN A RADIATION-SCARRED PLANET TURNED CIVILIZED --
-- A WORLD BEATEN INTO SUBMISSION BY AN EVEN MORE RUGGED PEOPLE, THEMSELVES EVOLVING TO SURVIVE AND THRIVE THERE.
THEY ARE A PEOPLE WHO VALUE TRADITION AND HONOR. AND WHILE A GENERAL RETURNING FROM A STALEMATE MIGHT NOT NORMALLY EXPECT A HERO'S WELCOME --

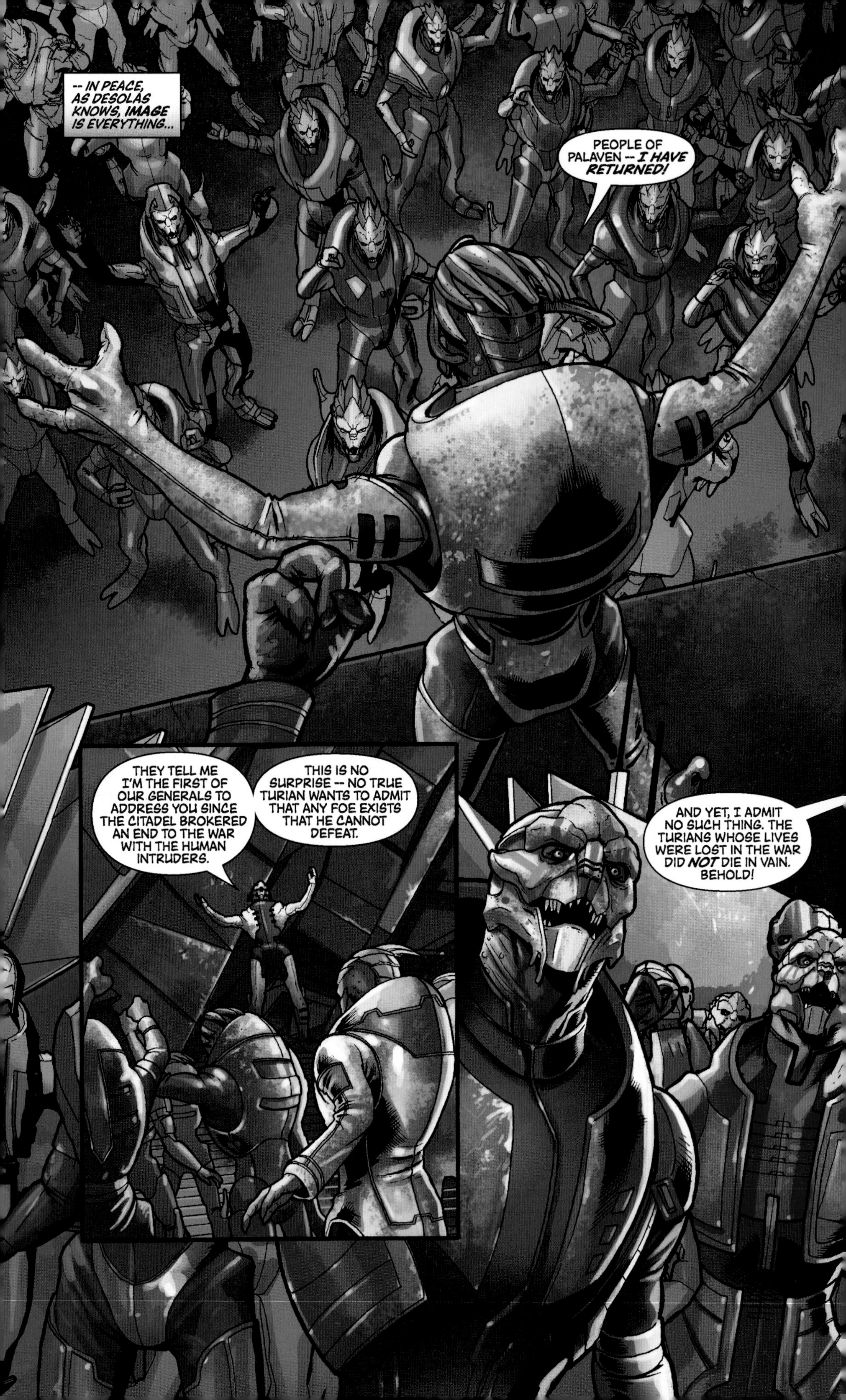
-- IN PEACE, AS DESOLAS KNOWS, IMAGE IS EVERYTHING...
PEOPLE OF PALAVEN -- I HAVE RETURNED!
THEY TELL ME I'M THE FIRST OF OUR GENERALS TO ADDRESS YOU SINCE THE CITADEL BROKERED AN END TO THE WAR WITH THE HUMAN INTRUDERS.
THIS IS NO SURPRISE -- NO TRUE TURIAN WANTS TO ADMIT THAT ANY FOE EXISTS THAT HE CANNOT DEFEAT.
AND YET, I ADMIT NO SUCH THING. THE TURIANS WHOSE LIVES WERE LOST IN THE WAR DID NOT DIE IN VAIN. BEHOLD!

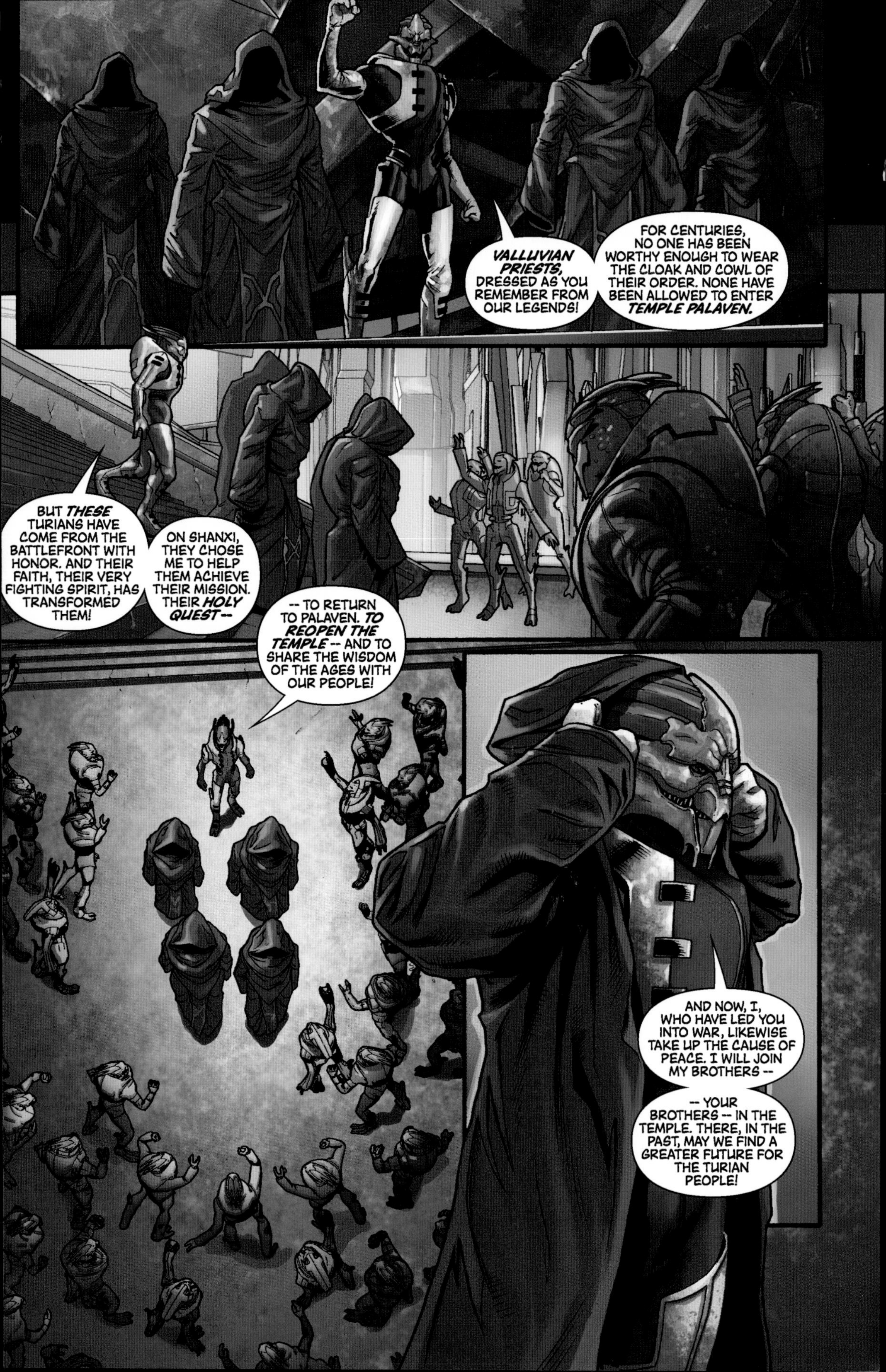
VALLUVIAN PRIESTS, DRESSED AS YOU REMEMBER FROM OUR LEGENDS!
FOR CENTURIES, NO ONE HAS BEEN WORTHY ENOUGH TO WEAR THE CLOAK AND COWL OF THEIR ORDER. NONE HAVE BEEN ALLOWED TO ENTER TEMPLE PALAVEN.
BUT THESE TURIANS HAVE COME FROM THE BATTLEFRONT WITH HONOR. AND THEIR FAITH, THEIR VERY FIGHTING SPIRIT, HAS TRANSFORMED THEM!
ON SHANXI, THEY CHOSE ME TO HELP THEM ACHIEVE THEIR MISSION. THEIR HOLY QUEST --
-- TO RETURN TO PALAVEN. TO REOPEN THE TEMPLE -- AND TO SHARE THE WISDOM OF THE AGES WITH OUR PEOPLE!
AND NOW, I, WHO HAVE LED YOU INTO WAR, LIKEWISE TAKE UP THE CAUSE OF PEACE. I WILL JOIN MY BROTHERS --
-- YOUR BROTHERS -- IN THE TEMPLE. THERE, IN THE PAST, MAY WE FIND A GREATER FUTURE FOR THE TURIAN PEOPLE!

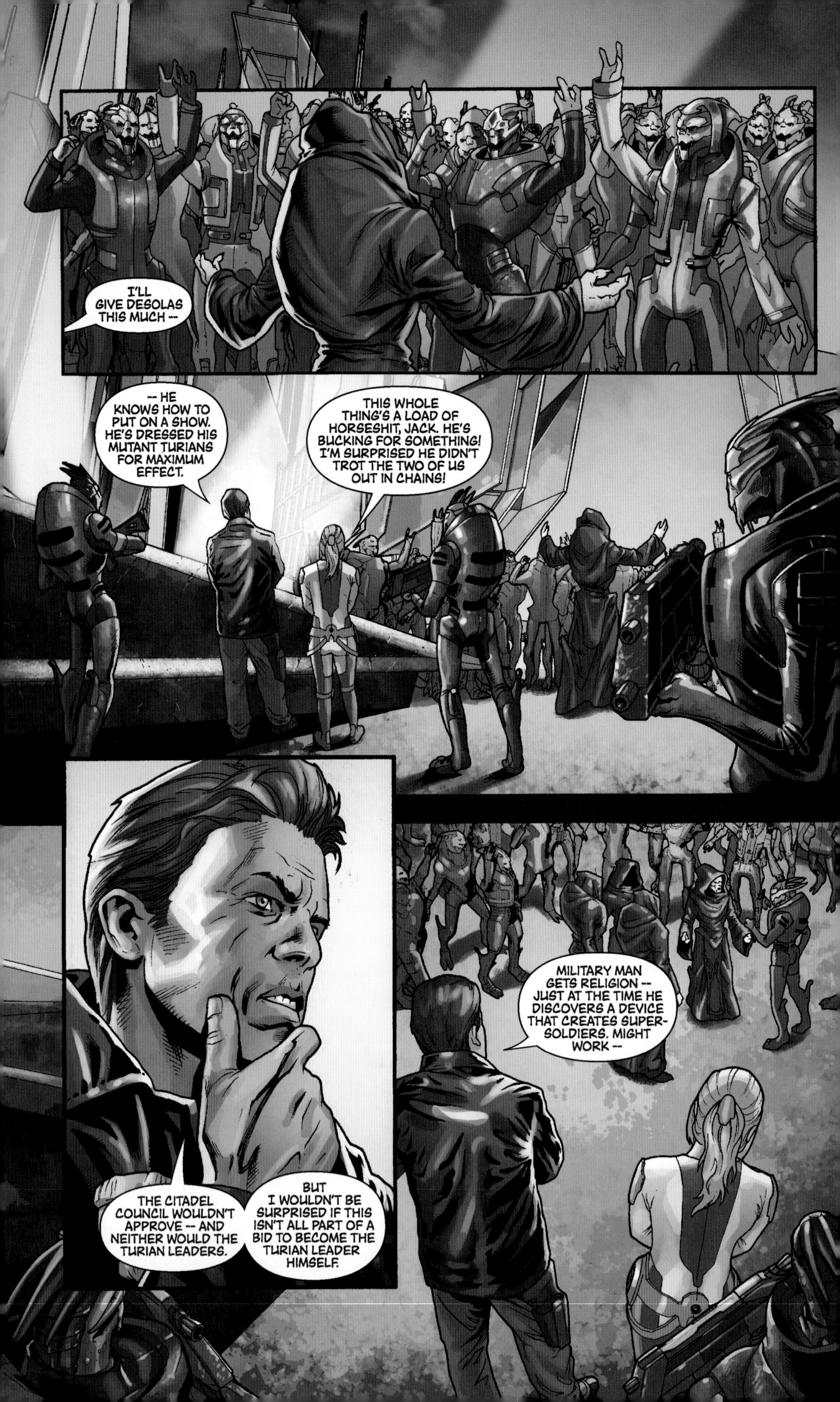

I'LL GIVE DESOLAS THIS MUCH --
-- HE KNOWS HOW TO PUT ON A SHOW. HE'S DRESSED HIS MUTANT TURIANS FOR MAXIMUM EFFECT.
THIS WHOLE THING'S A LOAD OF HORSESHIT, JACK. HE'S BUCKING FOR SOMETHING! I'M SURPRISED HE DIDN'T TROT THE TWO OF US OUT IN CHAINS!
MILITARY MAN GETS RELIGION -- JUST AT THE TIME HE DISCOVERS A DEVICE THAT CREATES SUPER-SOLDIERS. MIGHT WORK --
THE CITADEL COUNCIL WOULDN'T APPROVE -- AND NEITHER WOULD THE TURIAN LEADERS.
BUT I WOULDN'T BE SURPRISED IF THIS ISN'T ALL PART OF A BID TO BECOME THE TURIAN LEADER HIMSELF.

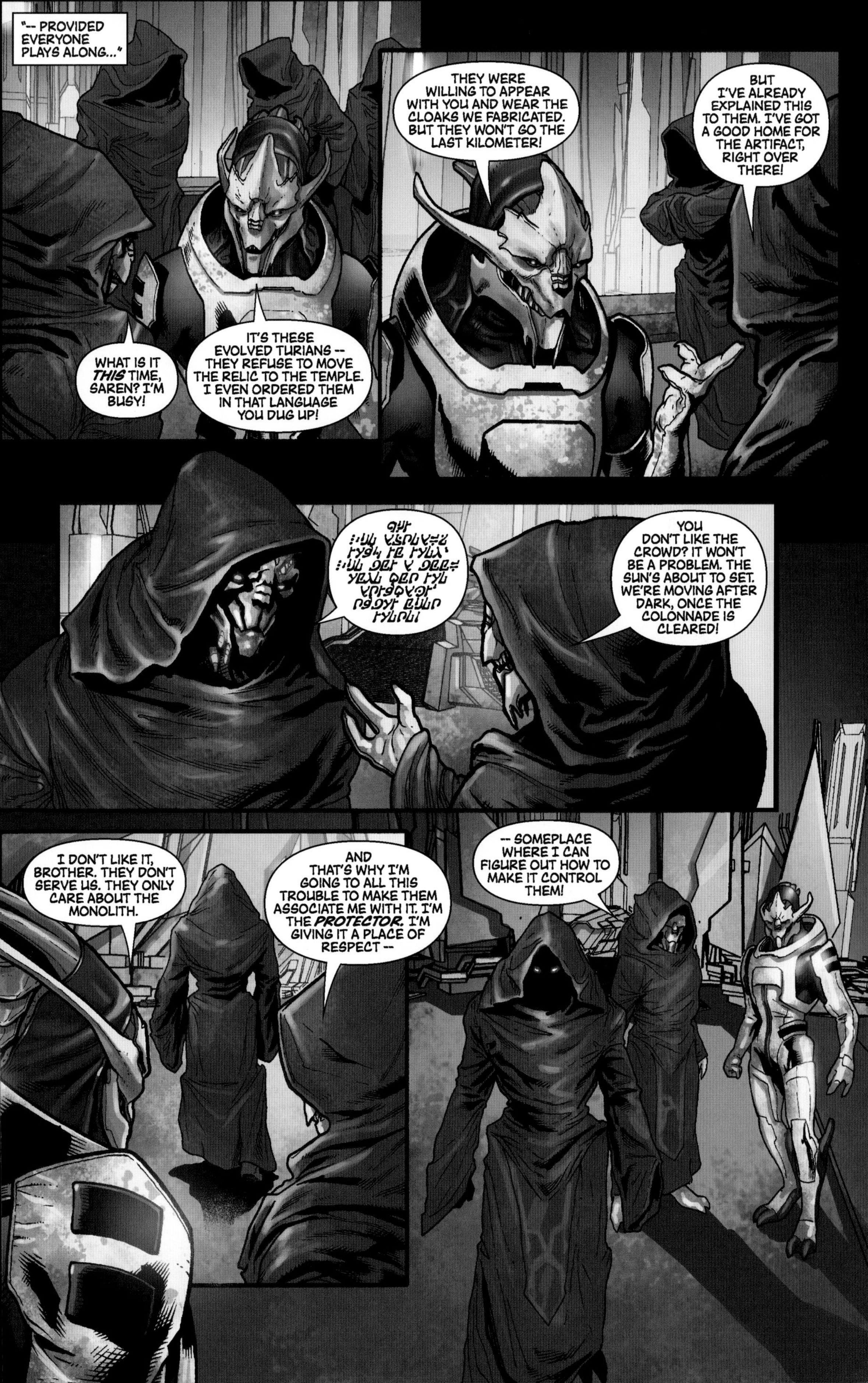
"-- PROVIDED EVERYONE PLAYS ALONG..."
WHAT IS IT *THIS* TIME, SAREN? I'M BUSY!
IT'S THESE EVOLVED TURIANS -- THEY REFUSE TO MOVE THE RELIC TO THE TEMPLE. I EVEN ORDERED THEM IN THAT LANGUAGE YOU DUG UP!
THEY WERE WILLING TO APPEAR WITH YOU AND WEAR THE CLOAKS WE FABRICATED. BUT THEY WON'T GO THE LAST KILOMETER!
BUT I'VE ALREADY EXPLAINED THIS TO THEM. I'VE GOT A GOOD HOME FOR THE ARTIFACT, RIGHT OVER THERE!
YOU DON'T LIKE THE CROWD? IT WON'T BE A PROBLEM. THE SUN'S ABOUT TO SET. WE'RE MOVING AFTER DARK, ONCE THE COLONNADE IS CLEARED!
I DON'T LIKE IT, BROTHER. THEY DON'T SERVE US. THEY ONLY CARE ABOUT THE MONOLITH.
AND THAT'S WHY I'M GOING TO ALL THIS TROUBLE TO MAKE THEM ASSOCIATE ME WITH IT. I'M THE *PROTECTOR*. I'M GIVING IT A PLACE OF RESPECT --
-- SOMEPLACE WHERE I CAN FIGURE OUT HOW TO MAKE IT CONTROL THEM!

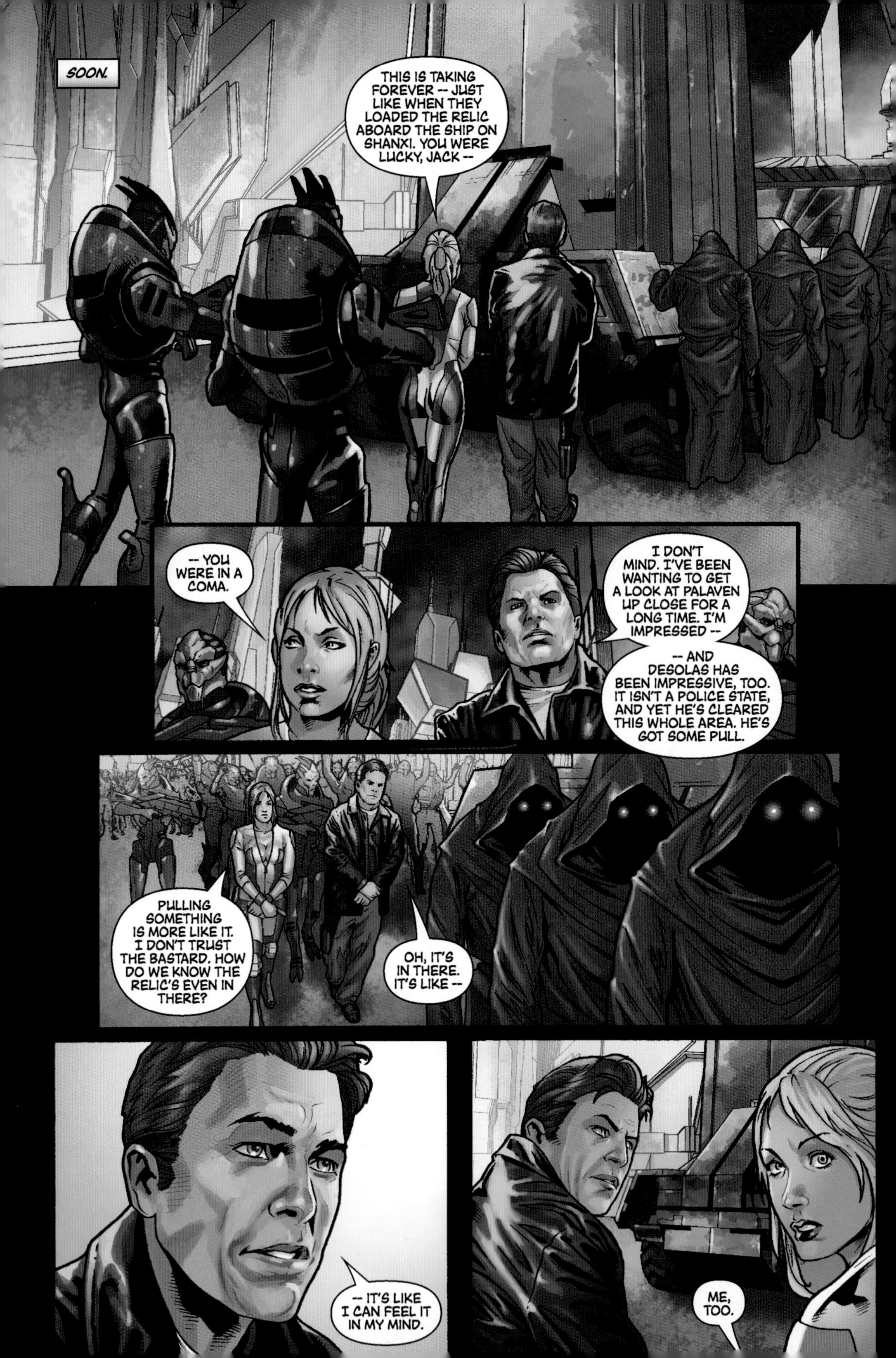
SOON.
THIS IS TAKING FOREVER -- JUST LIKE WHEN THEY LOADED THE RELIC ABOARD THE SHIP ON SHANXI. YOU WERE LUCKY, JACK --
-- YOU WERE IN A COMA.
I DON'T MIND. I'VE BEEN WANTING TO GET A LOOK AT PALAVEN UP CLOSE FOR A LONG TIME. I'M IMPRESSED --
-- AND DESOLAS HAS BEEN IMPRESSIVE, TOO. IT ISN'T A POLICE STATE, AND YET HE'S CLEARED THIS WHOLE AREA. HE'S GOT SOME PULL.
PULLING SOMETHING IS MORE LIKE IT. I DON'T TRUST THE BASTARD. HOW DO WE KNOW THE RELIC'S EVEN IN THERE?
OH, IT'S IN THERE. IT'S LIKE --
-- IT'S LIKE I CAN FEEL IT IN MY MIND.
ME, TOO.

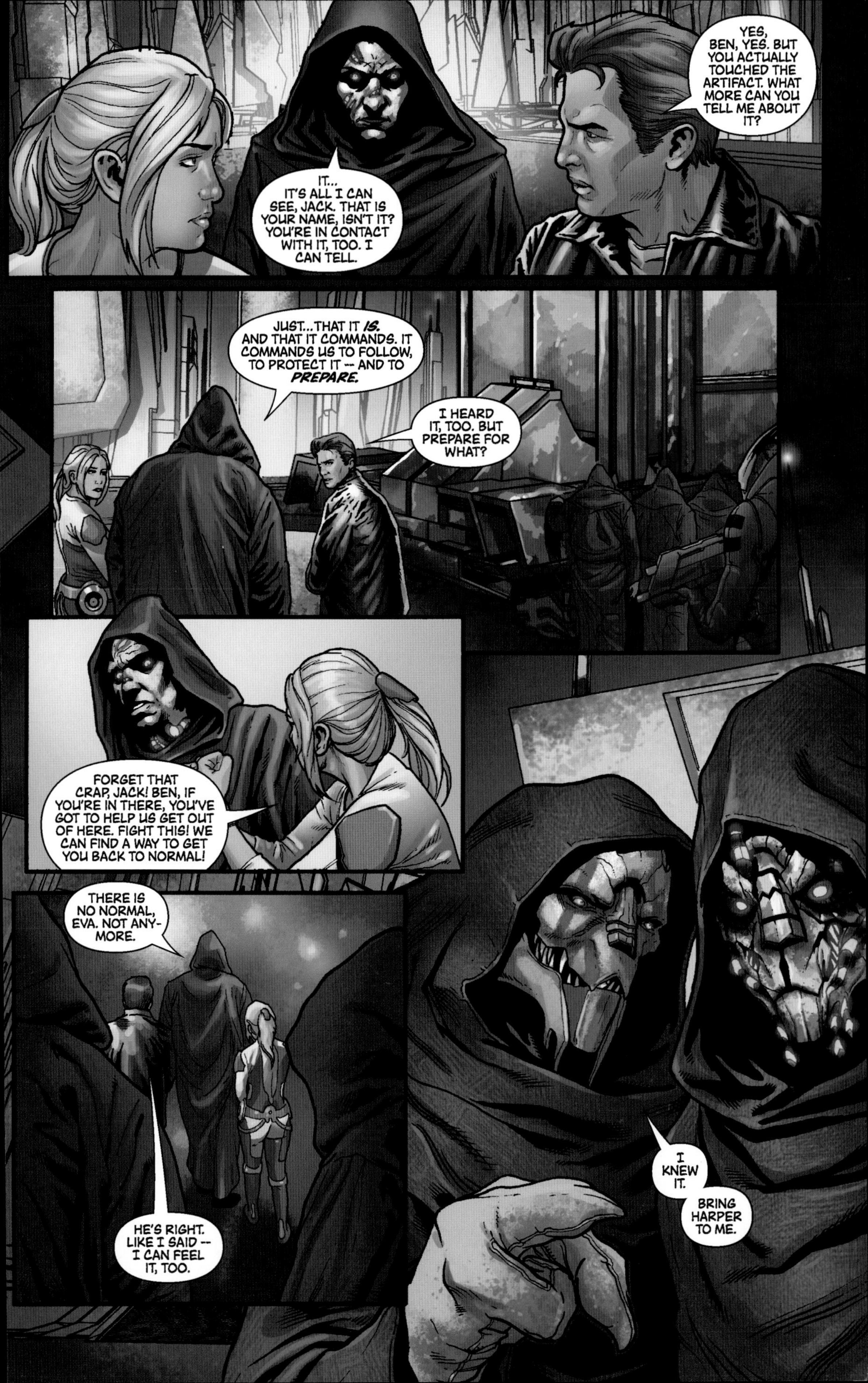
YES, BEN, YES. BUT YOU ACTUALLY TOUCHED THE ARTIFACT. WHAT MORE CAN YOU TELL ME ABOUT IT?
IT... IT'S ALL I CAN SEE, JACK. THAT IS YOUR NAME, ISN'T IT? YOU'RE IN CONTACT WITH IT, TOO. I CAN TELL.
JUST...THAT IT *IS.* AND THAT IT COMMANDS. IT COMMANDS US TO FOLLOW, TO PROTECT IT -- AND TO ***PREPARE.***
I HEARD IT, TOO. BUT PREPARE FOR WHAT?
FORGET THAT CRAP, JACK! BEN, IF YOU'RE IN THERE, YOU'VE GOT TO HELP US GET OUT OF HERE. FIGHT THIS! WE CAN FIND A WAY TO GET YOU BACK TO NORMAL!
THERE IS NO NORMAL, EVA. NOT ANY-MORE.
HE'S RIGHT. LIKE I SAID -- I CAN FEEL IT, TOO.
I KNEW IT.
BRING HARPER TO ME.

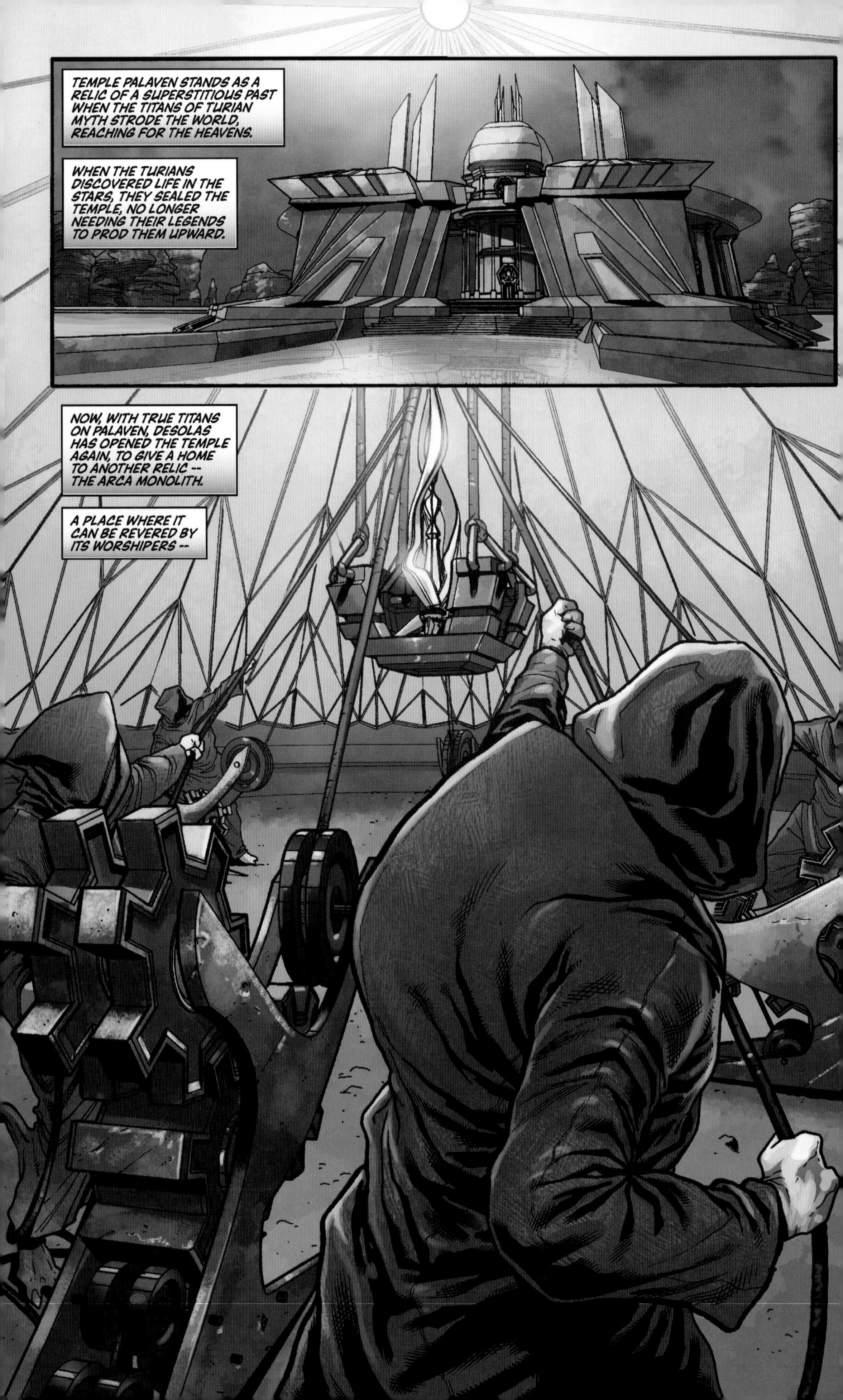
TEMPLE PALAVEN STANDS AS A RELIC OF A SUPERSTITIOUS PAST WHEN THE TITANS OF TURIAN MYTH STRODE THE WORLD, REACHING FOR THE HEAVENS.
WHEN THE TURIANS DISCOVERED LIFE IN THE STARS, THEY SEALED THE TEMPLE, NO LONGER NEEDING THEIR LEGENDS TO PROD THEM UPWARD.
NOW, WITH TRUE TITANS ON PALAVEN, DESOLAS HAS OPENED THE TEMPLE AGAIN, TO GIVE A HOME TO ANOTHER RELIC -- THE ARCA MONOLITH.
A PLACE WHERE IT CAN BE REVERED BY ITS WORSHIPERS --

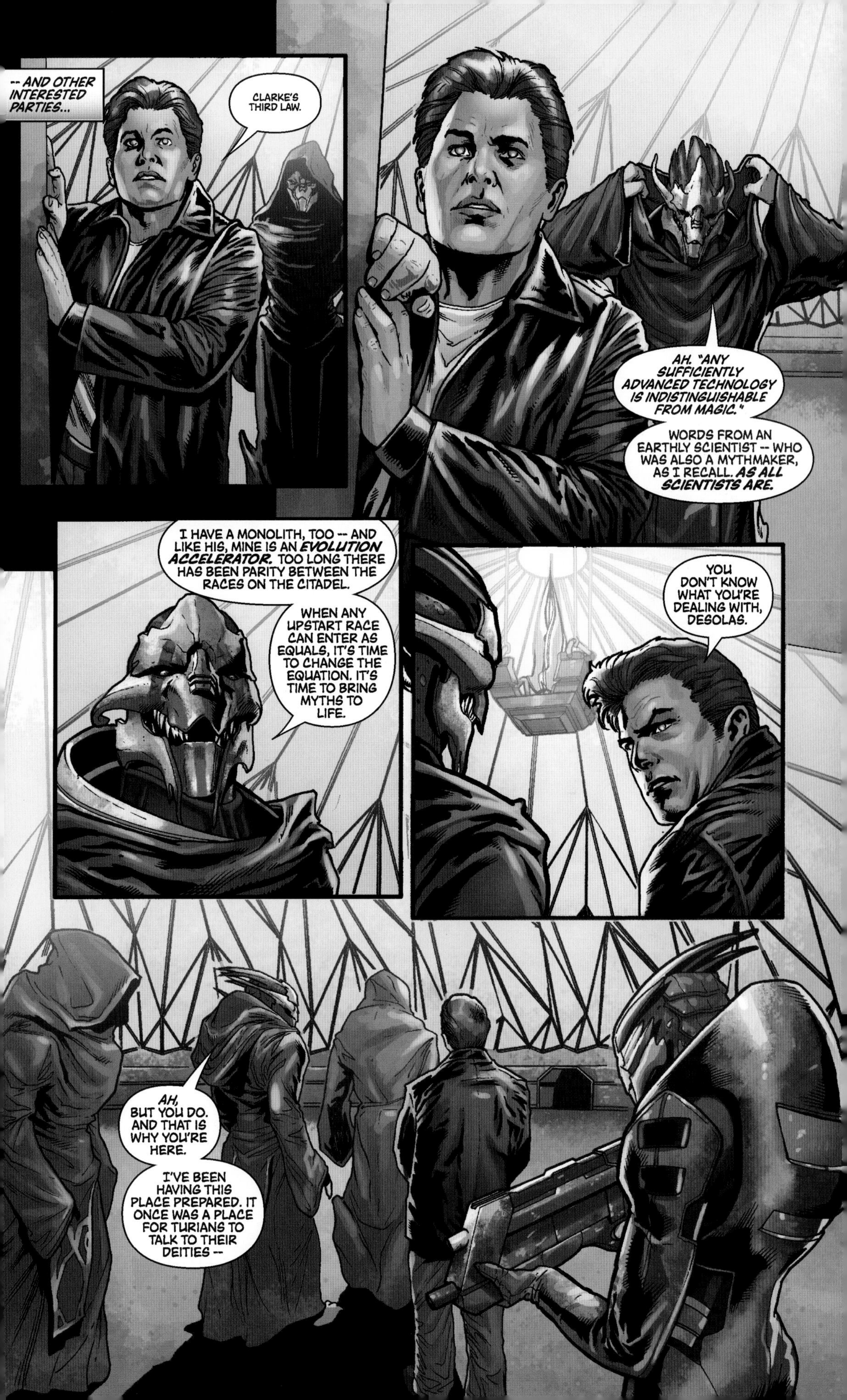
-- AND OTHER INTERESTED PARTIES...
CLARKE'S THIRD LAW.
AH. "ANY SUFFICIENTLY ADVANCED TECHNOLOGY IS INDISTINGUISHABLE FROM MAGIC."
WORDS FROM AN EARTHLY SCIENTIST -- WHO WAS ALSO A MYTHMAKER, AS I RECALL. AS ALL SCIENTISTS ARE.
I HAVE A MONOLITH, TOO -- AND LIKE HIS, MINE IS AN EVOLUTION ACCELERATOR. TOO LONG THERE HAS BEEN PARITY BETWEEN THE RACES ON THE CITADEL.
WHEN ANY UPSTART RACE CAN ENTER AS EQUALS, IT'S TIME TO CHANGE THE EQUATION. IT'S TIME TO BRING MYTHS TO LIFE.
YOU DON'T KNOW WHAT YOU'RE DEALING WITH, DESOLAS.
AH, BUT YOU DO. AND THAT IS WHY YOU'RE HERE.
I'VE BEEN HAVING THIS PLACE PREPARED. IT ONCE WAS A PLACE FOR TURIANS TO TALK TO THEIR DEITIES --

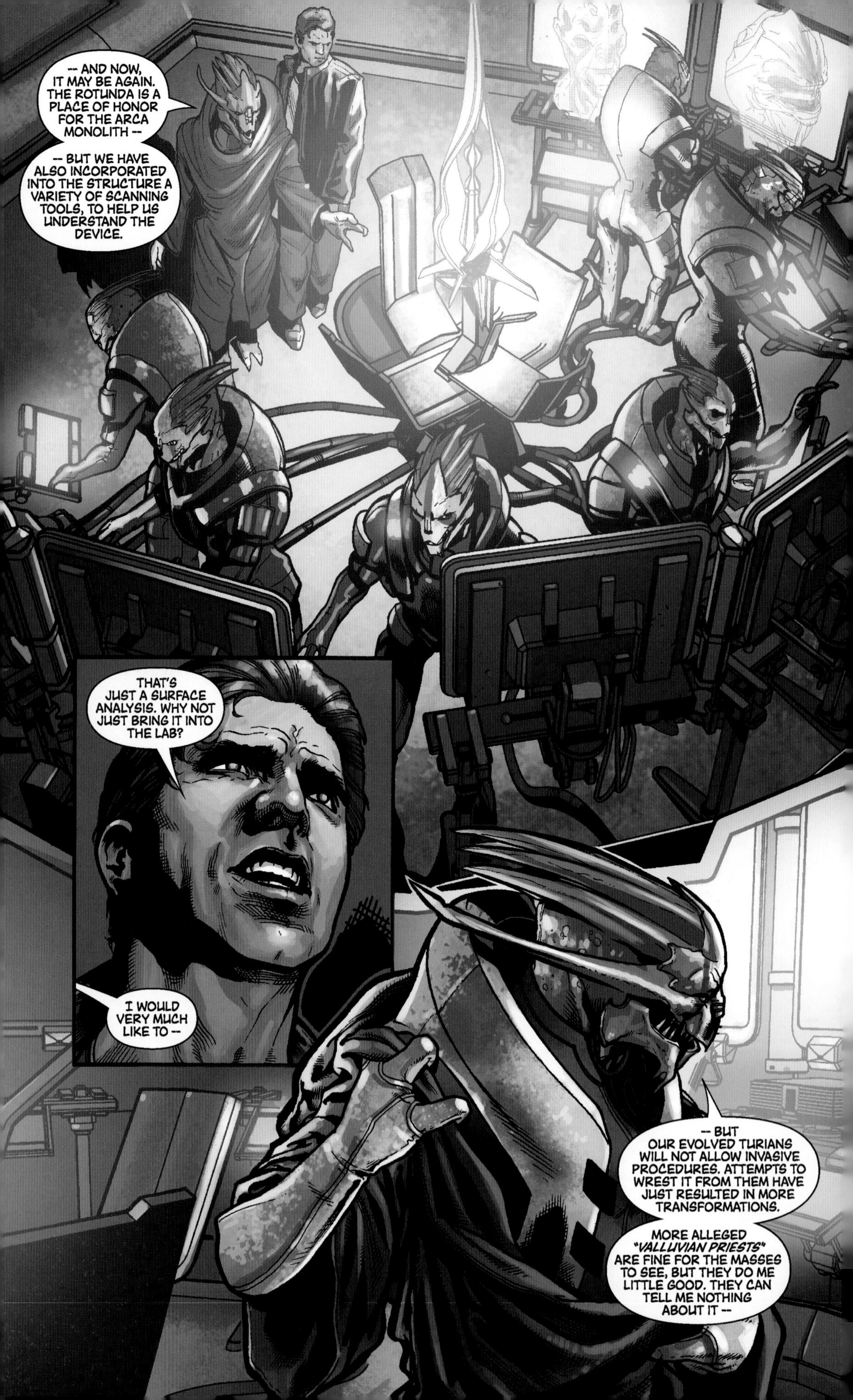
-- AND NOW, IT MAY BE AGAIN. THE ROTUNDA IS A PLACE OF HONOR FOR THE ARCA MONOLITH --
-- BUT WE HAVE ALSO INCORPORATED INTO THE STRUCTURE A VARIETY OF SCANNING TOOLS, TO HELP US UNDERSTAND THE DEVICE.
THAT'S JUST A SURFACE ANALYSIS. WHY NOT JUST BRING IT INTO THE LAB?
I WOULD VERY MUCH LIKE TO --
-- BUT OUR EVOLVED TURIANS WILL NOT ALLOW INVASIVE PROCEDURES. ATTEMPTS TO WREST IT FROM THEM HAVE JUST RESULTED IN MORE TRANSFORMATIONS.
MORE ALLEGED *"VALLUVIAN PRIESTS"* ARE FINE FOR THE MASSES TO SEE, BUT THEY DO ME LITTLE GOOD. THEY CAN TELL ME NOTHING ABOUT IT --

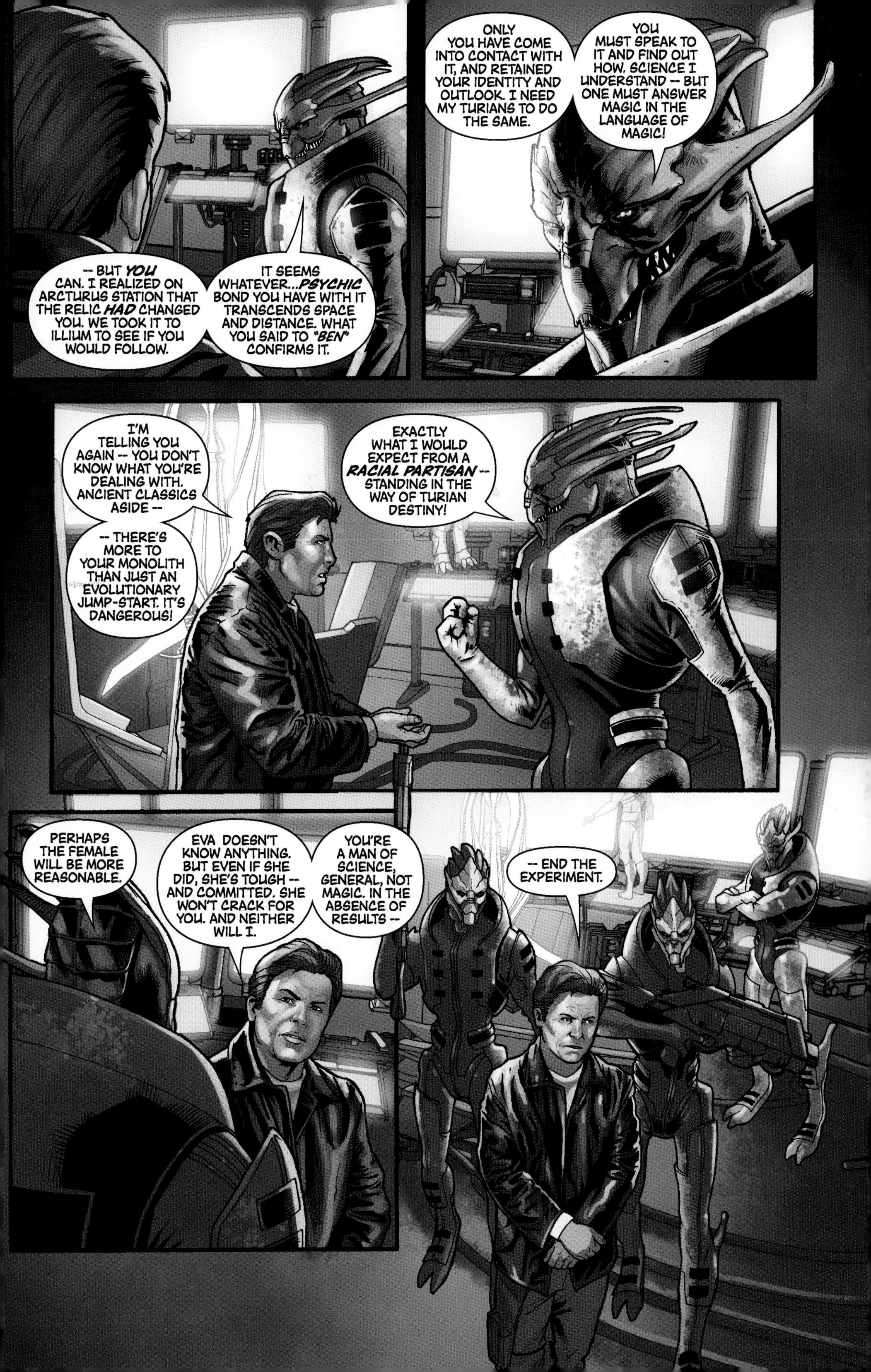
-- BUT YOU CAN. I REALIZED ON ARCTURUS STATION THAT THE RELIC HAD CHANGED YOU. WE TOOK IT TO ILLIUM TO SEE IF YOU WOULD FOLLOW.
IT SEEMS WHATEVER...PSYCHIC BOND YOU HAVE WITH IT TRANSCENDS SPACE AND DISTANCE. WHAT YOU SAID TO "BEN" CONFIRMS IT.
ONLY YOU HAVE COME INTO CONTACT WITH IT, AND RETAINED YOUR IDENTITY AND OUTLOOK. I NEED MY TURIANS TO DO THE SAME.
YOU MUST SPEAK TO IT AND FIND OUT HOW. SCIENCE I UNDERSTAND -- BUT ONE MUST ANSWER MAGIC IN THE LANGUAGE OF MAGIC!
I'M TELLING YOU AGAIN -- YOU DON'T KNOW WHAT YOU'RE DEALING WITH. ANCIENT CLASSICS ASIDE --
-- THERE'S MORE TO YOUR MONOLITH THAN JUST AN EVOLUTIONARY JUMP-START. IT'S DANGEROUS!
EXACTLY WHAT I WOULD EXPECT FROM A RACIAL PARTISAN -- STANDING IN THE WAY OF TURIAN DESTINY!
PERHAPS THE FEMALE WILL BE MORE REASONABLE.
EVA DOESN'T KNOW ANYTHING. BUT EVEN IF SHE DID, SHE'S TOUGH -- AND COMMITTED. SHE WON'T CRACK FOR YOU. AND NEITHER WILL I.
YOU'RE A MAN OF SCIENCE, GENERAL, NOT MAGIC. IN THE ABSENCE OF RESULTS --
-- END THE EXPERIMENT.

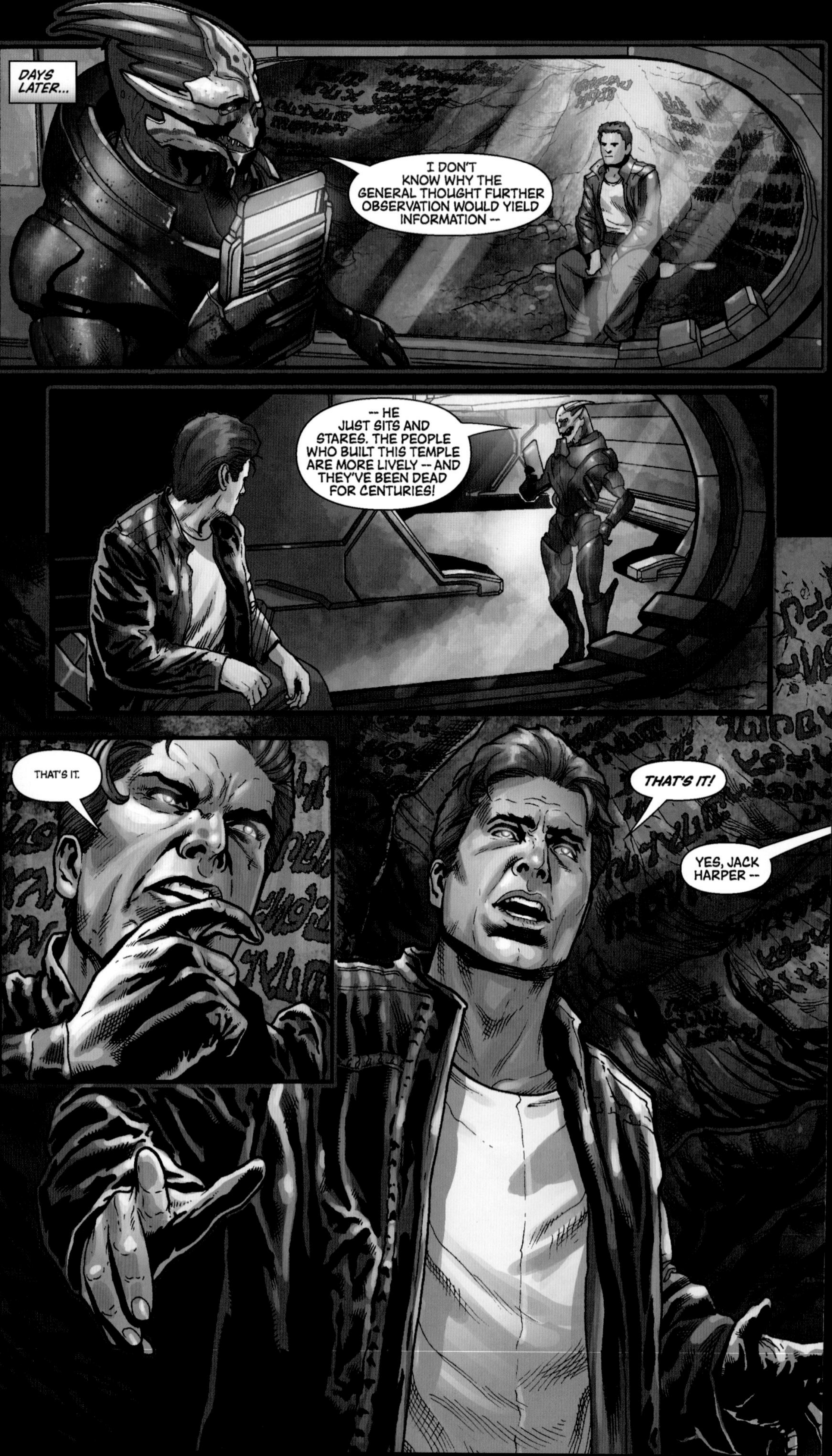
DAYS LATER...
I DON'T KNOW WHY THE GENERAL THOUGHT FURTHER OBSERVATION WOULD YIELD INFORMATION --
-- HE JUST SITS AND STARES. THE PEOPLE WHO BUILT THIS TEMPLE ARE MORE LIVELY -- AND THEY'VE BEEN DEAD FOR CENTURIES!
THAT'S IT.
THAT'S IT!
YES, JACK HARPER --

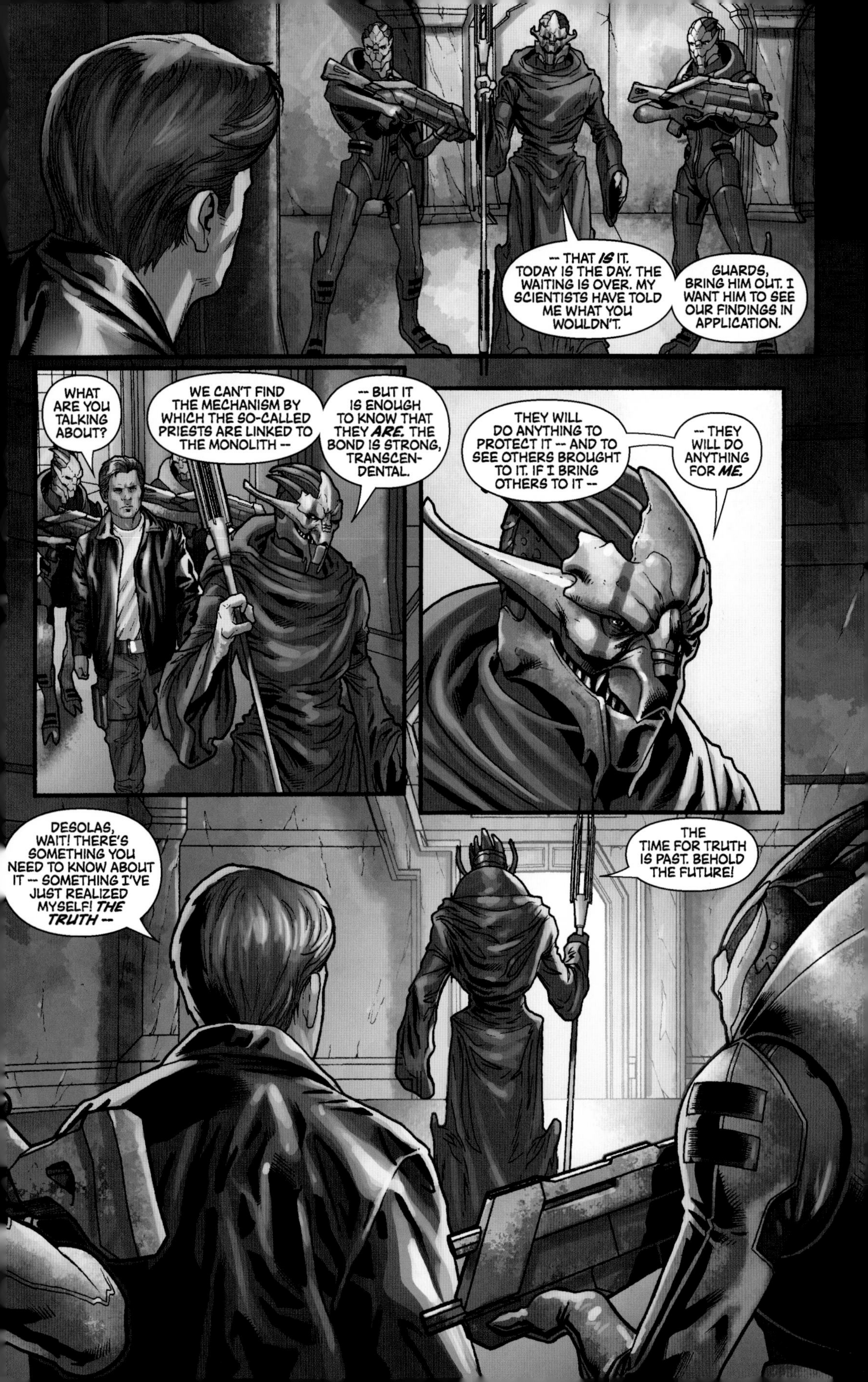
-- THAT *IS* IT. TODAY IS THE DAY. THE WAITING IS OVER. MY SCIENTISTS HAVE TOLD ME WHAT YOU WOULDN'T.
GUARDS, BRING HIM OUT. I WANT HIM TO SEE OUR FINDINGS IN APPLICATION.
WHAT ARE YOU TALKING ABOUT?
WE CAN'T FIND THE MECHANISM BY WHICH THE SO-CALLED PRIESTS ARE LINKED TO THE MONOLITH --
-- BUT IT IS ENOUGH TO KNOW THAT THEY *ARE.* THE BOND IS STRONG, TRANSCEN-DENTAL.
THEY WILL DO ANYTHING TO PROTECT IT -- AND TO SEE OTHERS BROUGHT TO IT. IF I BRING OTHERS TO IT --
-- THEY WILL DO ANYTHING FOR *ME.*
DESOLAS, WAIT! THERE'S SOMETHING YOU NEED TO KNOW ABOUT IT -- SOMETHING I'VE JUST REALIZED MYSELF! *THE TRUTH* --
THE TIME FOR TRUTH IS PAST. BEHOLD THE FUTURE!

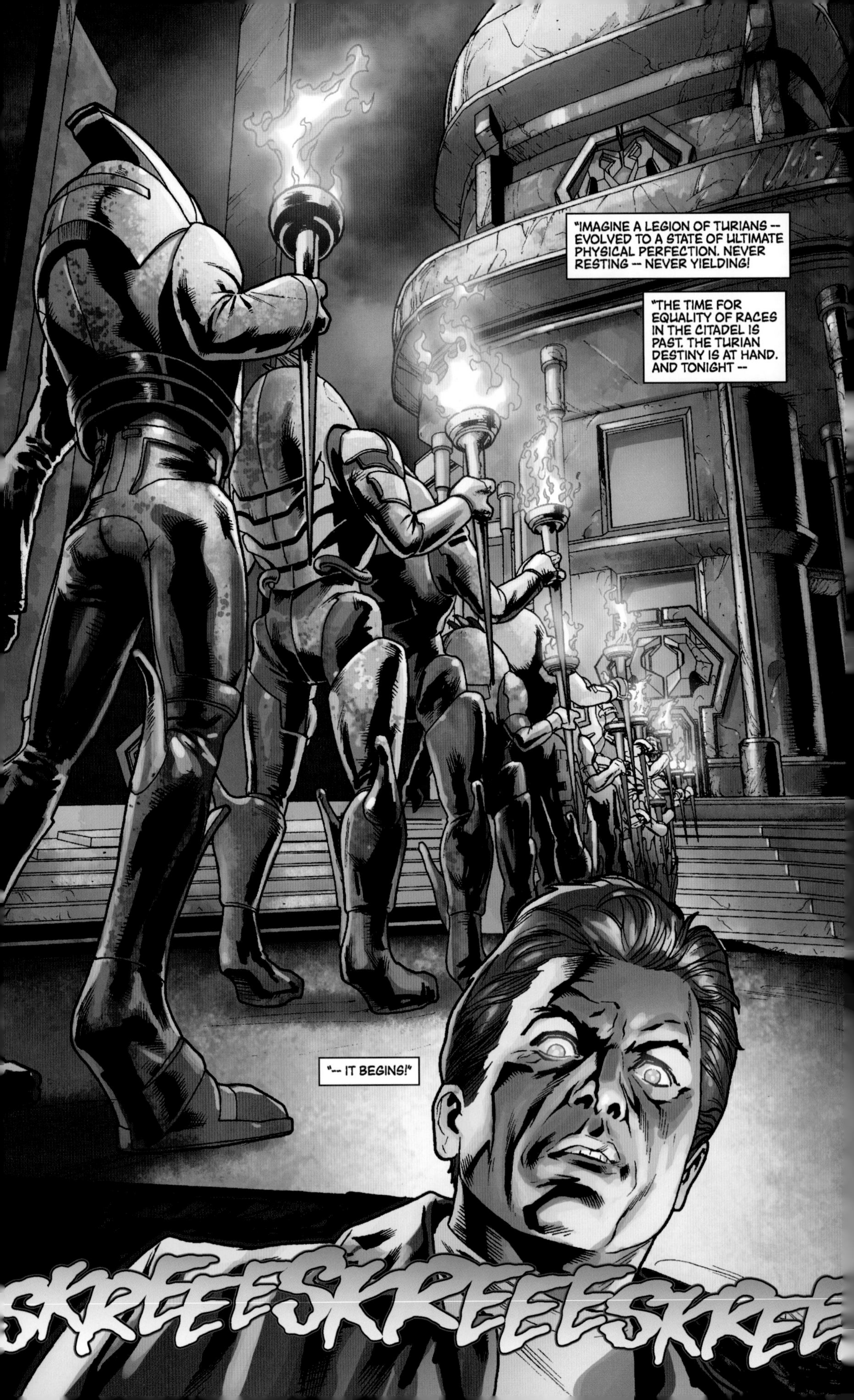
"IMAGINE A LEGION OF TURIANS -- EVOLVED TO A STATE OF ULTIMATE PHYSICAL PERFECTION. NEVER RESTING -- NEVER YIELDING!
"THE TIME FOR EQUALITY OF RACES IN THE CITADEL IS PAST. THE TURIAN DESTINY IS AT HAND. AND TONIGHT --
"-- IT BEGINS!"
SKREEESKREEESKREE

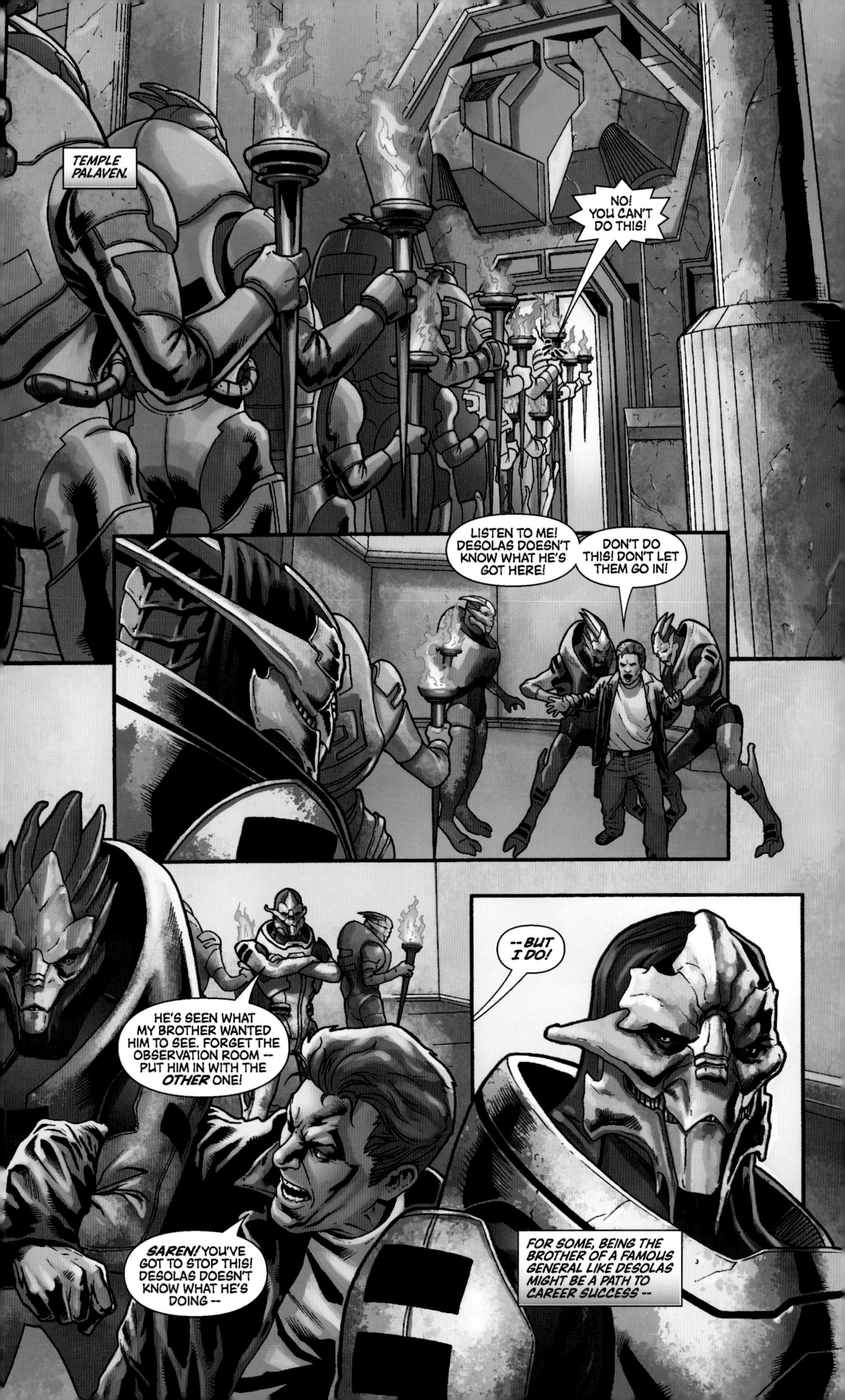
TEMPLE PALAVEN.
NO! YOU CAN'T DO THIS!
LISTEN TO ME! DESOLAS DOESN'T KNOW WHAT HE'S GOT HERE!
DON'T DO THIS! DON'T LET THEM GO IN!
HE'S SEEN WHAT MY BROTHER WANTED HIM TO SEE. FORGET THE OBSERVATION ROOM -- PUT HIM IN WITH THE OTHER ONE!
--BUT I DO!
SAREN! YOU'VE GOT TO STOP THIS! DESOLAS DOESN'T KNOW WHAT HE'S DOING --
FOR SOME, BEING THE BROTHER OF A FAMOUS GENERAL LIKE DESOLAS MIGHT BE A PATH TO CAREER SUCCESS --

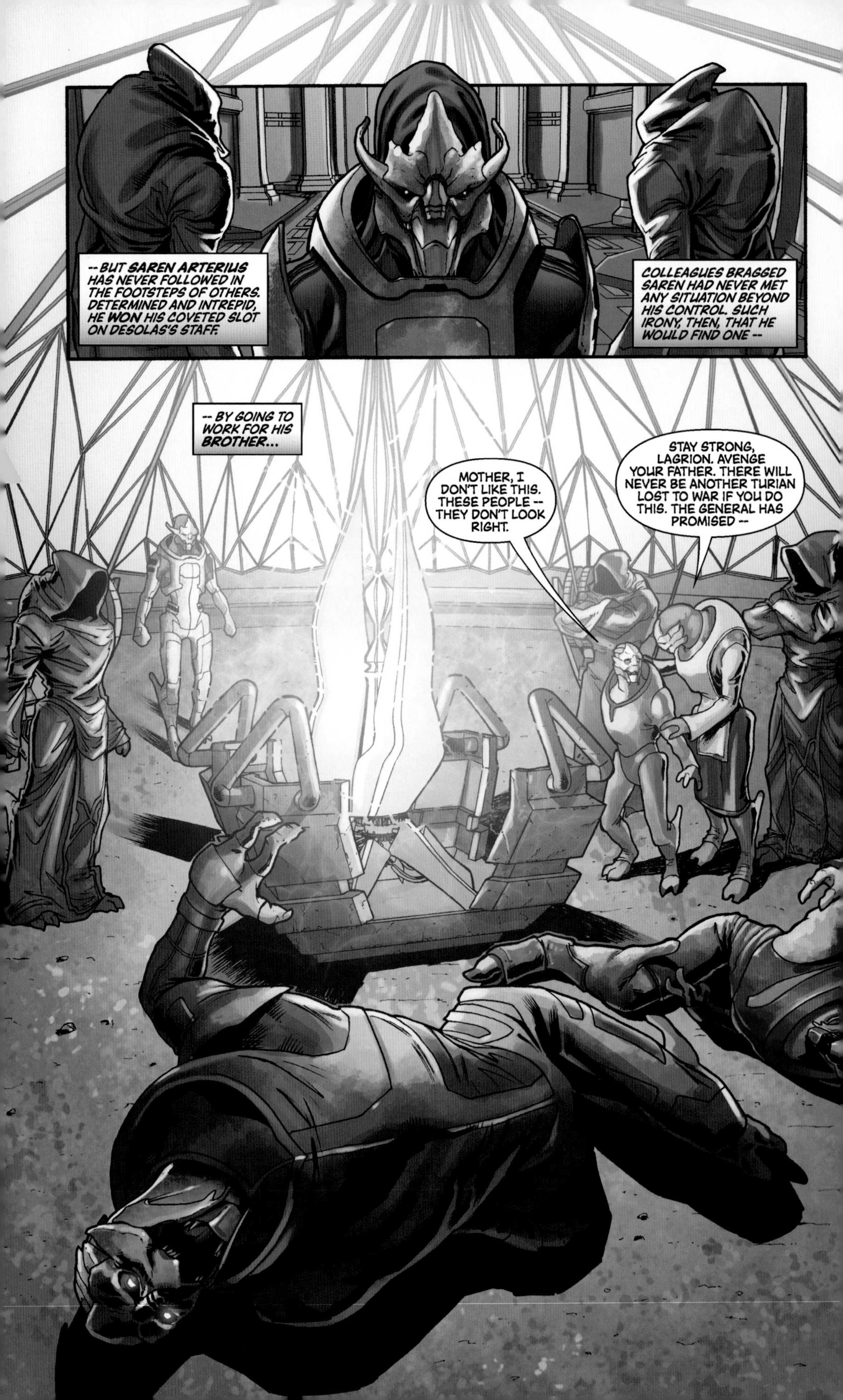
-- BUT SAREN ARTERIUS HAS NEVER FOLLOWED IN THE FOOTSTEPS OF OTHERS. DETERMINED AND INTREPID, HE WON HIS COVETED SLOT ON DESOLAS'S STAFF.
COLLEAGUES BRAGGED SAREN HAD NEVER MET ANY SITUATION BEYOND HIS CONTROL. SUCH IRONY, THEN, THAT HE WOULD FIND ONE --
-- BY GOING TO WORK FOR HIS BROTHER...
MOTHER, I DON'T LIKE THIS. THESE PEOPLE -- THEY DON'T LOOK RIGHT.
STAY STRONG, LAGRION. AVENGE YOUR FATHER. THERE WILL NEVER BE ANOTHER TURIAN LOST TO WAR IF YOU DO THIS. THE GENERAL HAS PROMISED --

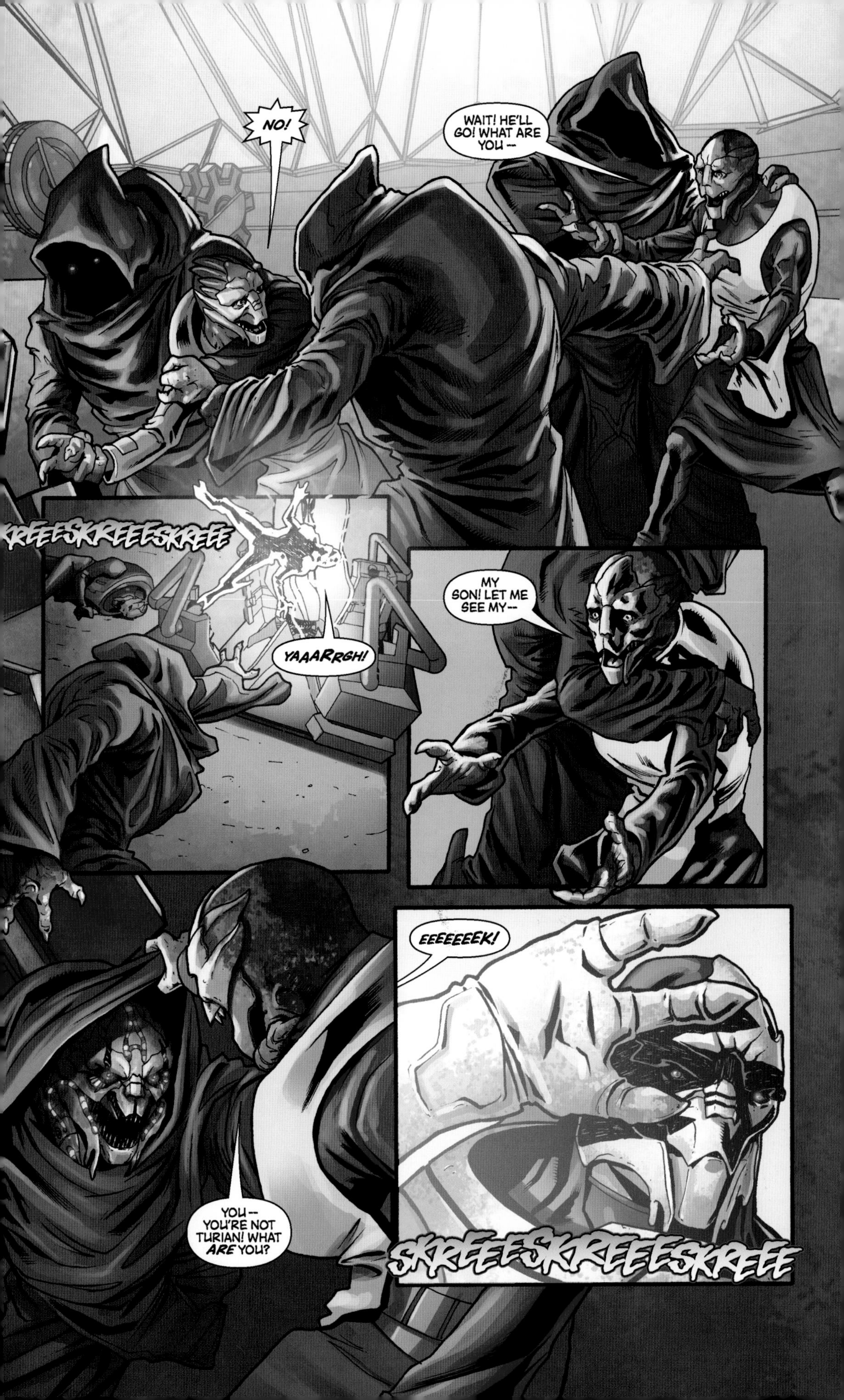
NO!
WAIT! HE'LL GO! WHAT ARE YOU --
SKREEESKREEESKREEE
YAAARRGH!
MY SON! LET ME SEE MY--
YOU -- YOU'RE NOT TURIAN! WHAT ARE YOU?
EEEEEEEK!
SKREEESKREEESKREEE

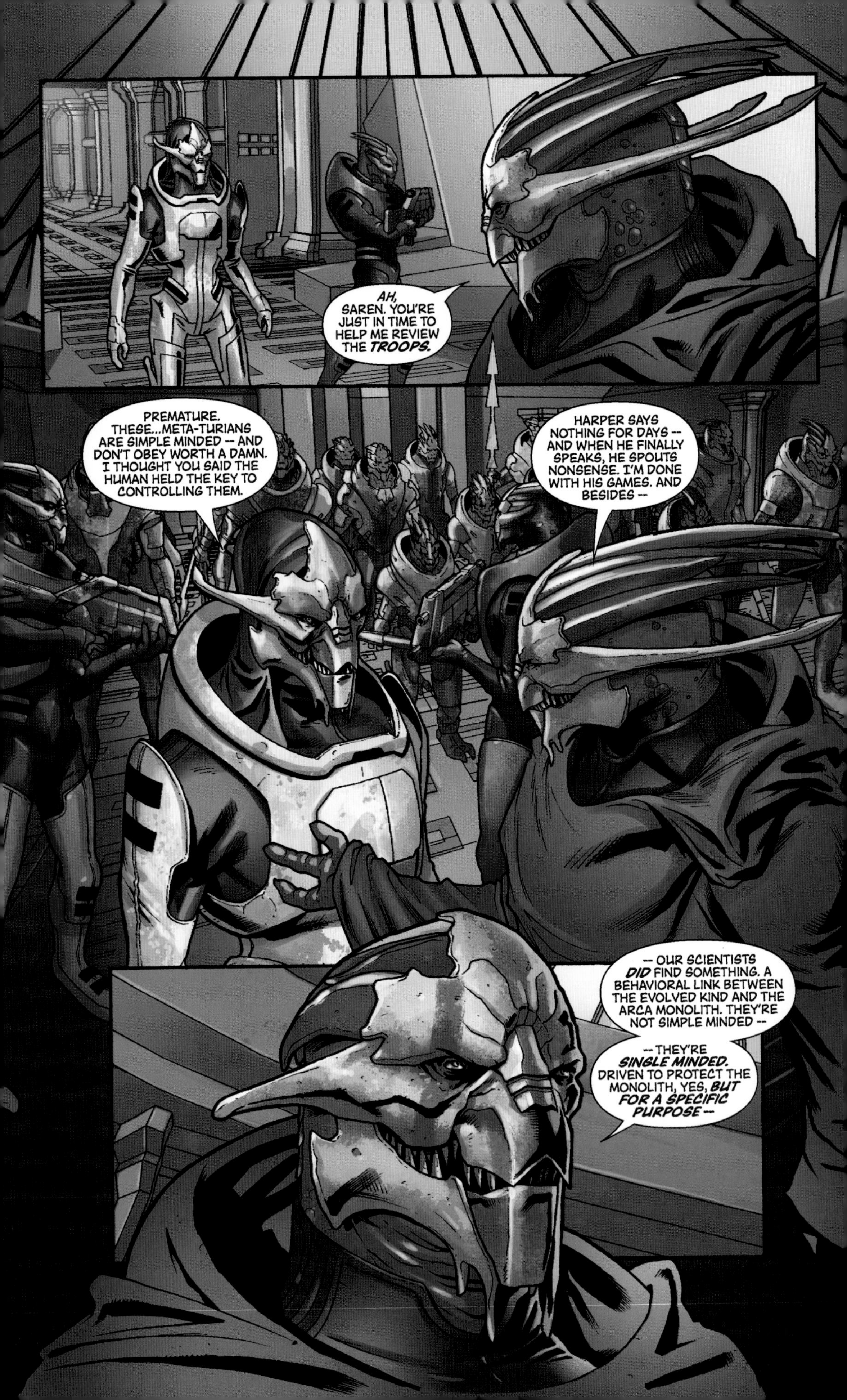
AH, SAREN. YOU'RE JUST IN TIME TO HELP ME REVIEW THE TROOPS.
PREMATURE. THESE...META-TURIANS ARE SIMPLE MINDED -- AND DON'T OBEY WORTH A DAMN. I THOUGHT YOU SAID THE HUMAN HELD THE KEY TO CONTROLLING THEM.
HARPER SAYS NOTHING FOR DAYS -- AND WHEN HE FINALLY SPEAKS, HE SPOUTS NONSENSE. I'M DONE WITH HIS GAMES. AND BESIDES --
-- OUR SCIENTISTS DID FIND SOMETHING. A BEHAVIORAL LINK BETWEEN THE EVOLVED KIND AND THE ARCA MONOLITH. THEY'RE NOT SIMPLE MINDED --
-- THEY'RE SINGLE MINDED. DRIVEN TO PROTECT THE MONOLITH, YES, BUT FOR A SPECIFIC PURPOSE --

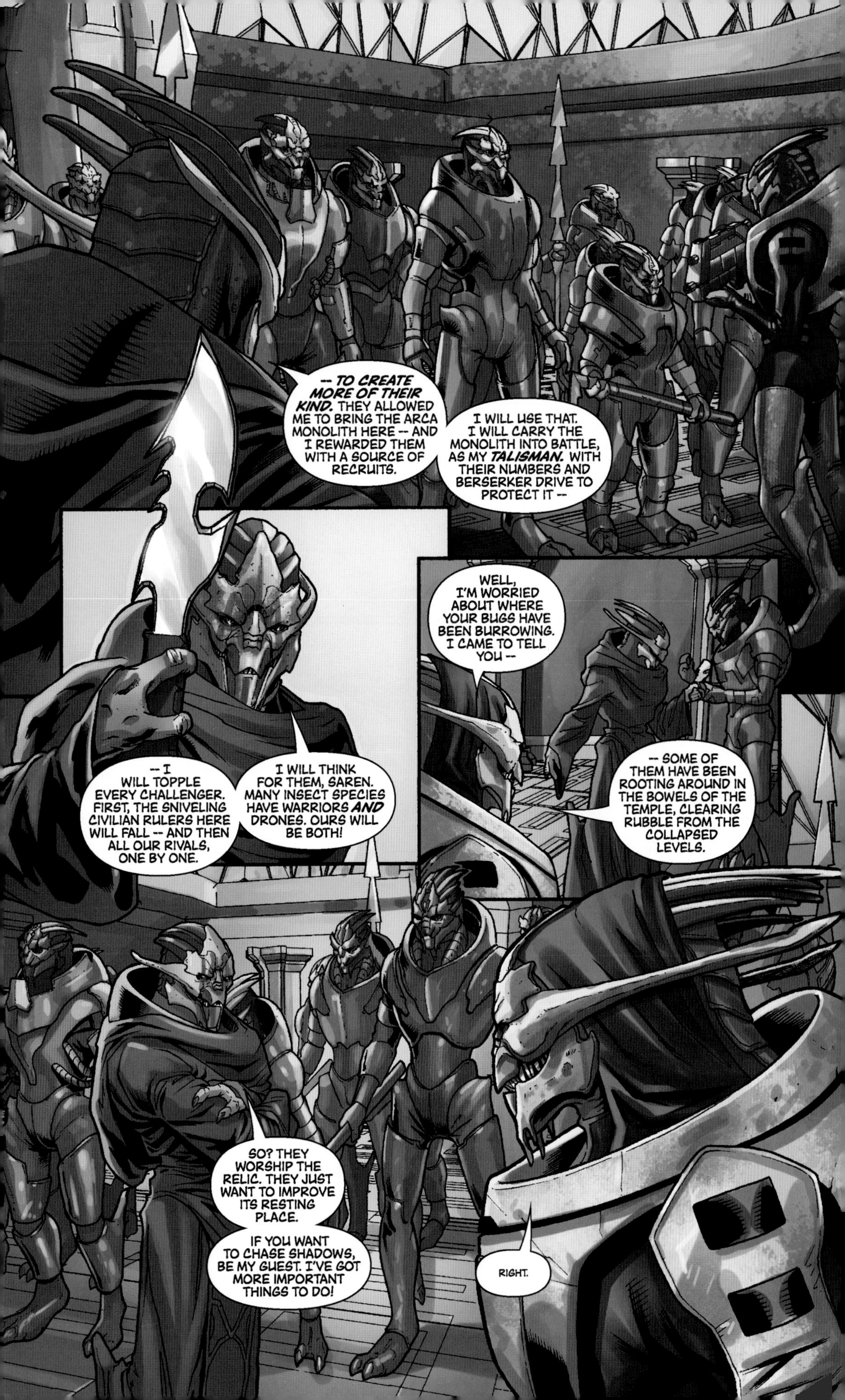
-- *TO CREATE MORE OF THEIR KIND.* THEY ALLOWED ME TO BRING THE ARCA MONOLITH HERE -- AND I REWARDED THEM WITH A SOURCE OF RECRUITS.
I WILL USE THAT. I WILL CARRY THE MONOLITH INTO BATTLE, AS MY *TALISMAN.* WITH THEIR NUMBERS AND BERSERKER DRIVE TO PROTECT IT --
-- I WILL TOPPLE EVERY CHALLENGER. FIRST, THE SNIVELING CIVILIAN RULERS HERE WILL FALL -- AND THEN ALL OUR RIVALS, ONE BY ONE.
I WILL THINK FOR THEM, SAREN. MANY INSECT SPECIES HAVE WARRIORS *AND* DRONES. OURS WILL BE BOTH!
WELL, I'M WORRIED ABOUT WHERE YOUR BUGS HAVE BEEN BURROWING. I CAME TO TELL YOU --
-- SOME OF THEM HAVE BEEN ROOTING AROUND IN THE BOWELS OF THE TEMPLE, CLEARING RUBBLE FROM THE COLLAPSED LEVELS.
SO? THEY WORSHIP THE RELIC. THEY JUST WANT TO IMPROVE ITS RESTING PLACE.
IF YOU WANT TO CHASE SHADOWS, BE MY GUEST. I'VE GOT MORE IMPORTANT THINGS TO DO!
RIGHT.

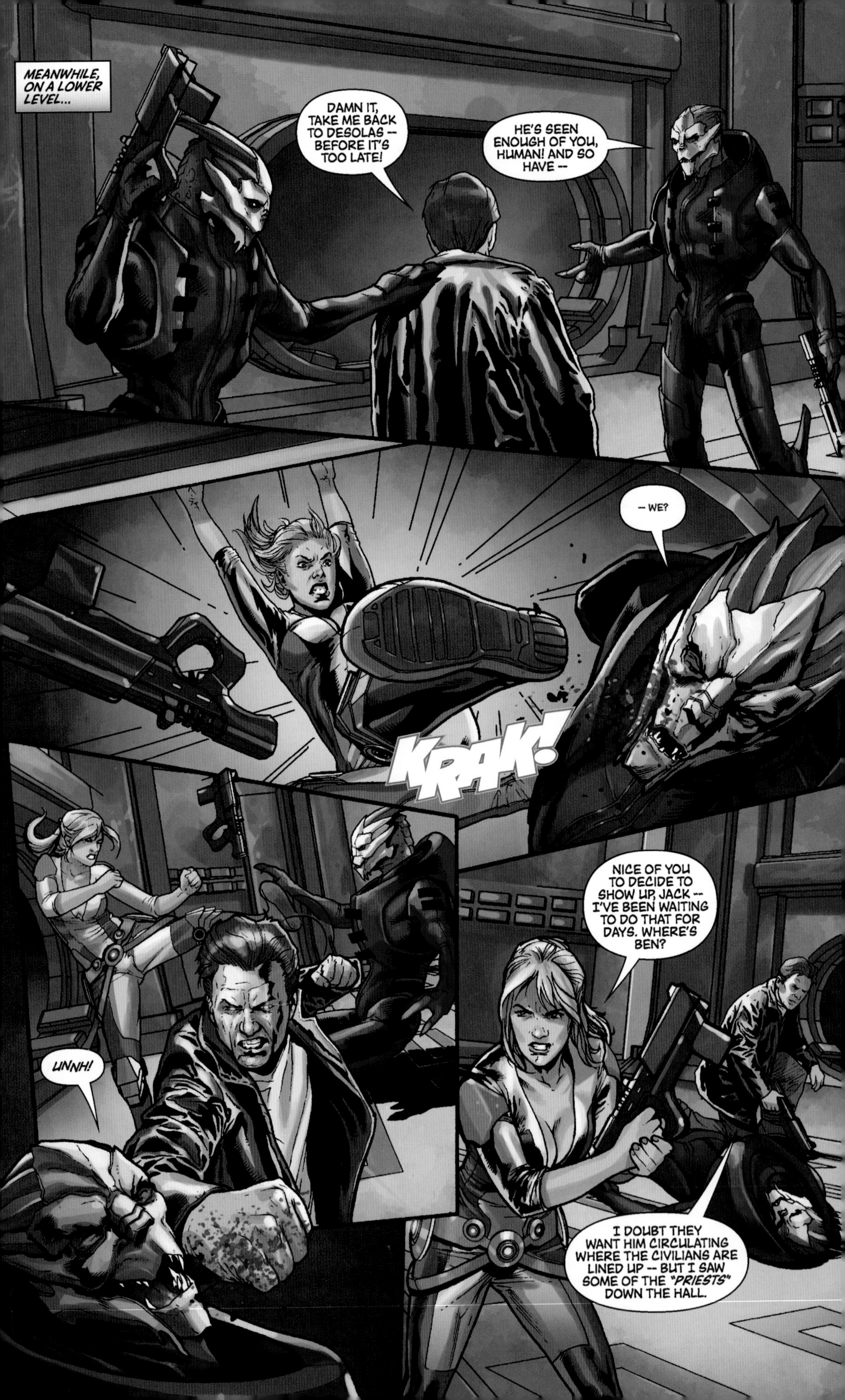
MEANWHILE, ON A LOWER LEVEL...
DAMN IT, TAKE ME BACK TO DESOLAS -- BEFORE IT'S TOO LATE!
HE'S SEEN ENOUGH OF YOU, HUMAN! AND SO HAVE --
-- WE?
KRAK!
UNNH!
NICE OF YOU TO DECIDE TO SHOW UP, JACK -- I'VE BEEN WAITING TO DO THAT FOR DAYS. WHERE'S BEN?
I DOUBT THEY WANT HIM CIRCULATING WHERE THE CIVILIANS ARE LINED UP -- BUT I SAW SOME OF THE "PRIESTS" DOWN THE HALL.

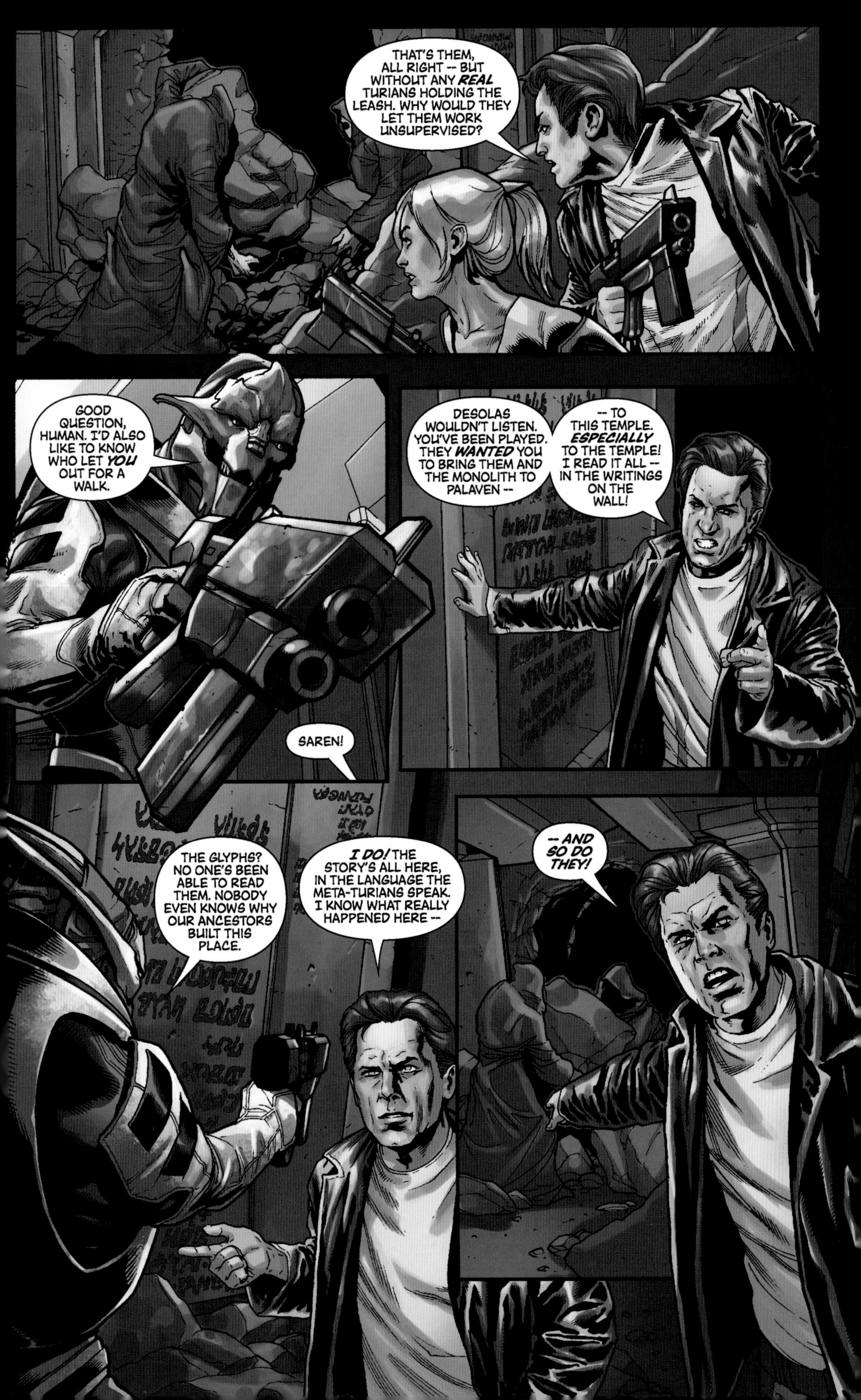
THAT'S THEM, ALL RIGHT -- BUT WITHOUT ANY REAL TURIANS HOLDING THE LEASH. WHY WOULD THEY LET THEM WORK UNSUPERVISED?
GOOD QUESTION, HUMAN. I'D ALSO LIKE TO KNOW WHO LET YOU OUT FOR A WALK.
SAREN!
DESOLAS WOULDN'T LISTEN. YOU'VE BEEN PLAYED. THEY WANTED YOU TO BRING THEM AND THE MONOLITH TO PALAVEN --
-- TO THIS TEMPLE. ESPECIALLY TO THE TEMPLE! I READ IT ALL -- IN THE WRITINGS ON THE WALL!
THE GLYPHS? NO ONE'S BEEN ABLE TO READ THEM. NOBODY EVEN KNOWS WHY OUR ANCESTORS BUILT THIS PLACE.
I DO! THE STORY'S ALL HERE, IN THE LANGUAGE THE META-TURIANS SPEAK. I KNOW WHAT REALLY HAPPENED HERE --
-- AND SO DO THEY!

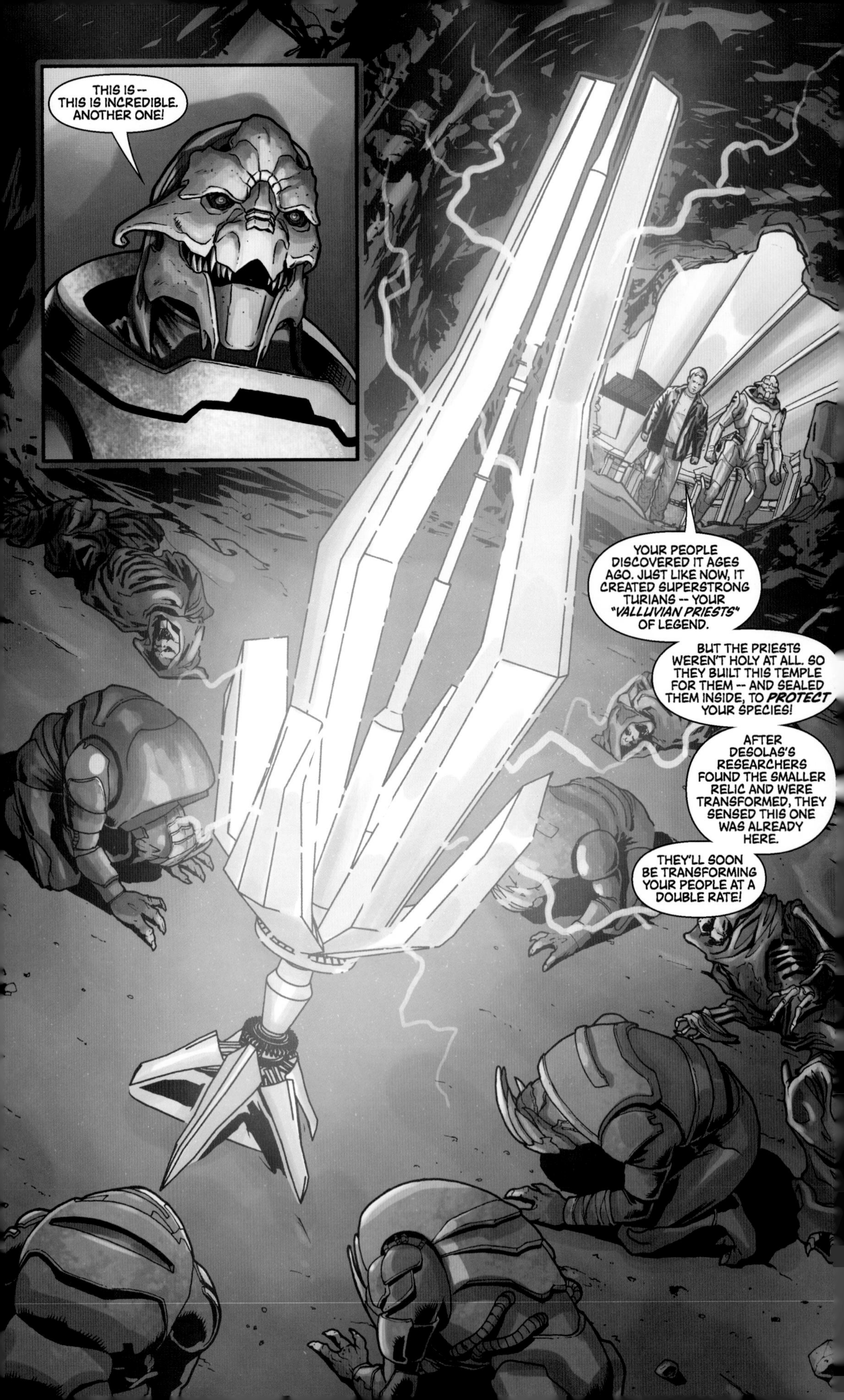
THIS IS -- THIS IS INCREDIBLE. ANOTHER ONE!
YOUR PEOPLE DISCOVERED IT AGES AGO. JUST LIKE NOW, IT CREATED SUPERSTRONG TURIANS -- YOUR "VALLUVIAN PRIESTS" OF LEGEND.
BUT THE PRIESTS WEREN'T HOLY AT ALL. SO THEY BUILT THIS TEMPLE FOR THEM -- AND SEALED THEM INSIDE, TO PROTECT YOUR SPECIES!
AFTER DESOLAS'S RESEARCHERS FOUND THE SMALLER RELIC AND WERE TRANSFORMED, THEY SENSED THIS ONE WAS ALREADY HERE.
THEY'LL SOON BE TRANSFORMING YOUR PEOPLE AT A DOUBLE RATE!

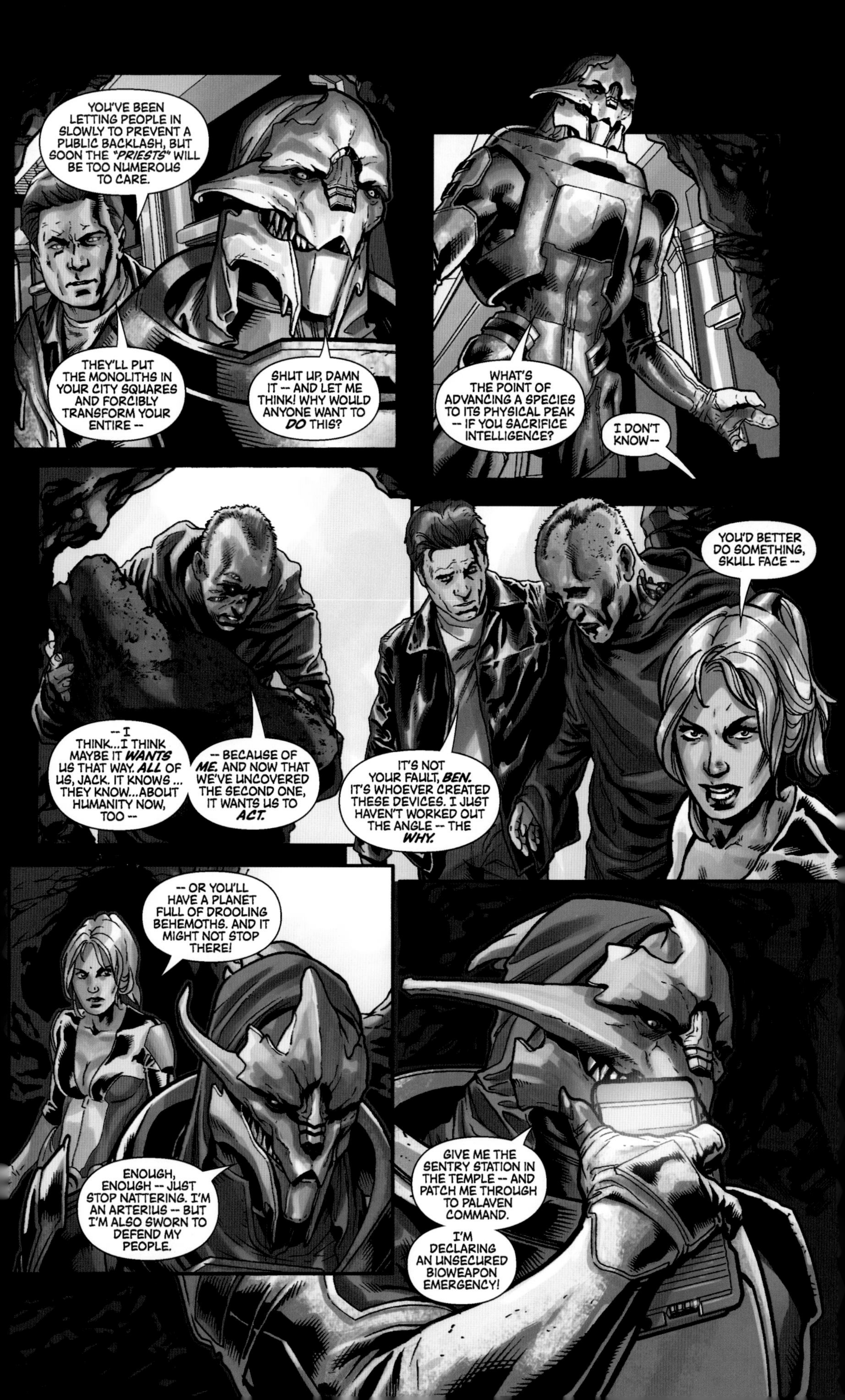
YOU'VE BEEN LETTING PEOPLE IN SLOWLY TO PREVENT A PUBLIC BACKLASH, BUT SOON THE "PRIESTS" WILL BE TOO NUMEROUS TO CARE.
THEY'LL PUT THE MONOLITHS IN YOUR CITY SQUARES AND FORCIBLY TRANSFORM YOUR ENTIRE --
SHUT UP, DAMN IT -- AND LET ME THINK! WHY WOULD ANYONE WANT TO DO THIS?
WHAT'S THE POINT OF ADVANCING A SPECIES TO ITS PHYSICAL PEAK -- IF YOU SACRIFICE INTELLIGENCE?
I DON'T KNOW--
-- I THINK...I THINK MAYBE IT WANTS US THAT WAY. ALL OF US, JACK. IT KNOWS ... THEY KNOW...ABOUT HUMANITY NOW, TOO --
-- BECAUSE OF ME. AND NOW THAT WE'VE UNCOVERED THE SECOND ONE, IT WANTS US TO ACT.
IT'S NOT YOUR FAULT, BEN. IT'S WHOEVER CREATED THESE DEVICES. I JUST HAVEN'T WORKED OUT THE ANGLE -- THE WHY.
YOU'D BETTER DO SOMETHING, SKULL FACE --
-- OR YOU'LL HAVE A PLANET FULL OF DROOLING BEHEMOTHS. AND IT MIGHT NOT STOP THERE!
ENOUGH, ENOUGH -- JUST STOP NATTERING. I'M AN ARTERIUS -- BUT I'M ALSO SWORN TO DEFEND MY PEOPLE.
GIVE ME THE SENTRY STATION IN THE TEMPLE -- AND PATCH ME THROUGH TO PALAVEN COMMAND.
I'M DECLARING AN UNSECURED BIOWEAPON EMERGENCY!

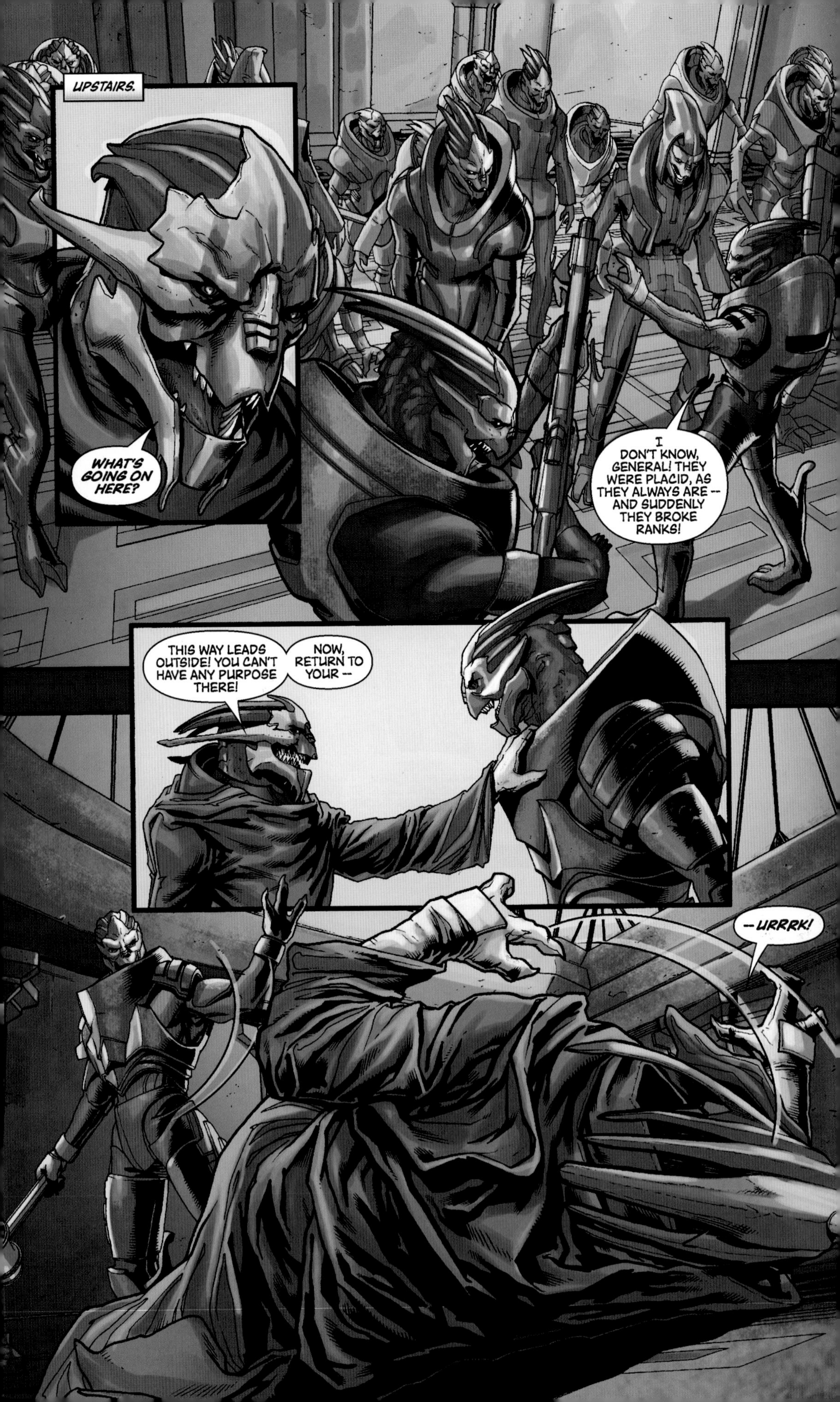
UPSTAIRS.
WHAT'S GOING ON HERE?
I DON'T KNOW, GENERAL! THEY WERE PLACID, AS THEY ALWAYS ARE -- AND SUDDENLY THEY BROKE RANKS!
THIS WAY LEADS OUTSIDE! YOU CAN'T HAVE ANY PURPOSE THERE!
NOW, RETURN TO YOUR --
--URRRK!

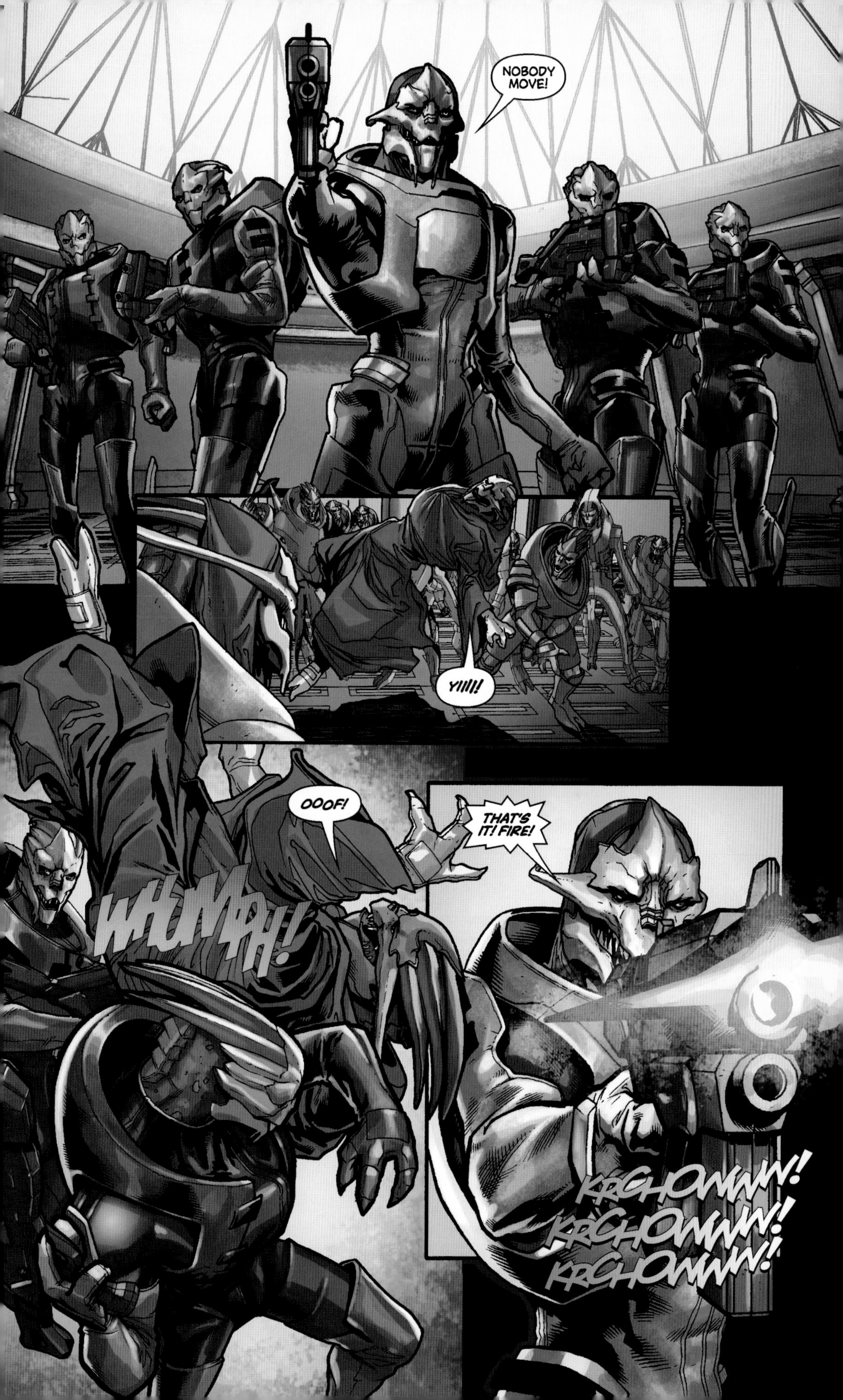
NOBODY MOVE!
YIIII!
OOOF!
WHUMPH!
THAT'S IT! FIRE!
KRGHOWWW!
KRGHOWWW!
KRGHOWWW!

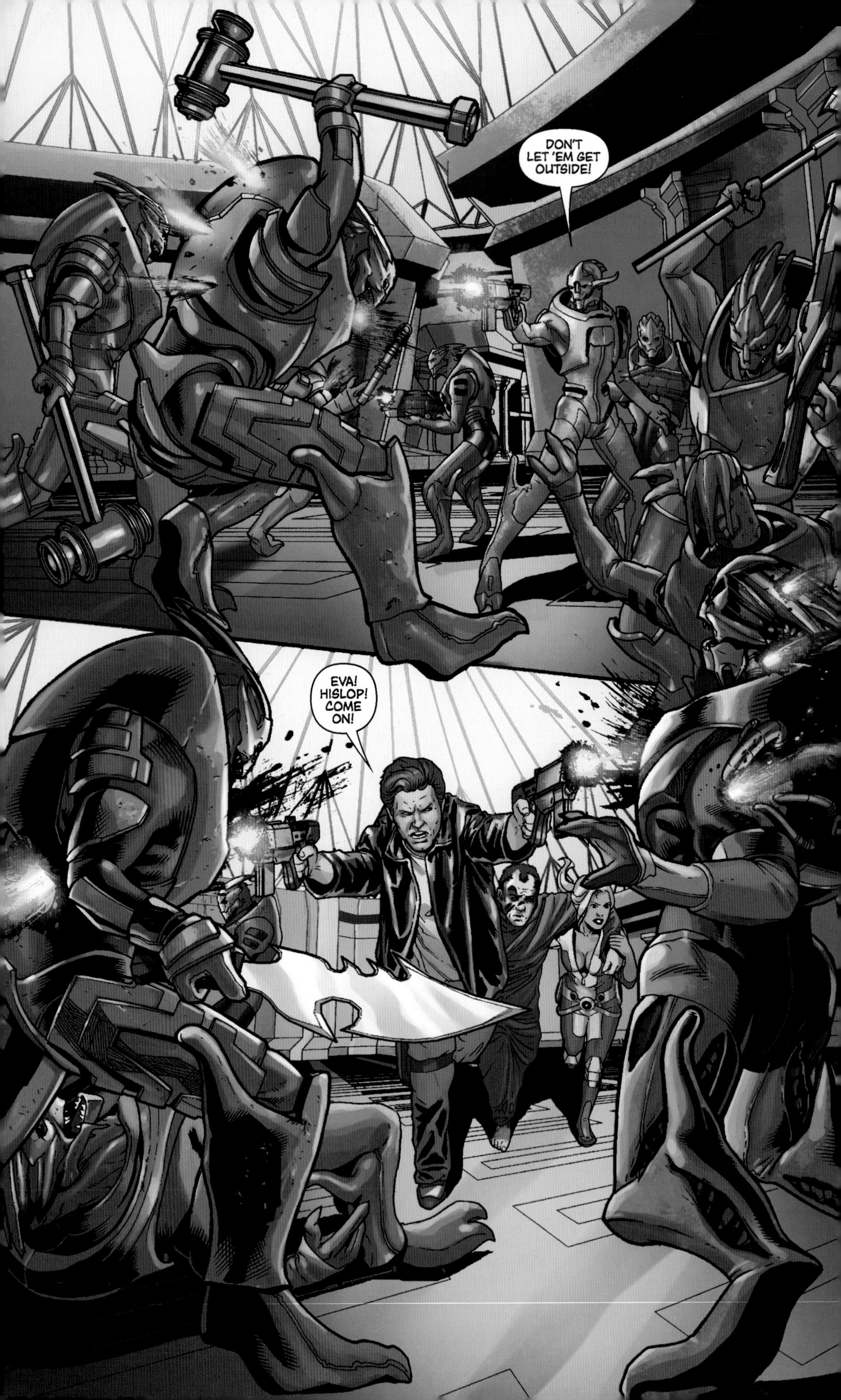
DON'T LET 'EM GET OUTSIDE!
EVA! HISLOP! COME ON!

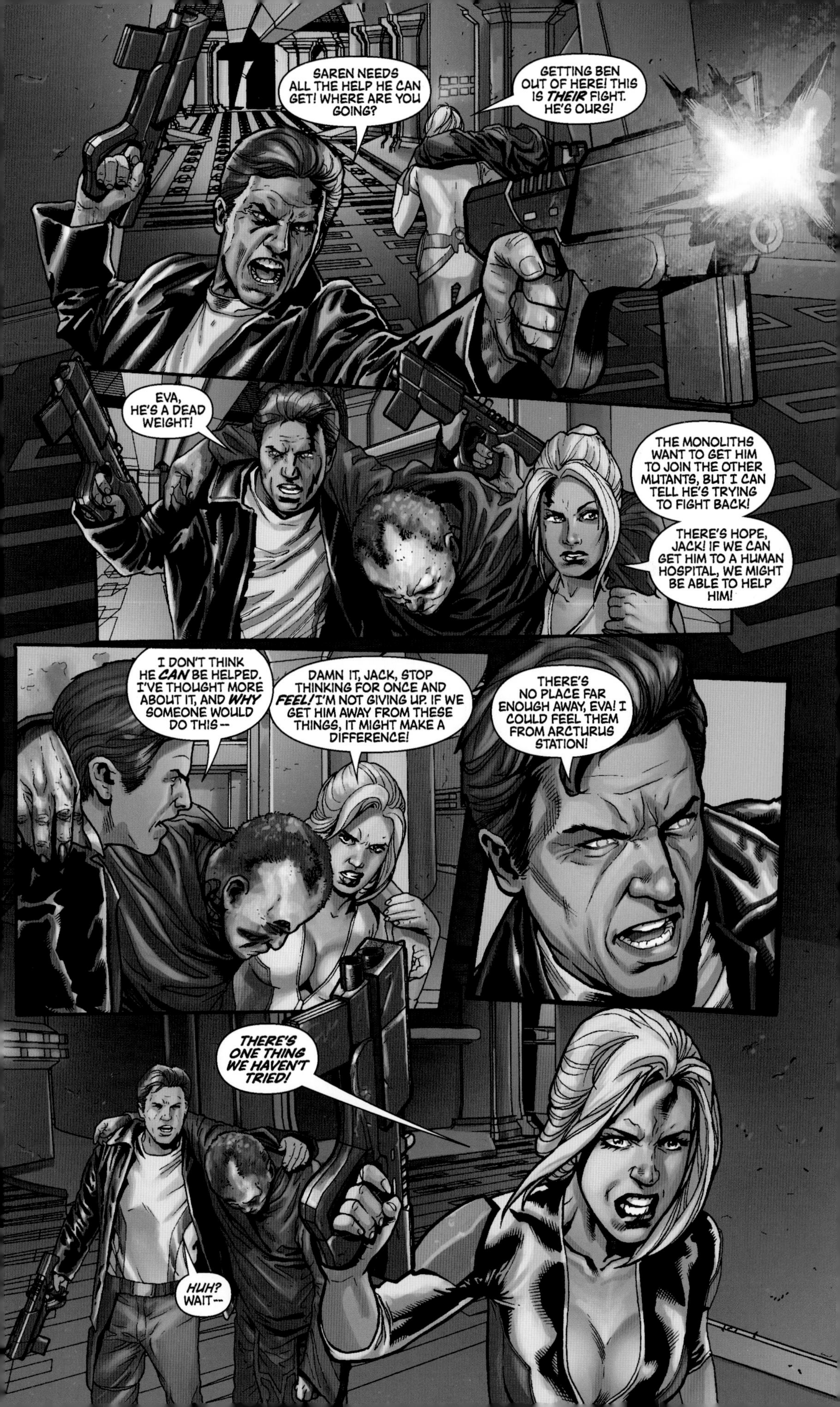
SAREN NEEDS ALL THE HELP HE CAN GET! WHERE ARE YOU GOING?
GETTING BEN OUT OF HERE! THIS IS *THEIR* FIGHT. HE'S OURS!
EVA, HE'S A DEAD WEIGHT!
THE MONOLITHS WANT TO GET HIM TO JOIN THE OTHER MUTANTS, BUT I CAN TELL HE'S TRYING TO FIGHT BACK!
THERE'S HOPE, JACK! IF WE CAN GET HIM TO A HUMAN HOSPITAL, WE MIGHT BE ABLE TO HELP HIM!
I DON'T THINK HE *CAN* BE HELPED. I'VE THOUGHT MORE ABOUT IT, AND *WHY* SOMEONE WOULD DO THIS--
DAMN IT, JACK, STOP THINKING FOR ONCE AND *FEEL!* I'M NOT GIVING UP. IF WE GET HIM AWAY FROM THESE THINGS, IT MIGHT MAKE A DIFFERENCE!
THERE'S NO PLACE FAR ENOUGH AWAY, EVA! I COULD FEEL THEM FROM ARCTURUS STATION!
THERE'S ONE THING WE HAVEN'T TRIED!
HUH? WAIT--

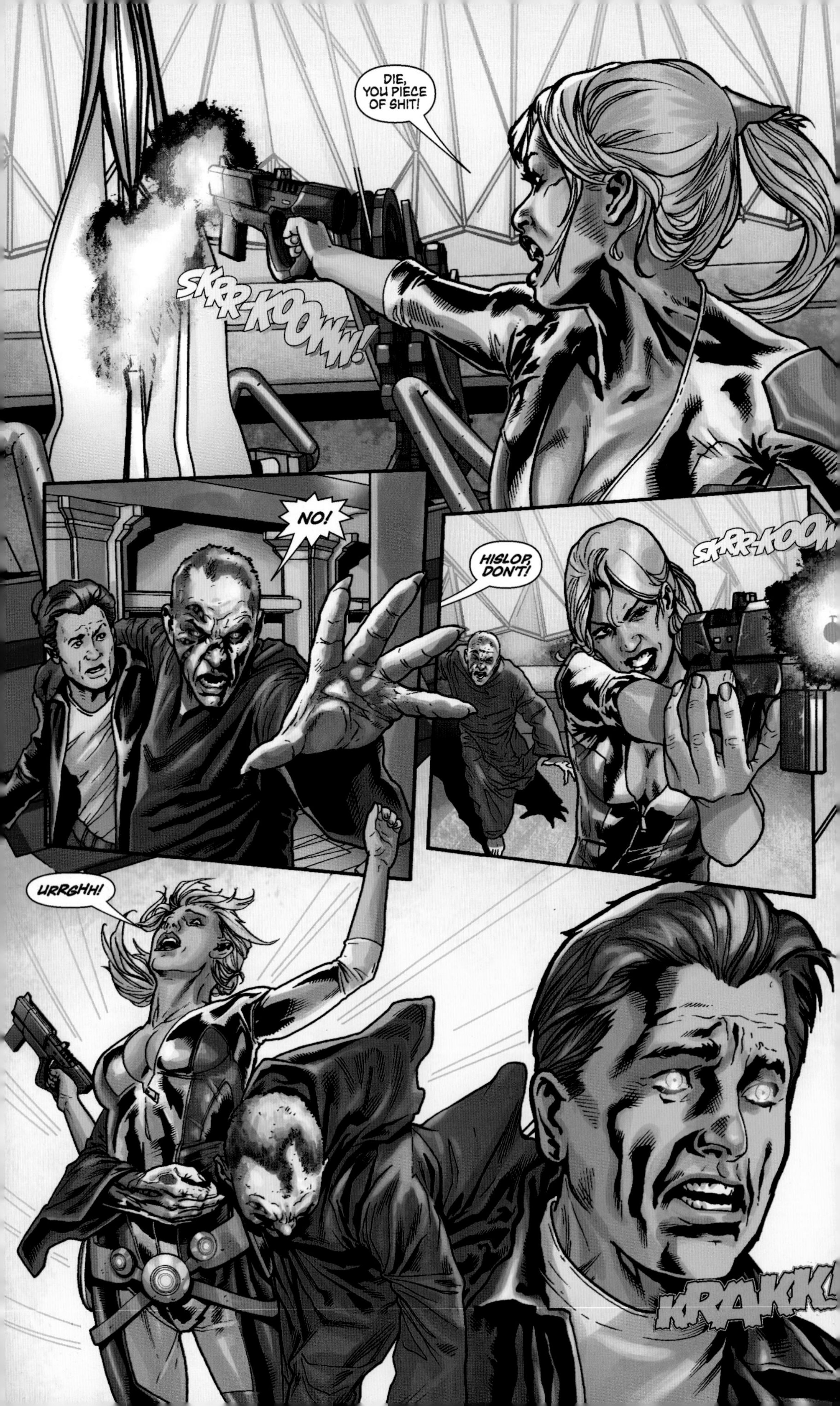
DIE, YOU PIECE OF SHIT!
SKRR-KOOWW!
NO!
HISLOP, DON'T!
SKRR-KOOW
URRGHH!
KRAKK!

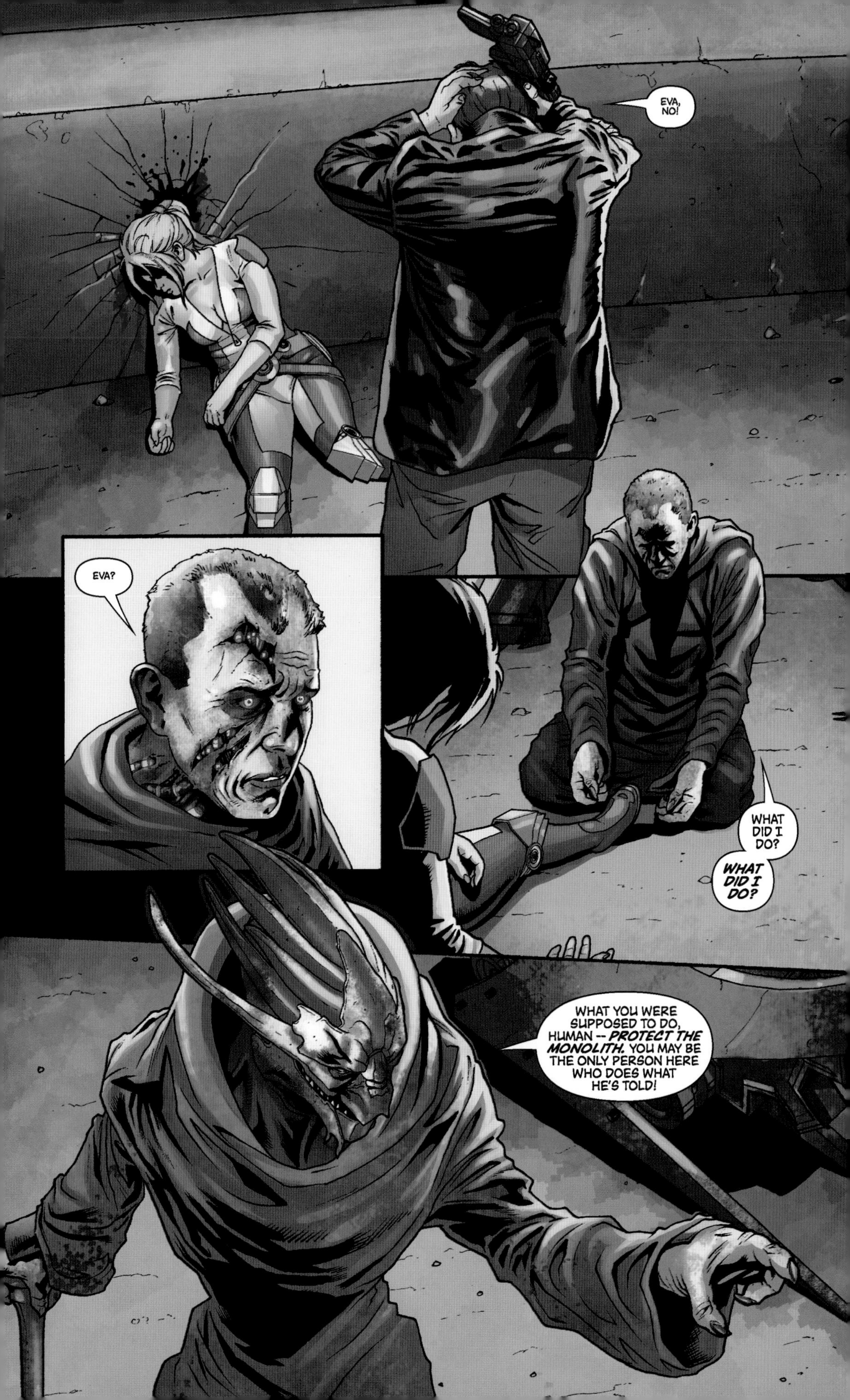
EVA, NO!
EVA?
WHAT DID I DO?
WHAT DID I DO?
WHAT YOU WERE SUPPOSED TO DO, HUMAN -- PROTECT THE MONOLITH. YOU MAY BE THE ONLY PERSON HERE WHO DOES WHAT HE'S TOLD!

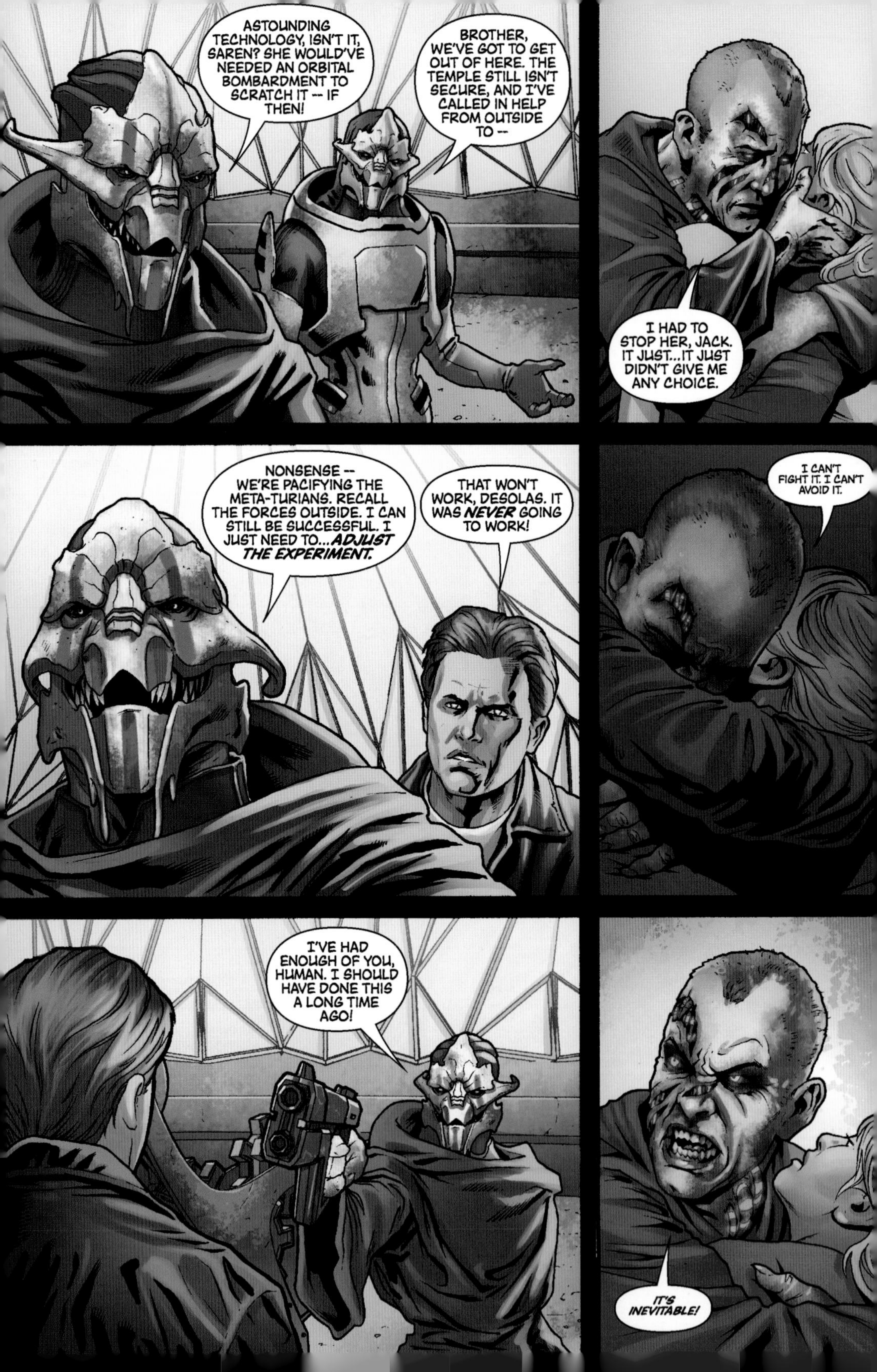
ASTOUNDING TECHNOLOGY, ISN'T IT, SAREN? SHE WOULD'VE NEEDED AN ORBITAL BOMBARDMENT TO SCRATCH IT -- IF THEN!
BROTHER, WE'VE GOT TO GET OUT OF HERE. THE TEMPLE STILL ISN'T SECURE, AND I'VE CALLED IN HELP FROM OUTSIDE TO --
I HAD TO STOP HER, JACK. IT JUST...IT JUST DIDN'T GIVE ME ANY CHOICE.
NONSENSE -- WE'RE PACIFYING THE META-TURIANS. RECALL THE FORCES OUTSIDE. I CAN STILL BE SUCCESSFUL. I JUST NEED TO...*ADJUST THE EXPERIMENT.*
THAT WON'T WORK, DESOLAS. IT WAS *NEVER* GOING TO WORK!
I CAN'T FIGHT IT. I CAN'T AVOID IT.
I'VE HAD ENOUGH OF YOU, HUMAN. I SHOULD HAVE DONE THIS A LONG TIME AGO!
IT'S INEVITABLE!

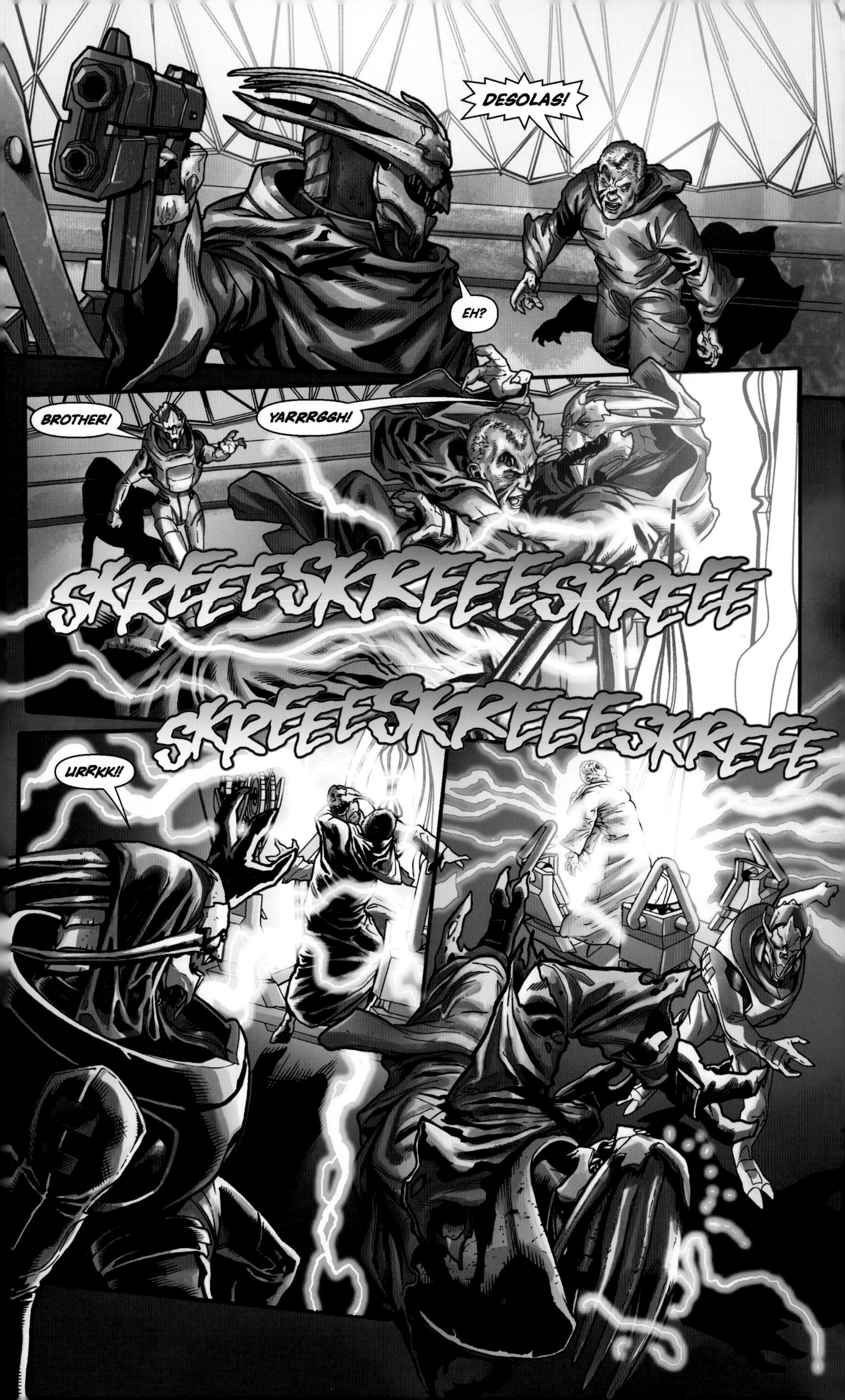
DESOLAS!
EH?
BROTHER!
YARRRGGH!
SKREEESKREEESKREEE
SKREEESKREEESKREEE
URRKK!!

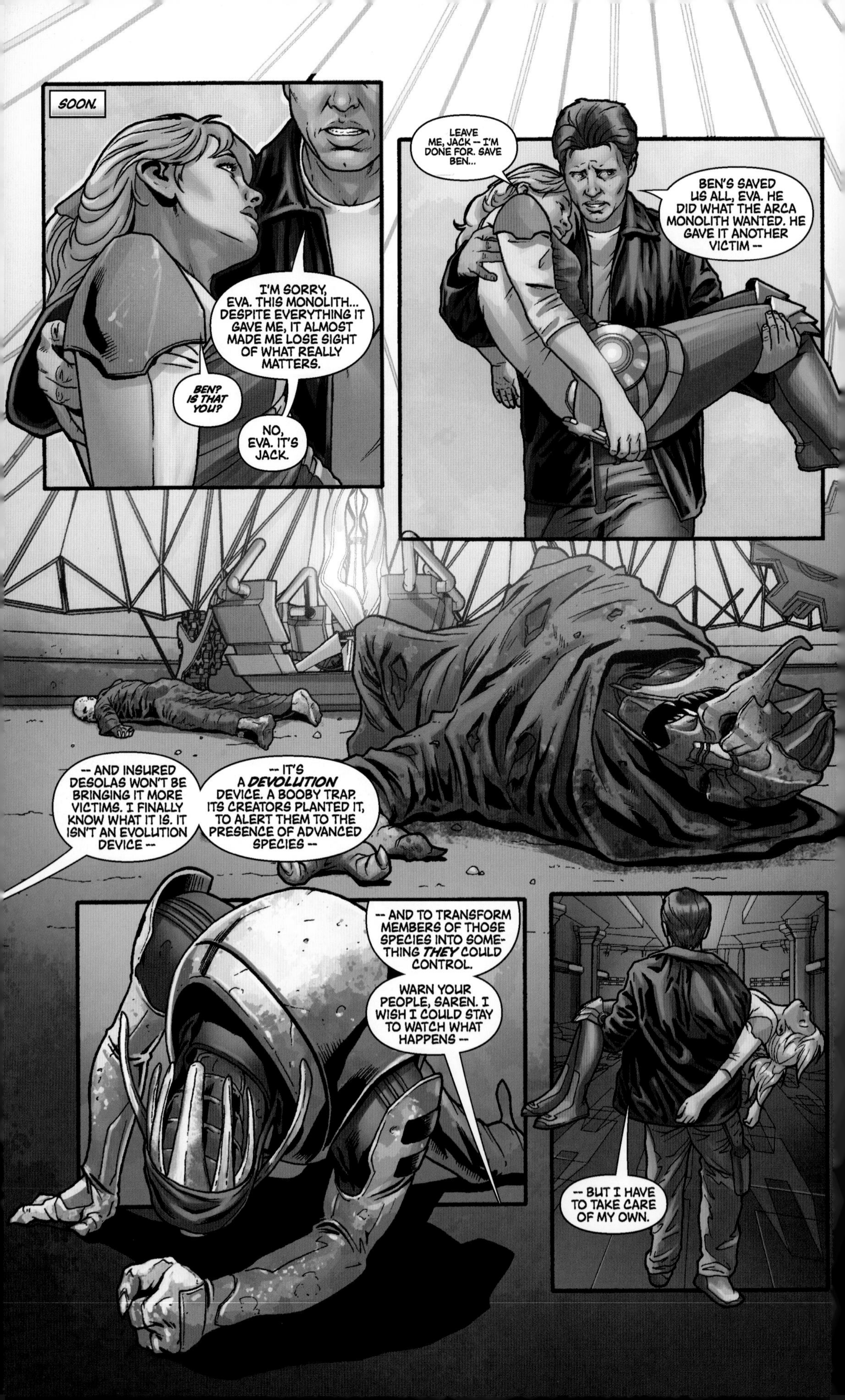
SOON.
BEN? IS THAT YOU?
I'M SORRY, EVA. THIS MONOLITH... DESPITE EVERYTHING IT GAVE ME, IT ALMOST MADE ME LOSE SIGHT OF WHAT REALLY MATTERS.
NO, EVA. IT'S JACK.
LEAVE ME, JACK -- I'M DONE FOR. SAVE BEN...
BEN'S SAVED US ALL, EVA. HE DID WHAT THE ARCA MONOLITH WANTED. HE GAVE IT ANOTHER VICTIM --
-- AND INSURED DESOLAS WON'T BE BRINGING IT MORE VICTIMS. I FINALLY KNOW WHAT IT IS. IT ISN'T AN EVOLUTION DEVICE --
-- IT'S A *DEVOLUTION* DEVICE. A BOOBY TRAP. ITS CREATORS PLANTED IT, TO ALERT THEM TO THE PRESENCE OF ADVANCED SPECIES --
-- AND TO TRANSFORM MEMBERS OF THOSE SPECIES INTO SOMETHING *THEY* COULD CONTROL.
WARN YOUR PEOPLE, SAREN. I WISH I COULD STAY TO WATCH WHAT HAPPENS --
-- BUT I HAVE TO TAKE CARE OF MY OWN.

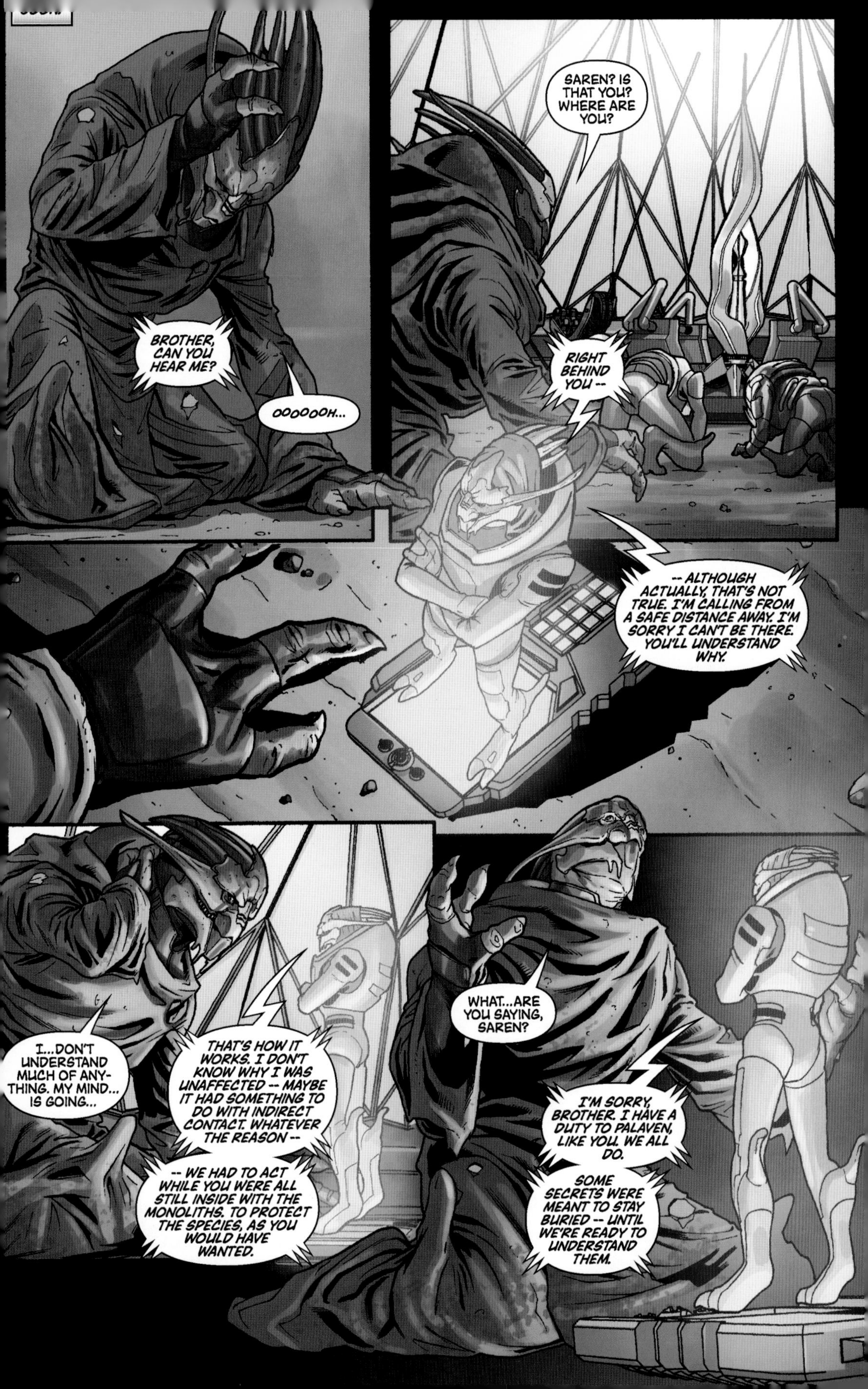
BROTHER, CAN YOU HEAR ME?
OOOOOOH...
SAREN? IS THAT YOU? WHERE ARE YOU?
RIGHT BEHIND YOU --
-- ALTHOUGH ACTUALLY, THAT'S NOT TRUE. I'M CALLING FROM A SAFE DISTANCE AWAY. I'M SORRY I CAN'T BE THERE. YOU'LL UNDERSTAND WHY.
I...DON'T UNDERSTAND MUCH OF ANY-THING. MY MIND... IS GOING...
THAT'S HOW IT WORKS. I DON'T KNOW WHY I WAS UNAFFECTED -- MAYBE IT HAD SOMETHING TO DO WITH INDIRECT CONTACT. WHATEVER THE REASON --
-- WE HAD TO ACT WHILE YOU WERE ALL STILL INSIDE WITH THE MONOLITHS. TO PROTECT THE SPECIES, AS YOU WOULD HAVE WANTED.
WHAT...ARE YOU SAYING, SAREN?
I'M SORRY, BROTHER. I HAVE A DUTY TO PALAVEN, LIKE YOU. WE ALL DO.
SOME SECRETS WERE MEANT TO STAY BURIED -- UNTIL WE'RE READY TO UNDERSTAND THEM.

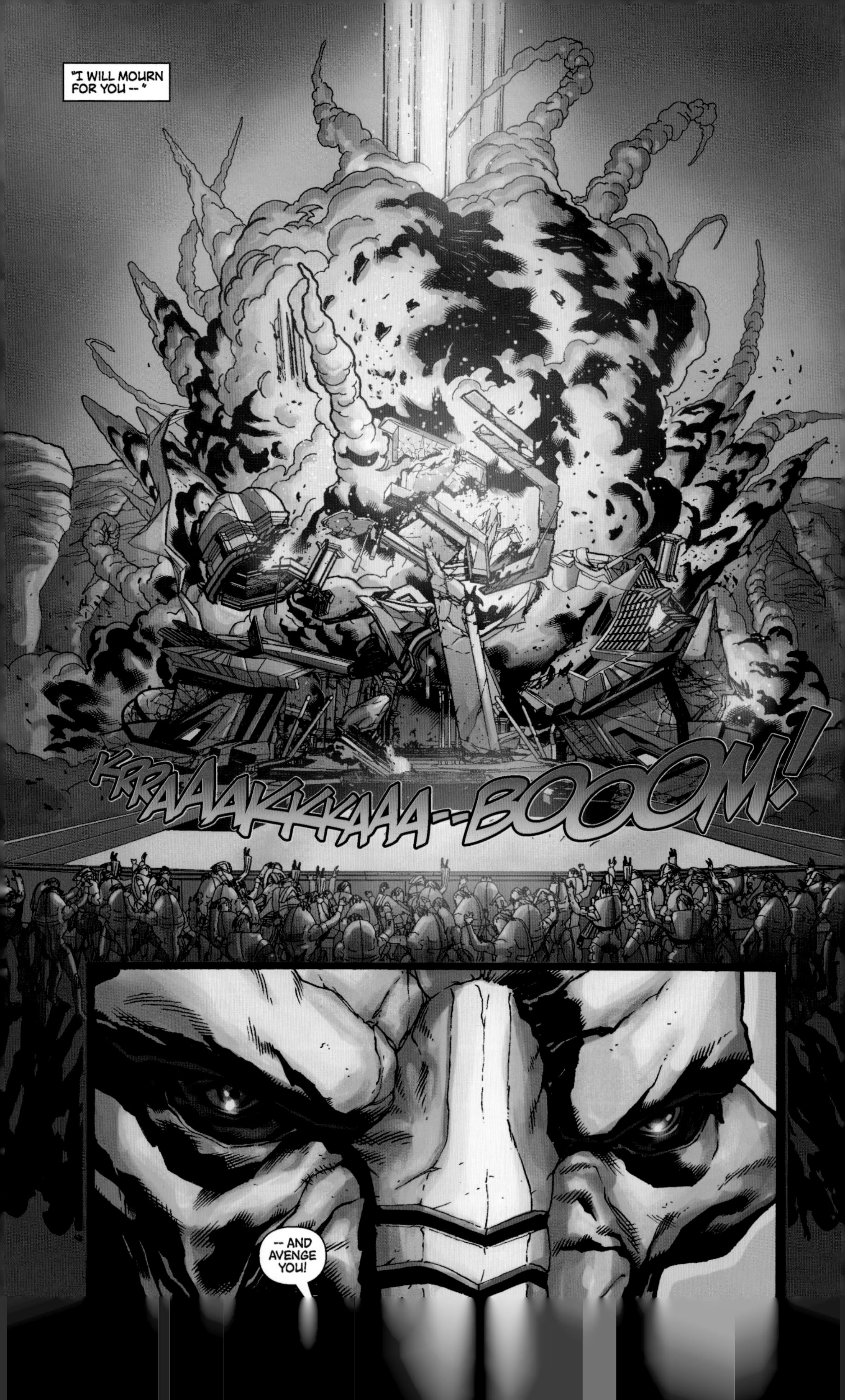
"I WILL MOURN FOR YOU --"
KRRAAAKKKAAA--BOOOM!
-- AND AVENGE YOU!

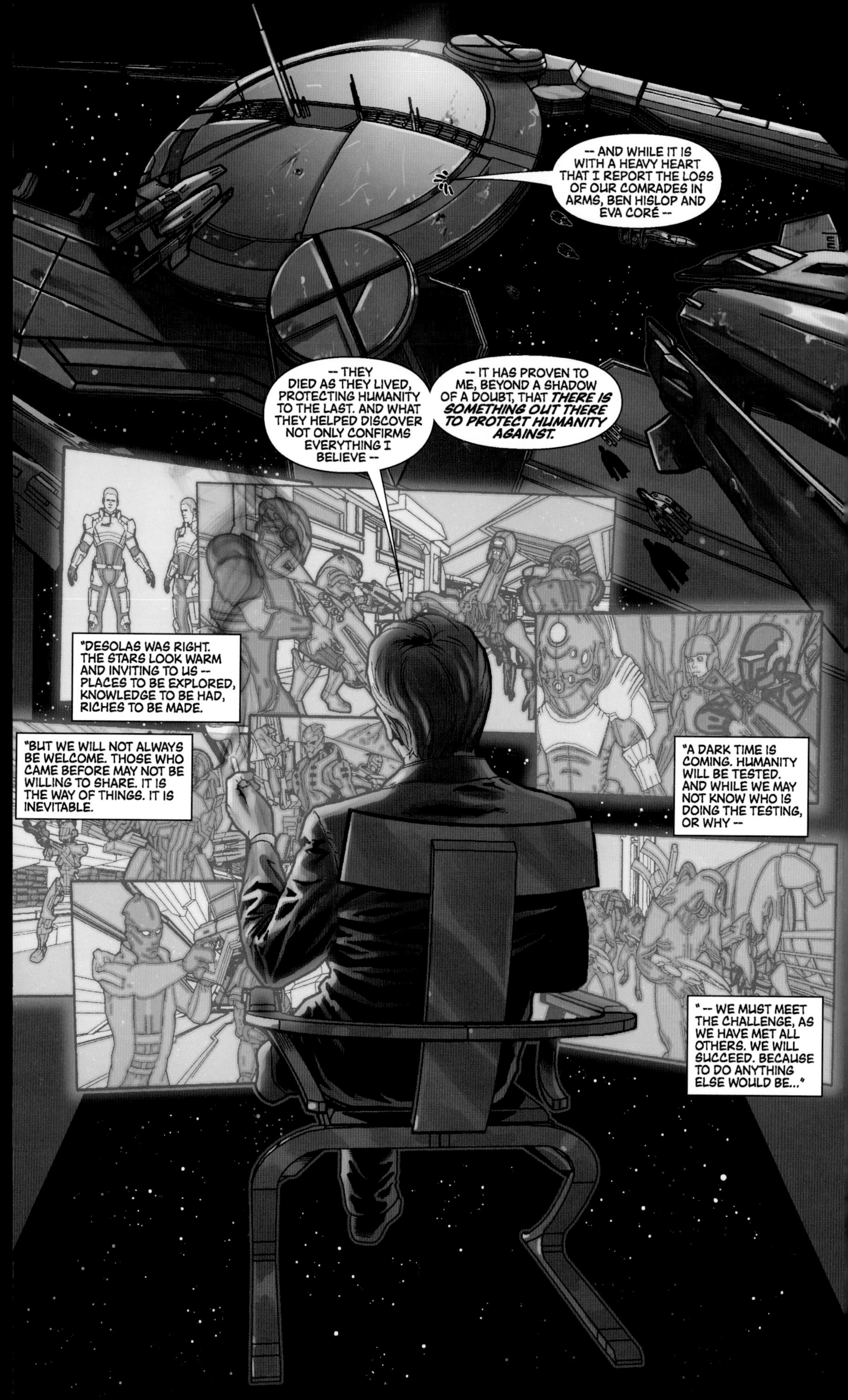
-- AND WHILE IT IS WITH A HEAVY HEART THAT I REPORT THE LOSS OF OUR COMRADES IN ARMS, BEN HISLOP AND EVA CORÉ --
-- THEY DIED AS THEY LIVED, PROTECTING HUMANITY TO THE LAST. AND WHAT THEY HELPED DISCOVER NOT ONLY CONFIRMS EVERYTHING I BELIEVE --
-- IT HAS PROVEN TO ME, BEYOND A SHADOW OF A DOUBT, THAT *THERE IS SOMETHING OUT THERE TO PROTECT HUMANITY AGAINST.*
"DESOLAS WAS RIGHT. THE STARS LOOK WARM AND INVITING TO US -- PLACES TO BE EXPLORED, KNOWLEDGE TO BE HAD, RICHES TO BE MADE.
"BUT WE WILL NOT ALWAYS BE WELCOME. THOSE WHO CAME BEFORE MAY NOT BE WILLING TO SHARE. IT IS THE WAY OF THINGS. IT IS INEVITABLE.
"A DARK TIME IS COMING. HUMANITY WILL BE TESTED. AND WHILE WE MAY NOT KNOW WHO IS DOING THE TESTING, OR WHY --
" -- WE MUST MEET THE CHALLENGE, AS WE HAVE MET ALL OTHERS. WE WILL SUCCEED. BECAUSE TO DO ANYTHING ELSE WOULD BE..."

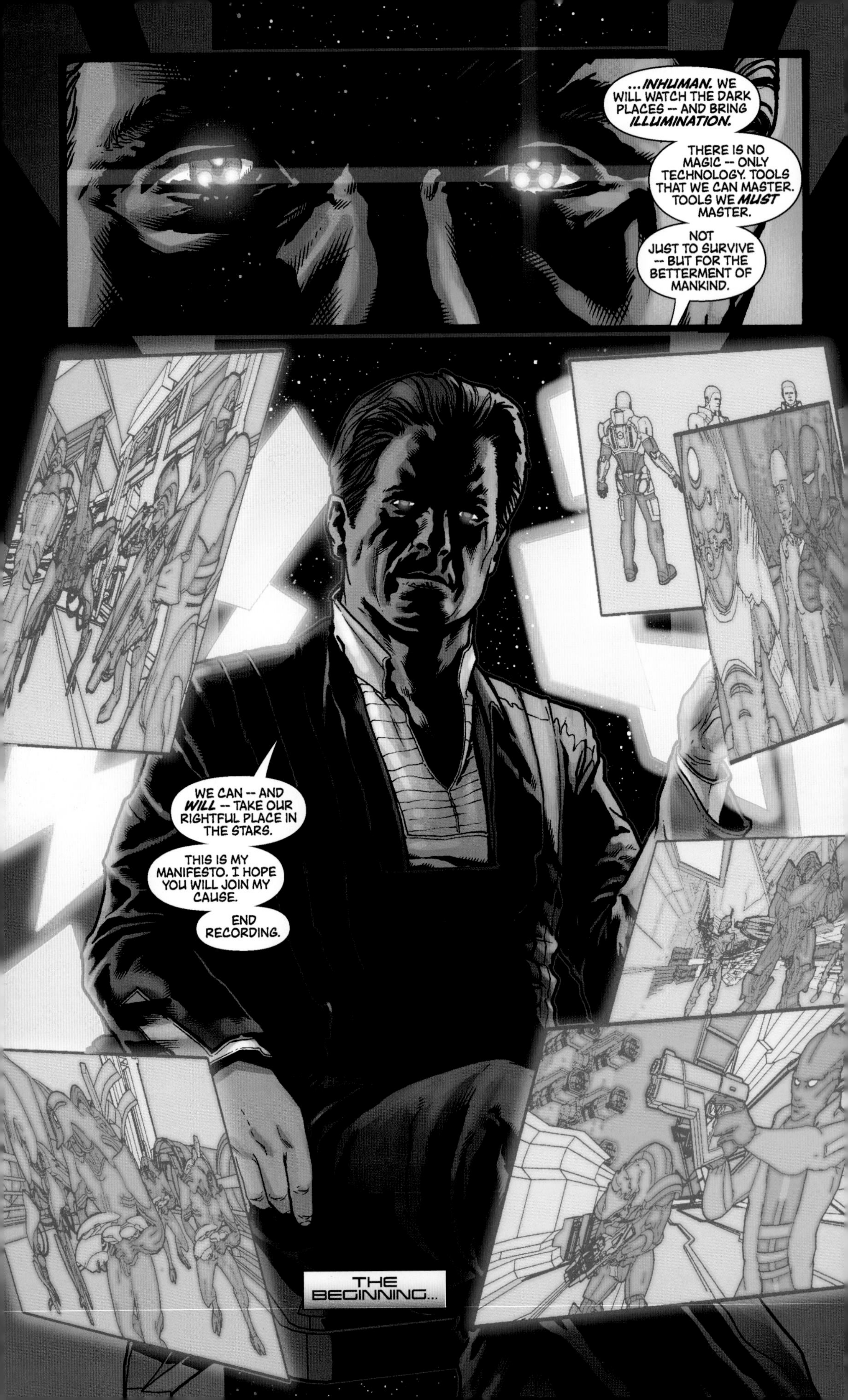
...INHUMAN. WE WILL WATCH THE DARK PLACES -- AND BRING ILLUMINATION.
THERE IS NO MAGIC -- ONLY TECHNOLOGY. TOOLS THAT WE CAN MASTER. TOOLS WE MUST MASTER.
NOT JUST TO SURVIVE -- BUT FOR THE BETTERMENT OF MANKIND.
WE CAN -- AND WILL -- TAKE OUR RIGHTFUL PLACE IN THE STARS.
THIS IS MY MANIFESTO. I HOPE YOU WILL JOIN MY CAUSE.
END RECORDING.
THE BEGINNING...

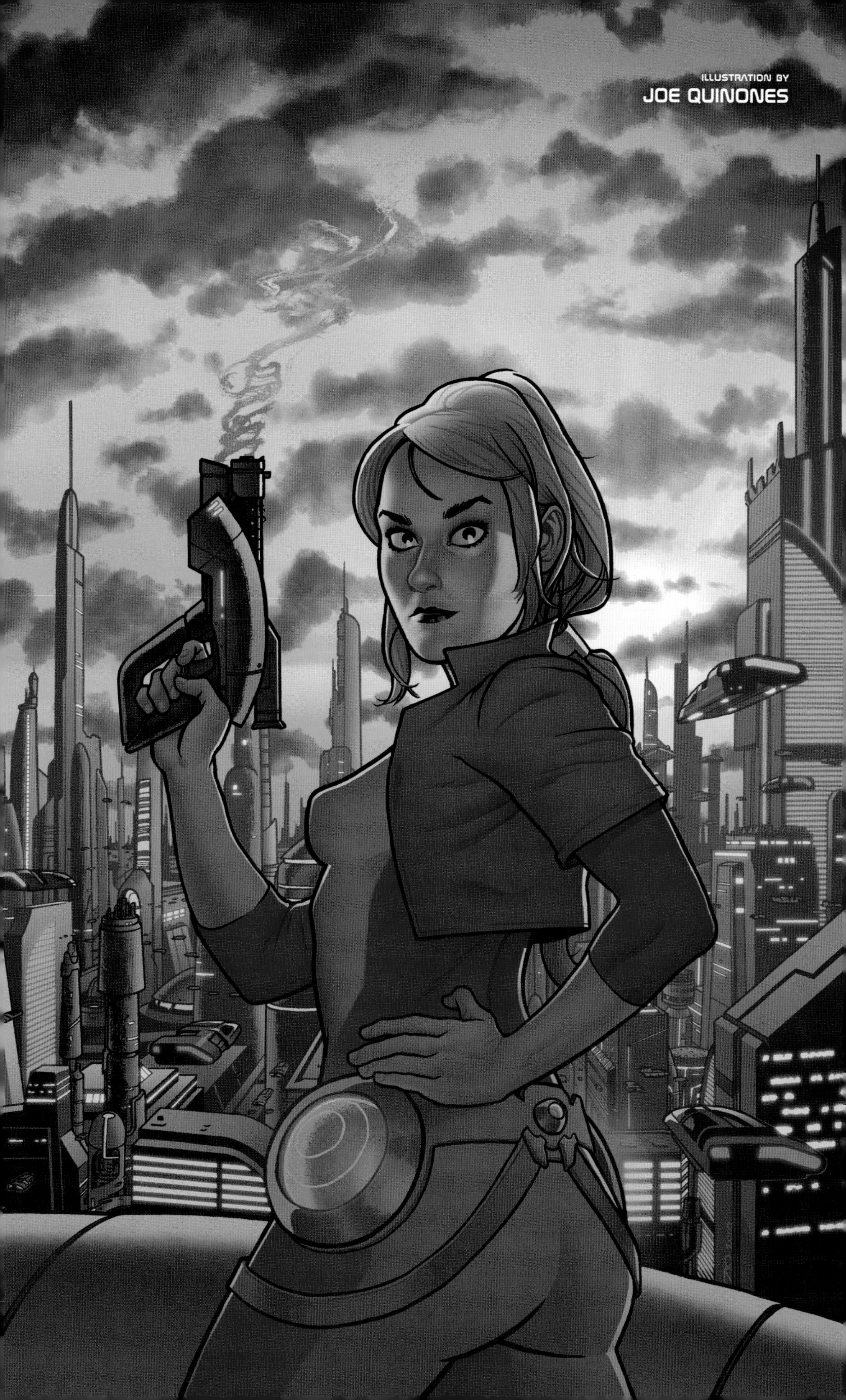
ILLUSTRATION BY
JOE QUINONES

INCURSION

SCRIPT
MAC WALTERS

ART
EDUARDO FRANCISCO

COLORS
MICHAEL ATIYEH

LETTERING
MICHAEL HEISLER

INQUISITION

SCRIPT
MAC WALTERS

ART
JEAN DIAZ

COLORS
MICHAEL ATIYEH

LETTERING
MICHAEL HEISLER

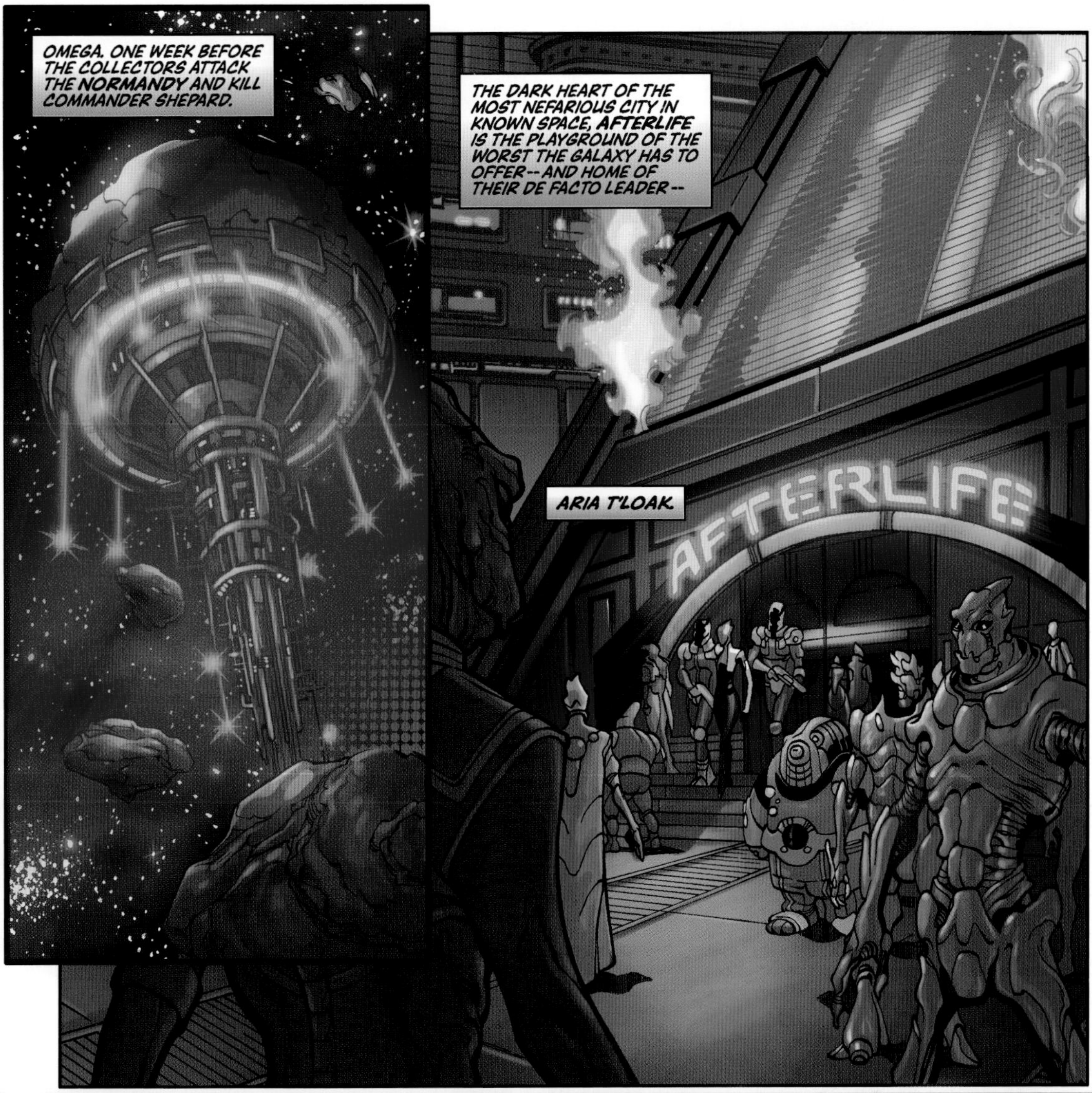
OMEGA. ONE WEEK BEFORE THE COLLECTORS ATTACK THE NORMANDY AND KILL COMMANDER SHEPARD.
THE DARK HEART OF THE MOST NEFARIOUS CITY IN KNOWN SPACE, AFTERLIFE IS THE PLAYGROUND OF THE WORST THE GALAXY HAS TO OFFER-- AND HOME OF THEIR DE FACTO LEADER --
ARIA T'LOAK.
AFTERLIFE

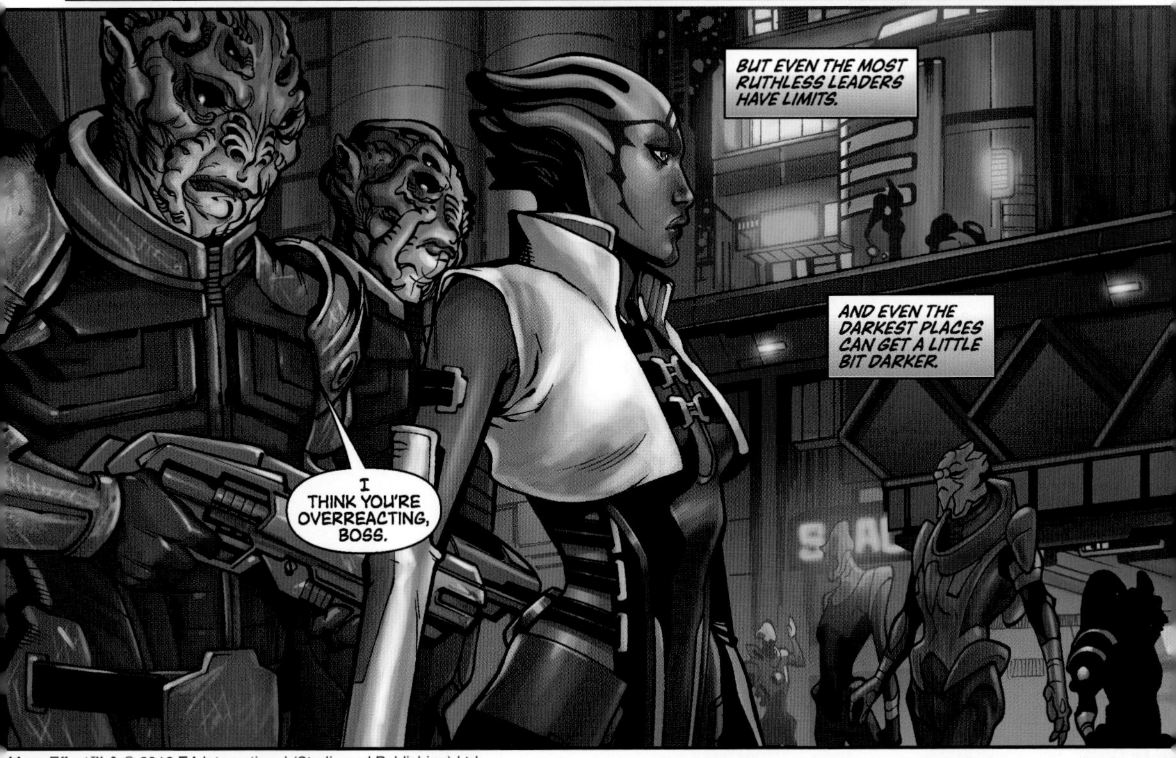
BUT EVEN THE MOST RUTHLESS LEADERS HAVE LIMITS.
AND EVEN THE DARKEST PLACES CAN GET A LITTLE BIT DARKER.
I THINK YOU'RE OVERREACTING, BOSS.

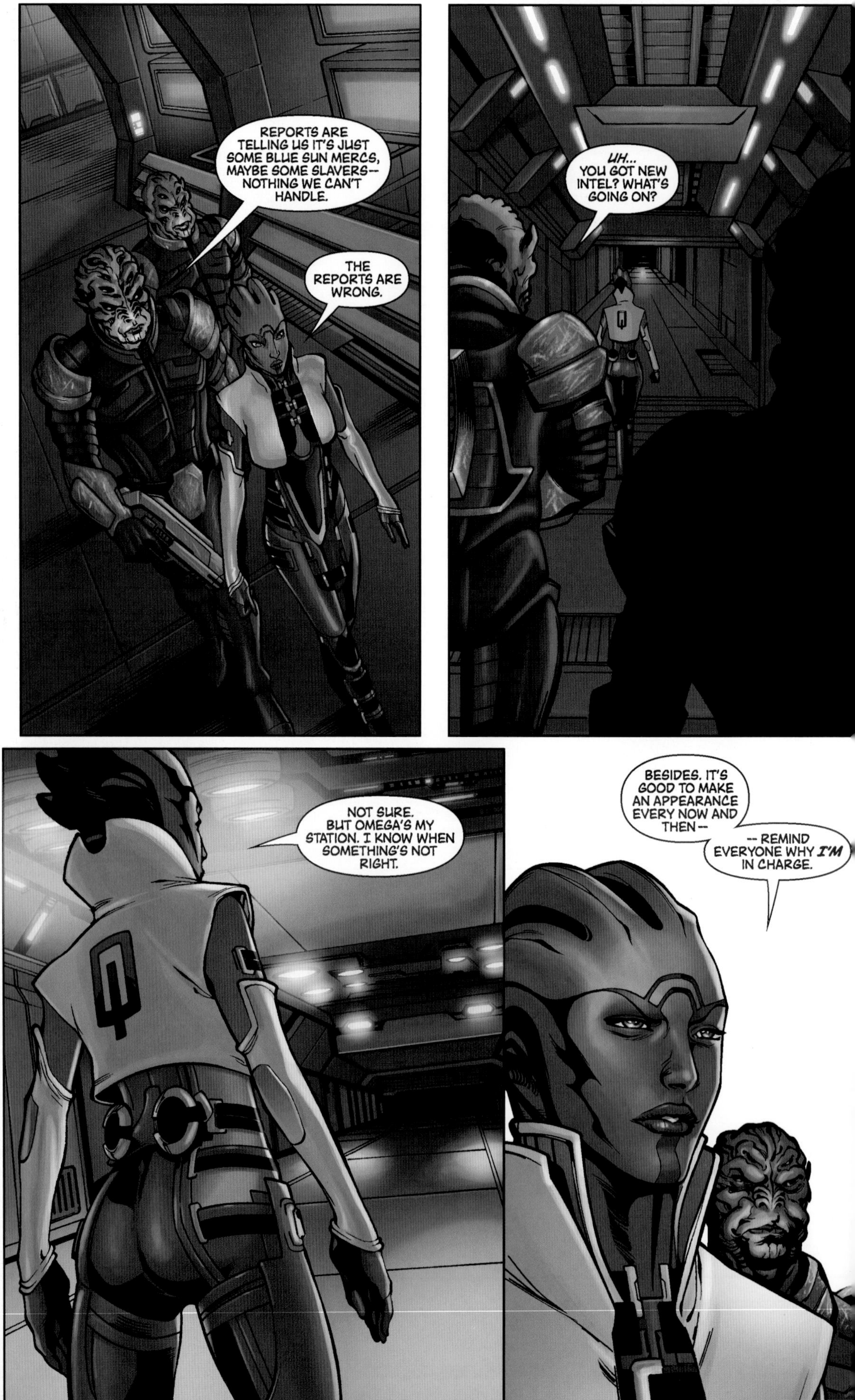
REPORTS ARE TELLING US IT'S JUST SOME BLUE SUN MERCS, MAYBE SOME SLAVERS-- NOTHING WE CAN'T HANDLE.
THE REPORTS ARE WRONG.
UH... YOU GOT NEW INTEL? WHAT'S GOING ON?
NOT SURE. BUT OMEGA'S MY STATION. I KNOW WHEN SOMETHING'S NOT RIGHT.
BESIDES. IT'S GOOD TO MAKE AN APPEARANCE EVERY NOW AND THEN--
-- REMIND EVERYONE WHY *I'M* IN CHARGE.

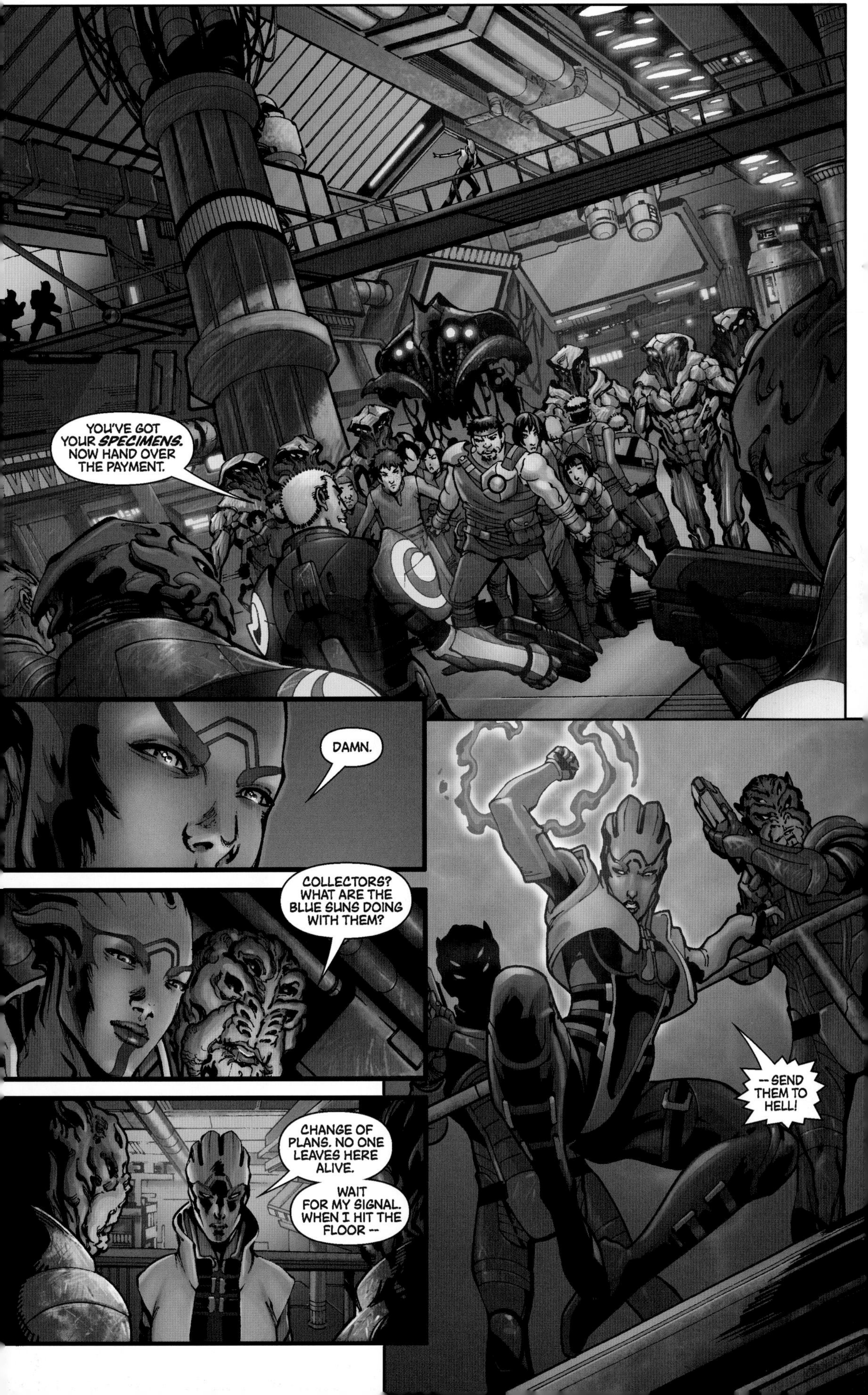
YOU'VE GOT YOUR *SPECIMENS.* NOW HAND OVER THE PAYMENT.
DAMN.
COLLECTORS? WHAT ARE THE BLUE SUNS DOING WITH THEM?
CHANGE OF PLANS. NO ONE LEAVES HERE ALIVE.
WAIT FOR MY SIGNAL. WHEN I HIT THE FLOOR --
-- SEND THEM TO HELL!

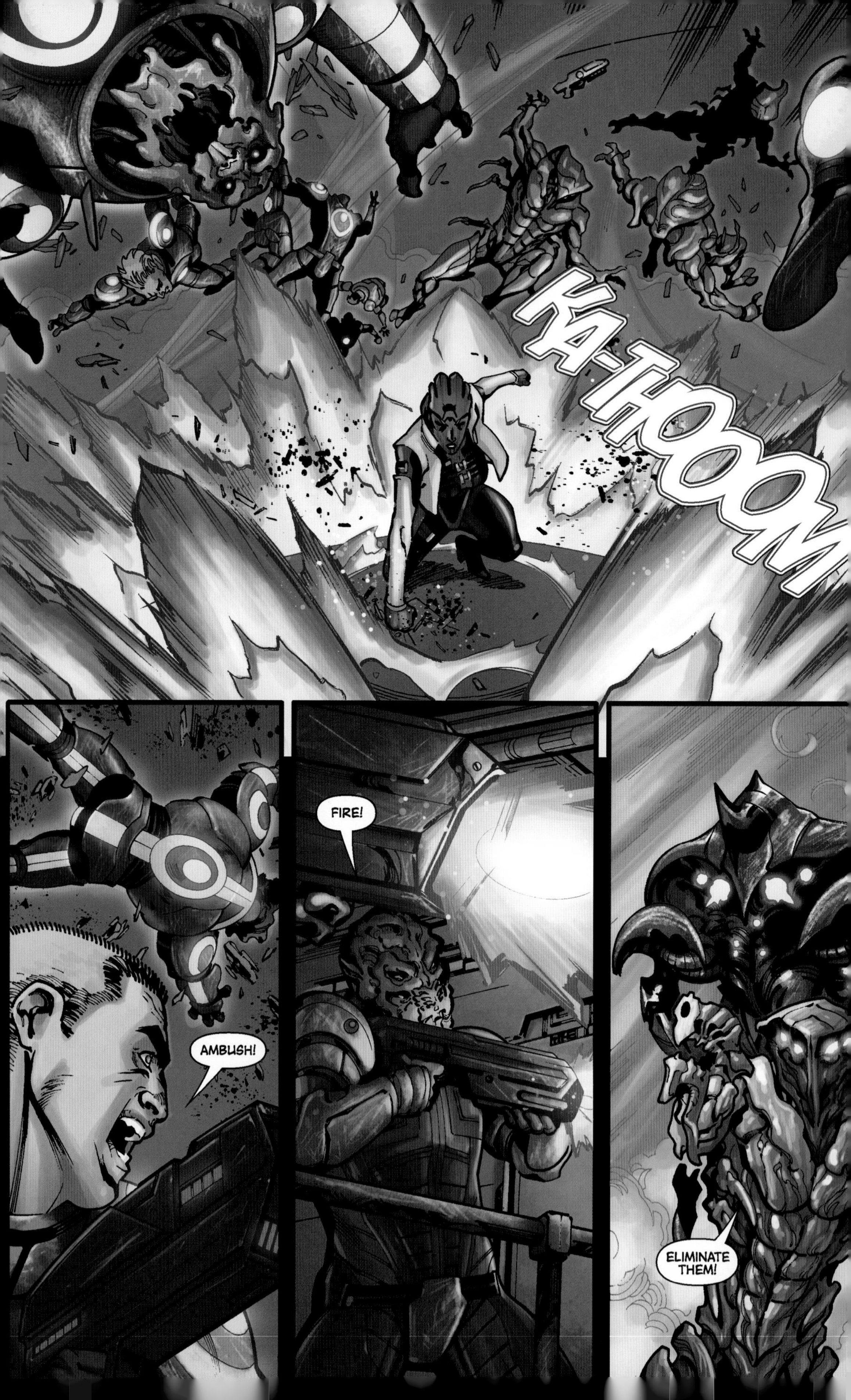
KA-THOOOM
AMBUSH!
FIRE!
ELIMINATE THEM!

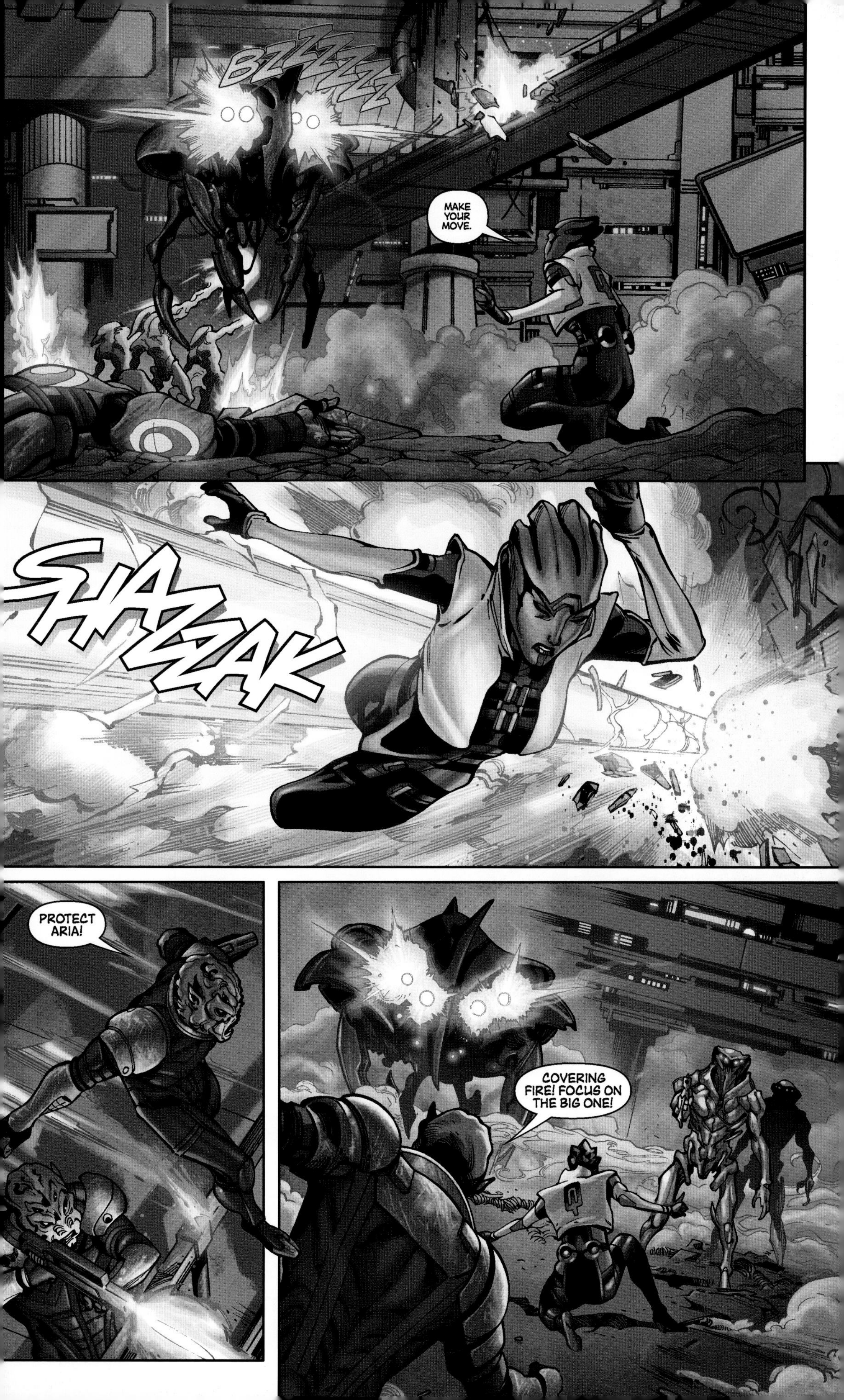
BZZZZZZZ
MAKE YOUR MOVE.
SHAZZAK
PROTECT ARIA!
COVERING FIRE! FOCUS ON THE BIG ONE!

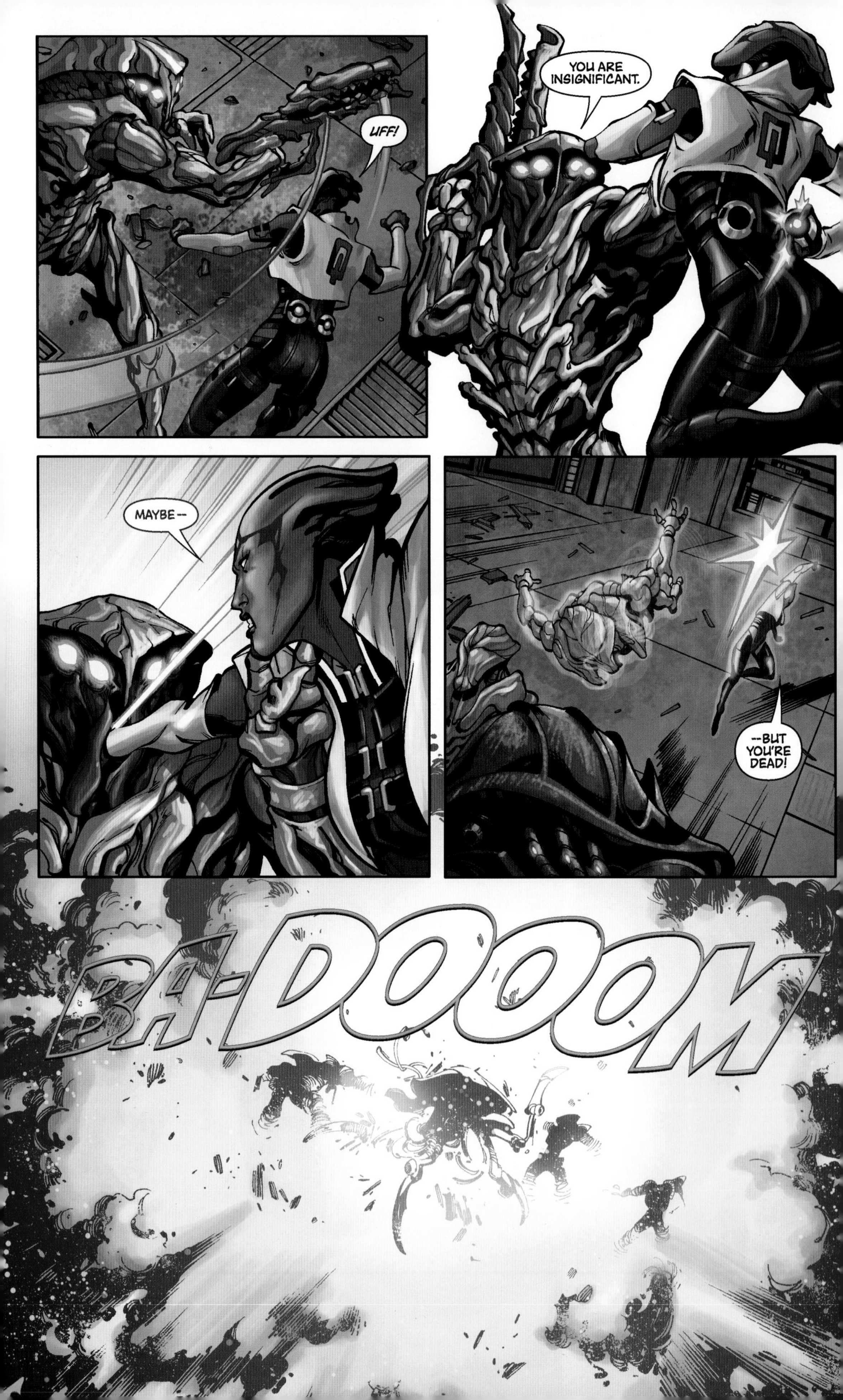
UFF!
YOU ARE INSIGNIFICANT.
MAYBE --
--BUT YOU'RE DEAD!
BA-DOOOM

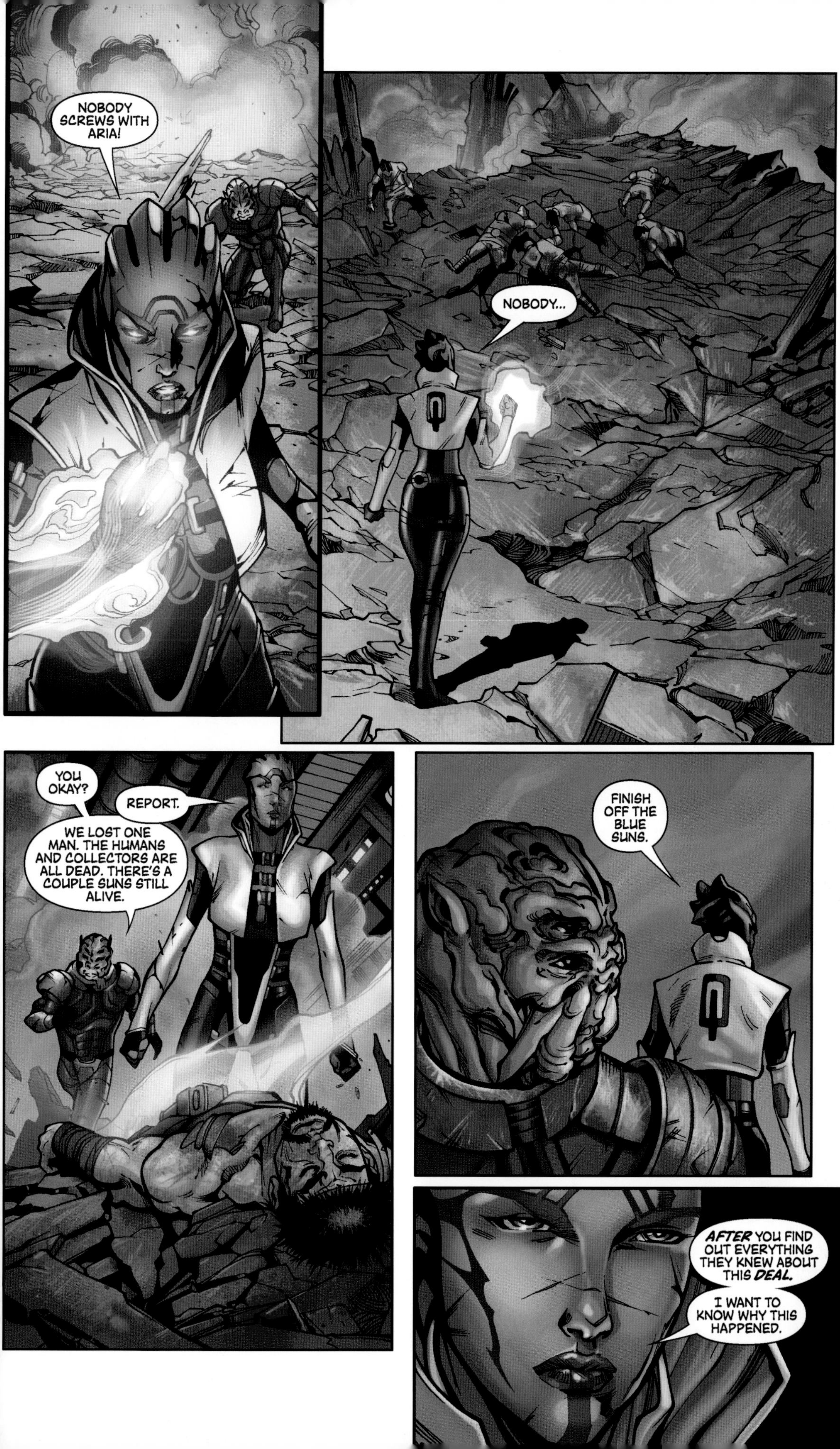
NOBODY SCREWS WITH ARIA!
NOBODY...
YOU OKAY?
REPORT.
WE LOST ONE MAN. THE HUMANS AND COLLECTORS ARE ALL DEAD. THERE'S A COUPLE SUNS STILL ALIVE.
FINISH OFF THE BLUE SUNS.
AFTER YOU FIND OUT EVERYTHING THEY KNEW ABOUT THIS *DEAL.*
I WANT TO KNOW WHY THIS HAPPENED.

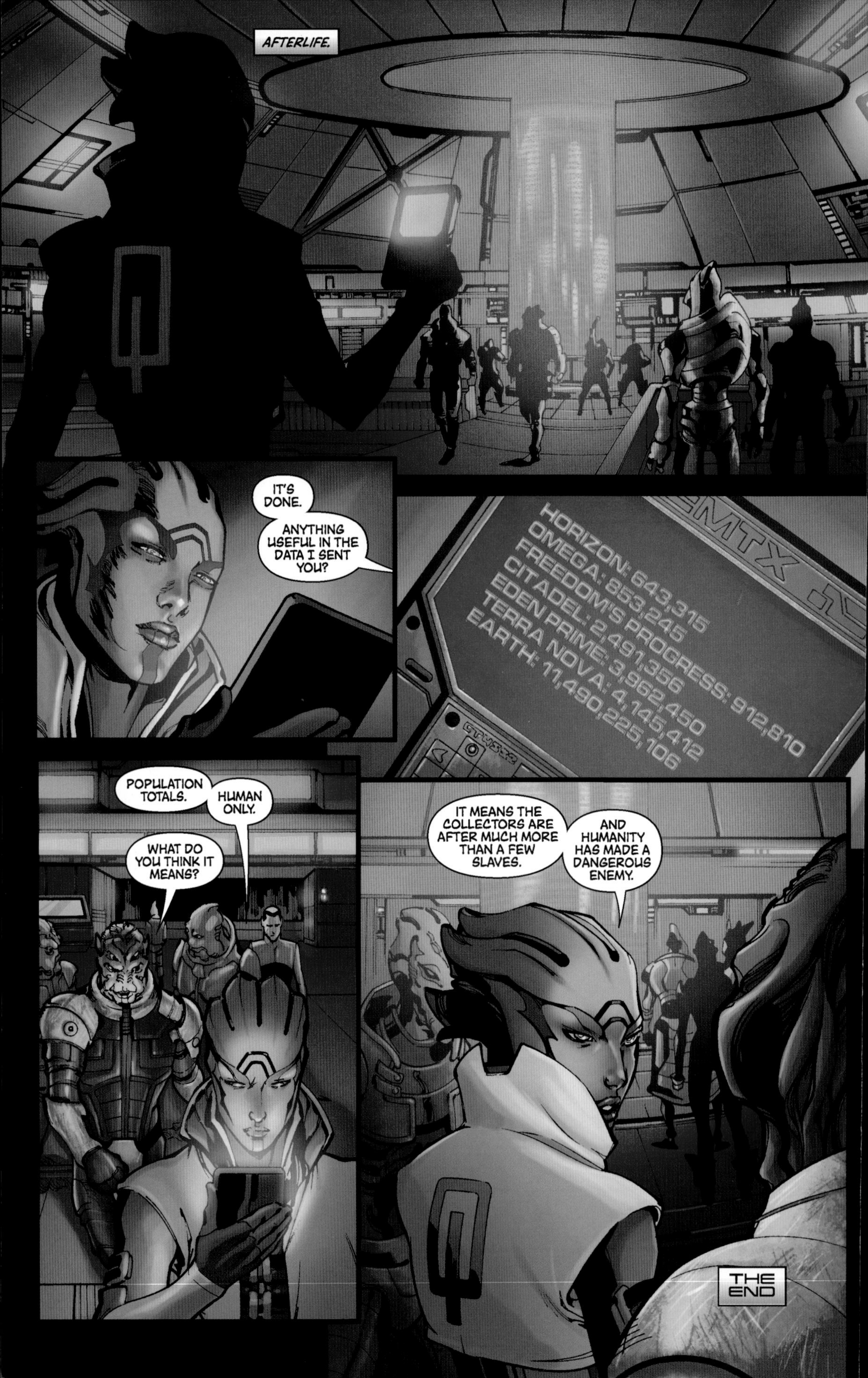
AFTERLIFE.
IT'S DONE.
ANYTHING USEFUL IN THE DATA I SENT YOU?
HORIZON: 643,315
OMEGA: 853,245
FREEDOM'S PROGRESS: 912,810
CITADEL: 2,491,356
EDEN PRIME: 3,962,450
TERRA NOVA: 4,145,412
EARTH: 11,490,225,106
POPULATION TOTALS.
HUMAN ONLY.
WHAT DO YOU THINK IT MEANS?
IT MEANS THE COLLECTORS ARE AFTER MUCH MORE THAN A FEW SLAVES.
AND HUMANITY HAS MADE A DANGEROUS ENEMY.
THE END

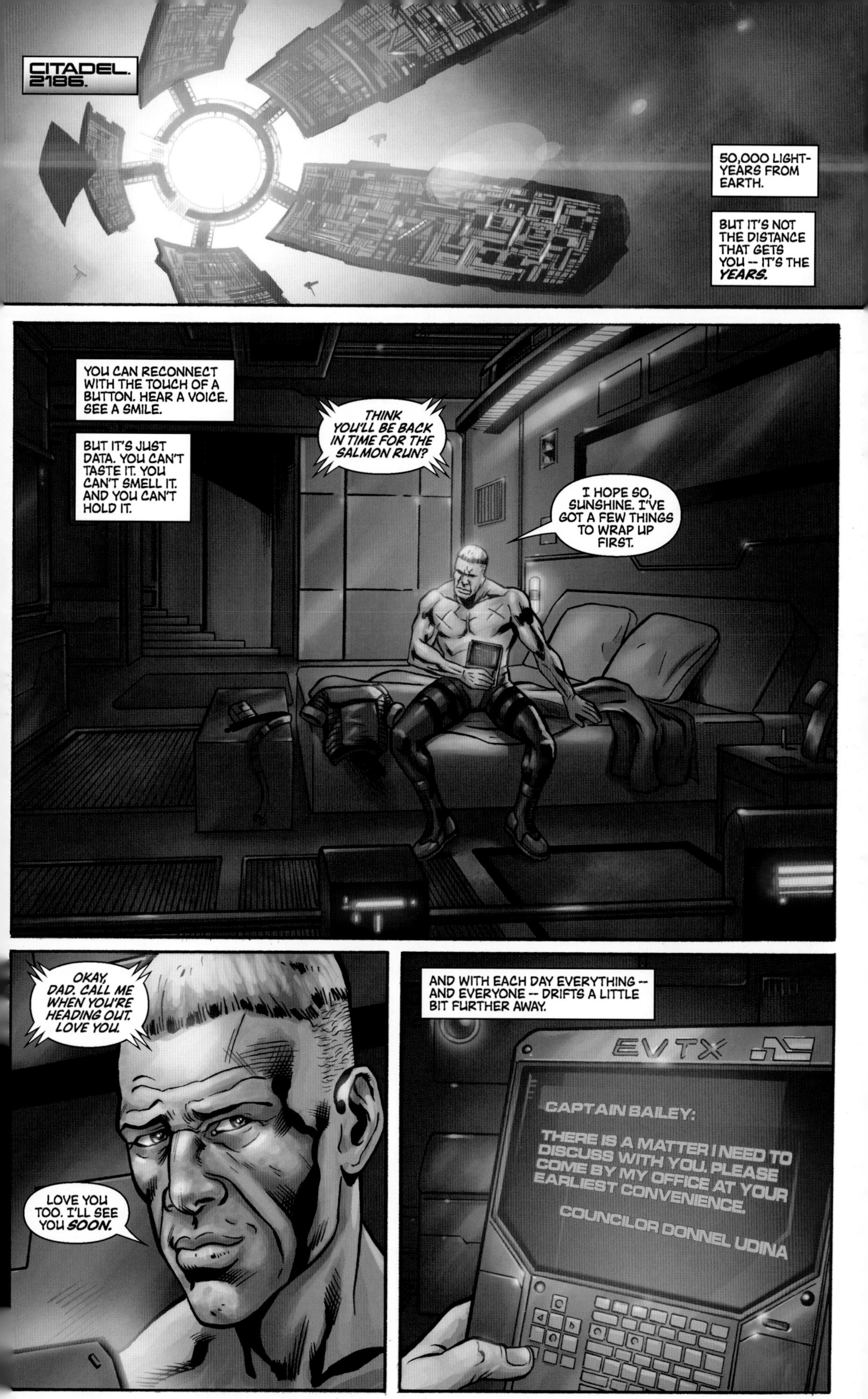
CITADEL. 2186.
50,000 LIGHT-YEARS FROM EARTH.
BUT IT'S NOT THE DISTANCE THAT GETS YOU -- IT'S THE *YEARS.*
YOU CAN RECONNECT WITH THE TOUCH OF A BUTTON. HEAR A VOICE. SEE A SMILE.
BUT IT'S JUST DATA. YOU CAN'T TASTE IT. YOU CAN'T SMELL IT. AND YOU CAN'T HOLD IT.
THINK YOU'LL BE BACK IN TIME FOR THE SALMON RUN?
I HOPE SO, SUNSHINE. I'VE GOT A FEW THINGS TO WRAP UP FIRST.
OKAY, DAD. CALL ME WHEN YOU'RE HEADING OUT. LOVE YOU.
LOVE YOU TOO. I'LL SEE YOU *SOON.*
AND WITH EACH DAY EVERYTHING -- AND EVERYONE -- DRIFTS A LITTLE BIT FURTHER AWAY.
EVTX
CAPTAIN BAILEY:
THERE IS A MATTER I NEED TO DISCUSS WITH YOU. PLEASE COME BY MY OFFICE AT YOUR EARLIEST CONVENIENCE.
COUNCILOR DONNEL UDINA

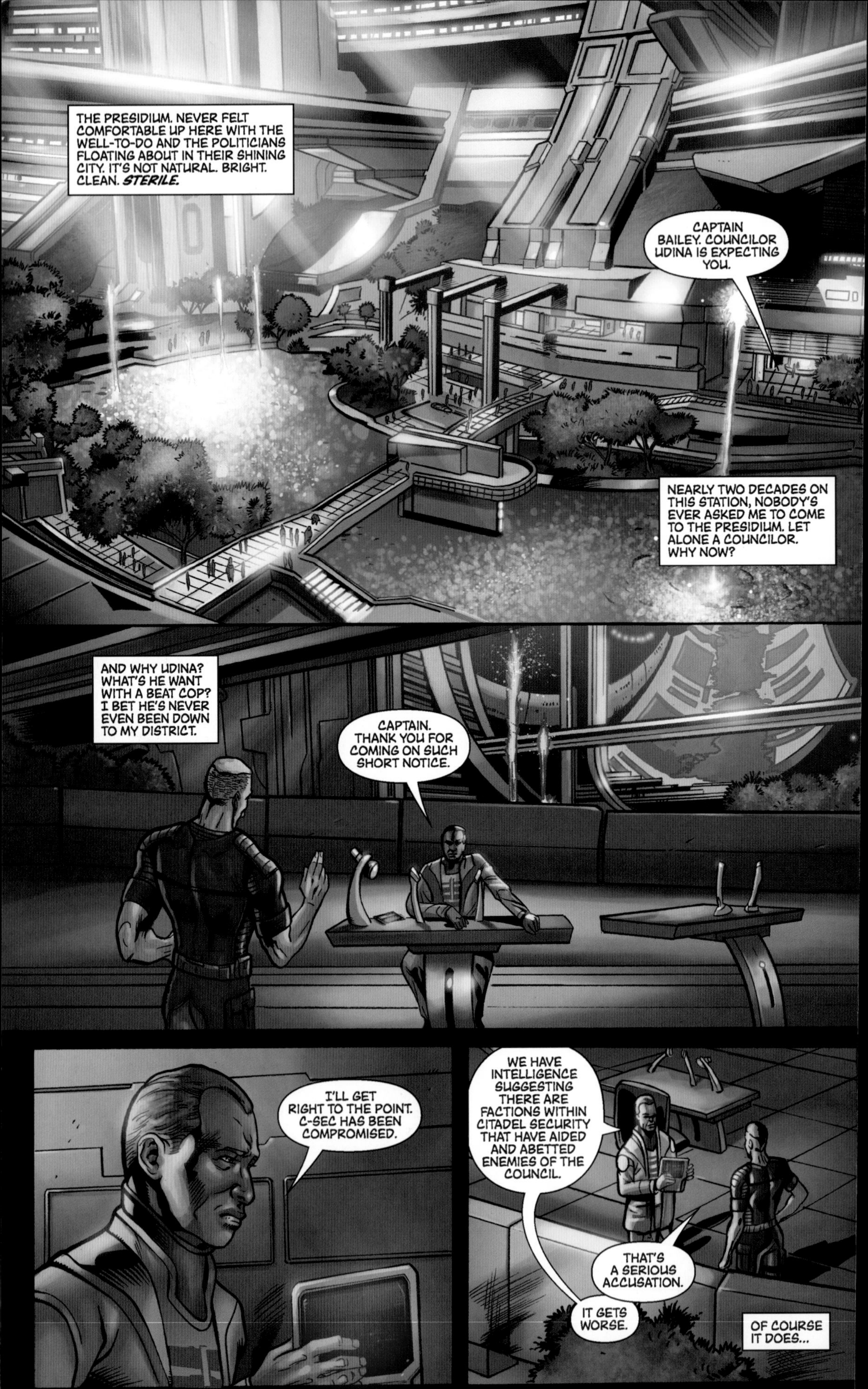
THE PRESIDIUM. NEVER FELT COMFORTABLE UP HERE WITH THE WELL-TO-DO AND THE POLITICIANS FLOATING ABOUT IN THEIR SHINING CITY. IT'S NOT NATURAL. BRIGHT. CLEAN. *STERILE.*
CAPTAIN BAILEY. COUNCILOR UDINA IS EXPECTING YOU.
NEARLY TWO DECADES ON THIS STATION, NOBODY'S EVER ASKED ME TO COME TO THE PRESIDIUM. LET ALONE A COUNCILOR. WHY NOW?
AND WHY UDINA? WHAT'S HE WANT WITH A BEAT COP? I BET HE'S NEVER EVEN BEEN DOWN TO MY DISTRICT.
CAPTAIN. THANK YOU FOR COMING ON SUCH SHORT NOTICE.
I'LL GET RIGHT TO THE POINT. C-SEC HAS BEEN COMPROMISED.
WE HAVE INTELLIGENCE SUGGESTING THERE ARE FACTIONS WITHIN CITADEL SECURITY THAT HAVE AIDED AND ABETTED ENEMIES OF THE COUNCIL.
THAT'S A SERIOUS ACCUSATION.
IT GETS WORSE.
OF COURSE IT DOES...

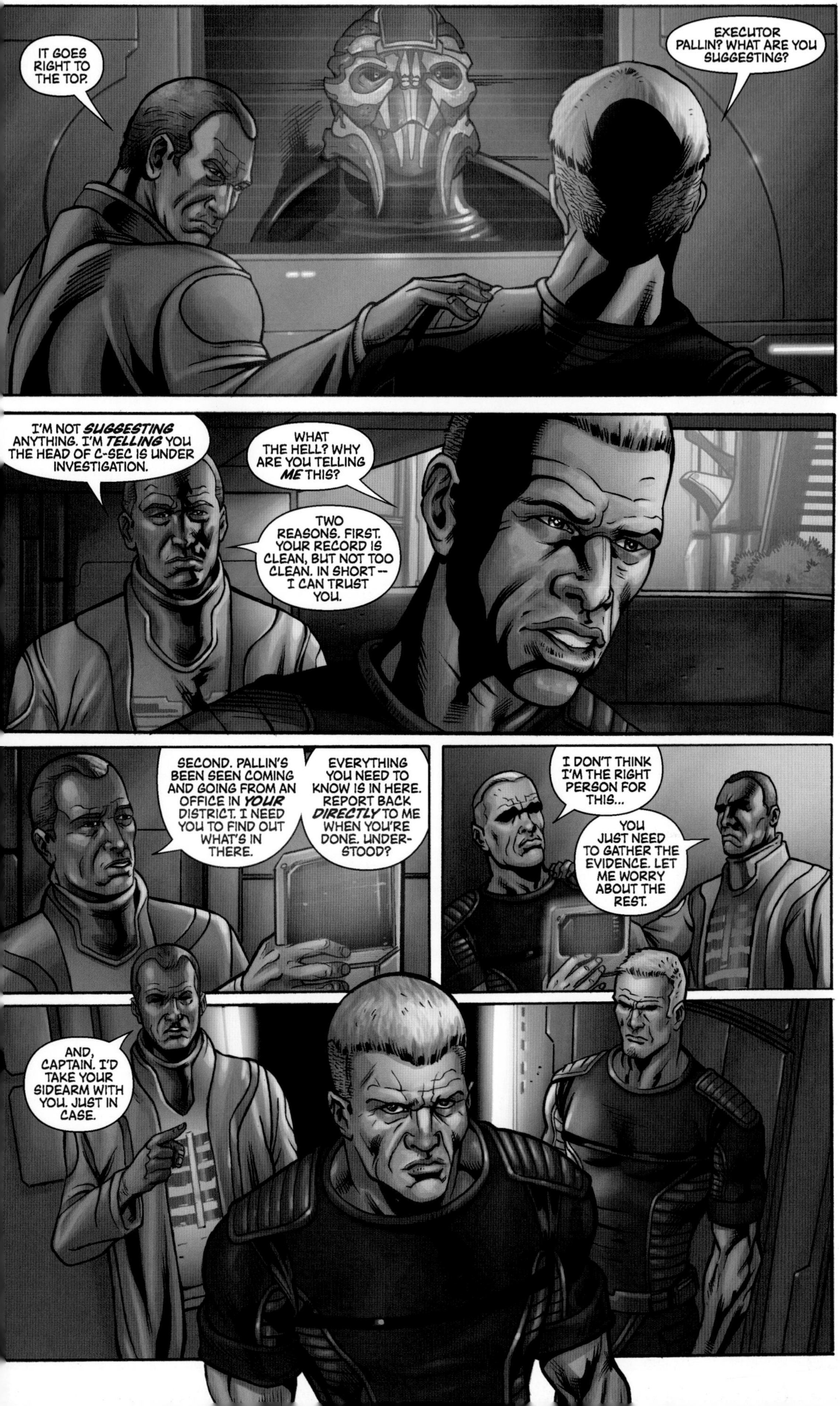
IT GOES RIGHT TO THE TOP.
EXECUTOR PALLIN? WHAT ARE YOU SUGGESTING?
I'M NOT SUGGESTING ANYTHING. I'M TELLING YOU THE HEAD OF C-SEC IS UNDER INVESTIGATION.
WHAT THE HELL? WHY ARE YOU TELLING ME THIS?
TWO REASONS. FIRST. YOUR RECORD IS CLEAN, BUT NOT TOO CLEAN. IN SHORT -- I CAN TRUST YOU.
SECOND. PALLIN'S BEEN SEEN COMING AND GOING FROM AN OFFICE IN YOUR DISTRICT. I NEED YOU TO FIND OUT WHAT'S IN THERE.
EVERYTHING YOU NEED TO KNOW IS IN HERE. REPORT BACK DIRECTLY TO ME WHEN YOU'RE DONE. UNDERSTOOD?
I DON'T THINK I'M THE RIGHT PERSON FOR THIS...
YOU JUST NEED TO GATHER THE EVIDENCE. LET ME WORRY ABOUT THE REST.
AND, CAPTAIN. I'D TAKE YOUR SIDEARM WITH YOU. JUST IN CASE.

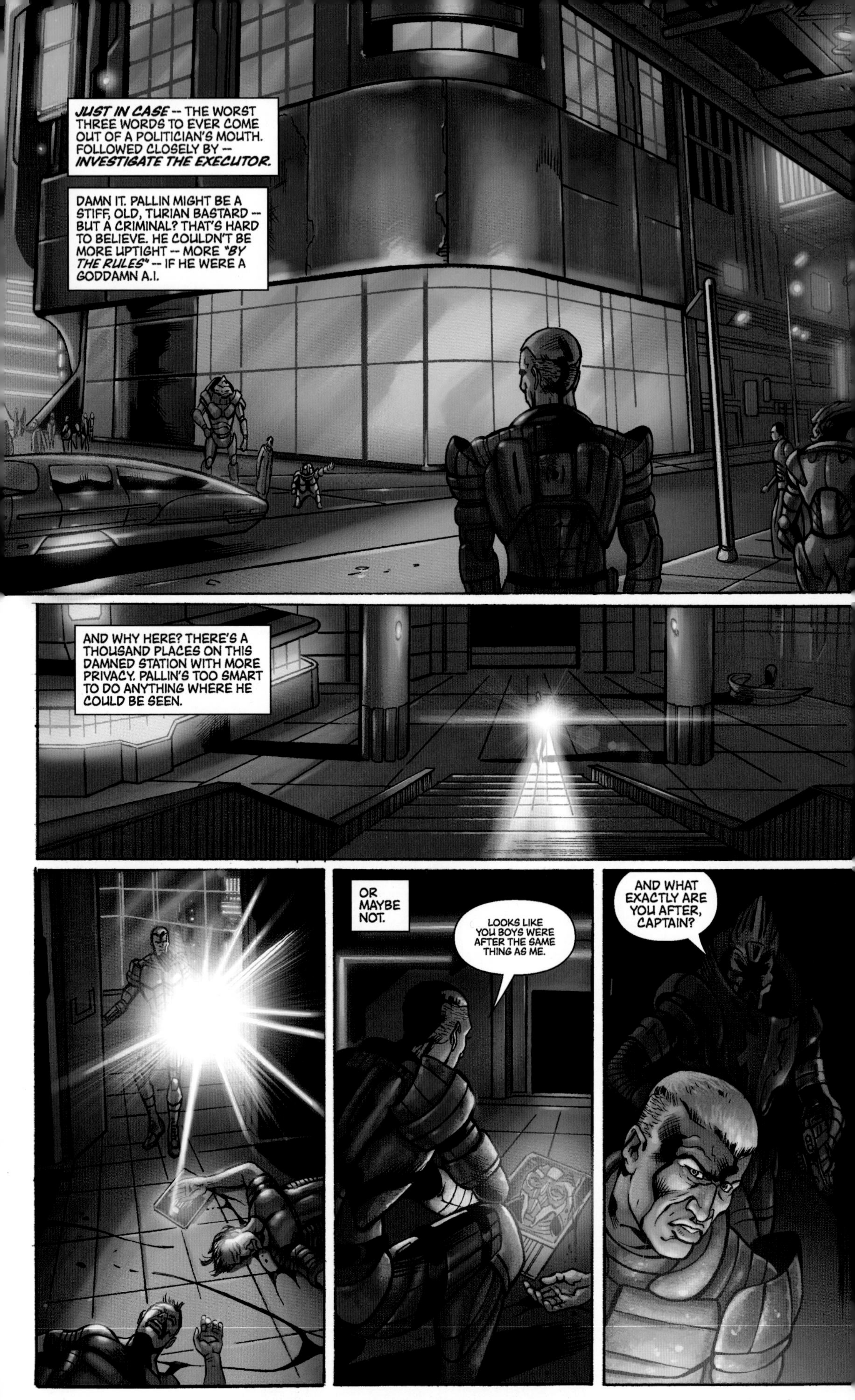
JUST IN CASE -- THE WORST THREE WORDS TO EVER COME OUT OF A POLITICIAN'S MOUTH. FOLLOWED CLOSELY BY -- INVESTIGATE THE EXECUTOR.
DAMN IT. PALLIN MIGHT BE A STIFF, OLD, TURIAN BASTARD -- BUT A CRIMINAL? THAT'S HARD TO BELIEVE. HE COULDN'T BE MORE UPTIGHT -- MORE "BY THE RULES" -- IF HE WERE A GODDAMN A.I.
AND WHY HERE? THERE'S A THOUSAND PLACES ON THIS DAMNED STATION WITH MORE PRIVACY. PALLIN'S TOO SMART TO DO ANYTHING WHERE HE COULD BE SEEN.
OR MAYBE NOT.
LOOKS LIKE YOU BOYS WERE AFTER THE SAME THING AS ME.
AND WHAT EXACTLY ARE YOU AFTER, CAPTAIN?

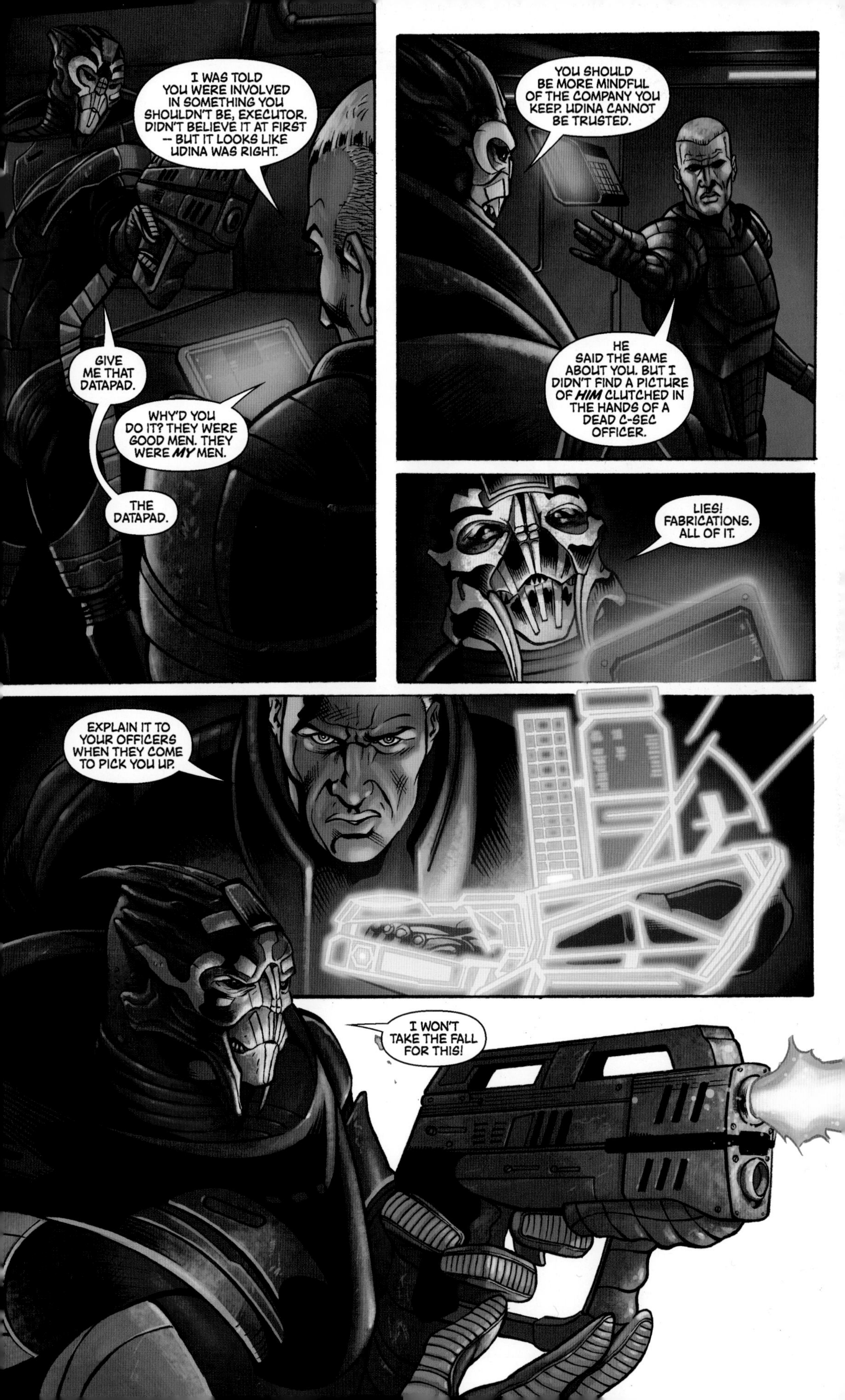
I WAS TOLD YOU WERE INVOLVED IN SOMETHING YOU SHOULDN'T BE, EXECUTOR. DIDN'T BELIEVE IT AT FIRST -- BUT IT LOOKS LIKE UDINA WAS RIGHT.
GIVE ME THAT DATAPAD.
WHY'D YOU DO IT? THEY WERE GOOD MEN. THEY WERE *MY* MEN.
THE DATAPAD.
YOU SHOULD BE MORE MINDFUL OF THE COMPANY YOU KEEP. UDINA CANNOT BE TRUSTED.
HE SAID THE SAME ABOUT YOU. BUT I DIDN'T FIND A PICTURE OF *HIM* CLUTCHED IN THE HANDS OF A DEAD C-SEC OFFICER.
LIES! FABRICATIONS. ALL OF IT.
EXPLAIN IT TO YOUR OFFICERS WHEN THEY COME TO PICK YOU UP.
I WON'T TAKE THE FALL FOR THIS!

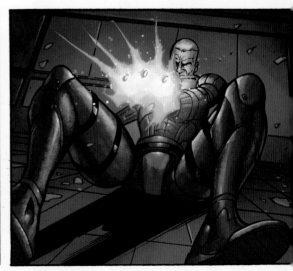

DROP IT.

YOU AND UDINA WON'T GET AWAY WITH THIS. I DIDN'T DO ANYTHING WRONG.

THAT'S NOT FOR US TO DECIDE.

WRONG!

NOBODY DECIDES MY FATE BUT *ME*.

NOBODY.

KRCHOWWW!

FATE... IS A BITCH, EXECUTOR.

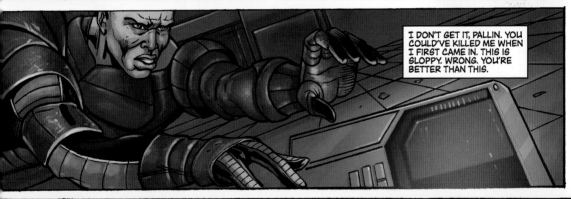

I DON'T GET IT, PALLIN. YOU COULD'VE KILLED ME WHEN I FIRST CAME IN. THIS IS SLOPPY. WRONG. YOU'RE BETTER THAN THIS.

AT LEAST I THOUGHT YOU WERE.

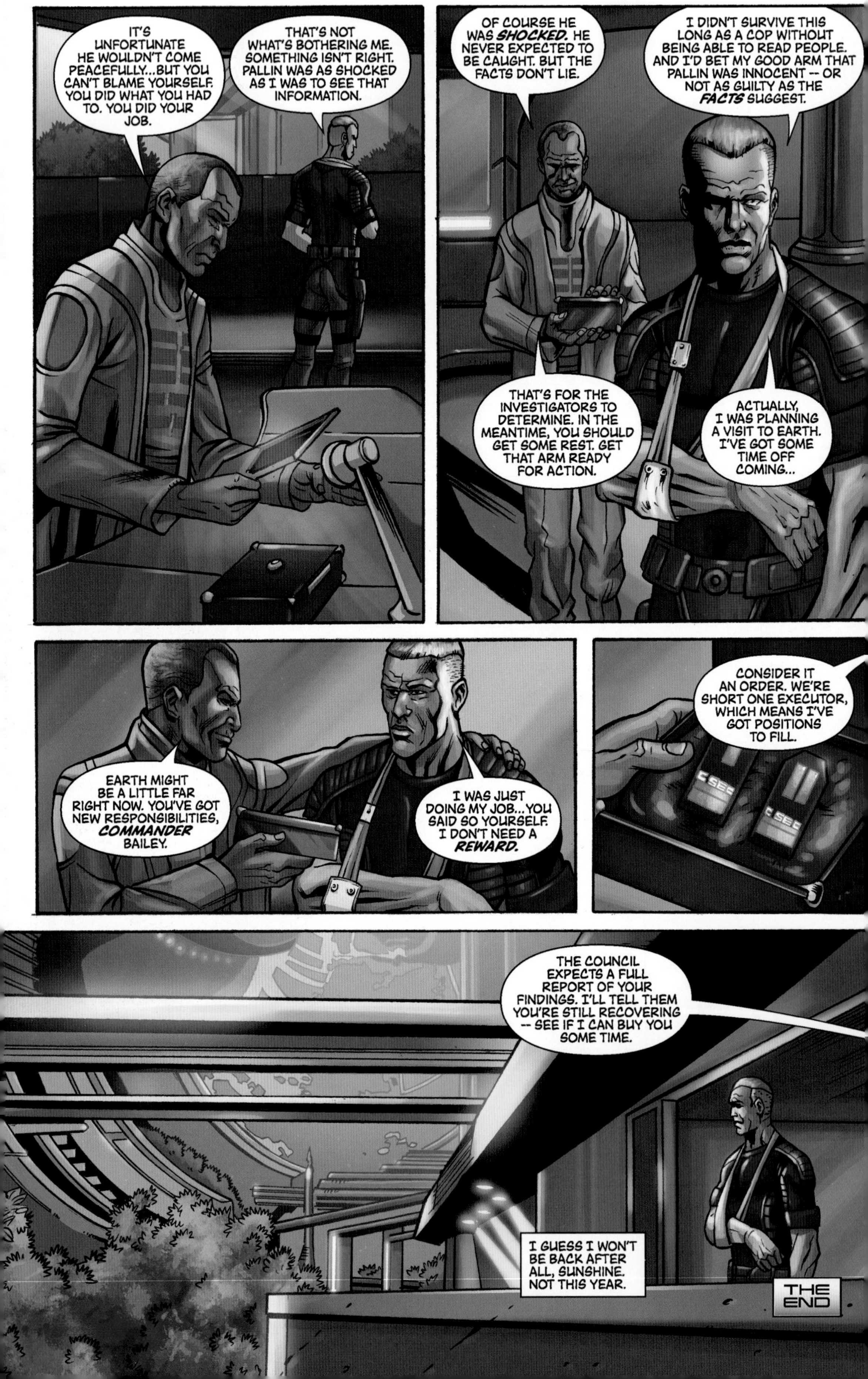
IT'S UNFORTUNATE HE WOULDN'T COME PEACEFULLY...BUT YOU CAN'T BLAME YOURSELF. YOU DID WHAT YOU HAD TO. YOU DID YOUR JOB.
THAT'S NOT WHAT'S BOTHERING ME. SOMETHING ISN'T RIGHT. PALLIN WAS AS SHOCKED AS I WAS TO SEE THAT INFORMATION.
OF COURSE HE WAS SHOCKED. HE NEVER EXPECTED TO BE CAUGHT. BUT THE FACTS DON'T LIE.
I DIDN'T SURVIVE THIS LONG AS A COP WITHOUT BEING ABLE TO READ PEOPLE. AND I'D BET MY GOOD ARM THAT PALLIN WAS INNOCENT -- OR NOT AS GUILTY AS THE FACTS SUGGEST.
THAT'S FOR THE INVESTIGATORS TO DETERMINE. IN THE MEANTIME, YOU SHOULD GET SOME REST. GET THAT ARM READY FOR ACTION.
ACTUALLY, I WAS PLANNING A VISIT TO EARTH. I'VE GOT SOME TIME OFF COMING...
EARTH MIGHT BE A LITTLE FAR RIGHT NOW. YOU'VE GOT NEW RESPONSIBILITIES, COMMANDER BAILEY.
I WAS JUST DOING MY JOB...YOU SAID SO YOURSELF. I DON'T NEED A REWARD.
CONSIDER IT AN ORDER. WE'RE SHORT ONE EXECUTOR, WHICH MEANS I'VE GOT POSITIONS TO FILL.
C-SEC
C-SEC
THE COUNCIL EXPECTS A FULL REPORT OF YOUR FINDINGS. I'LL TELL THEM YOU'RE STILL RECOVERING -- SEE IF I CAN BUY YOU SOME TIME.
I GUESS I WON'T BE BACK AFTER ALL, SUNSHINE. NOT THIS YEAR.
THE END

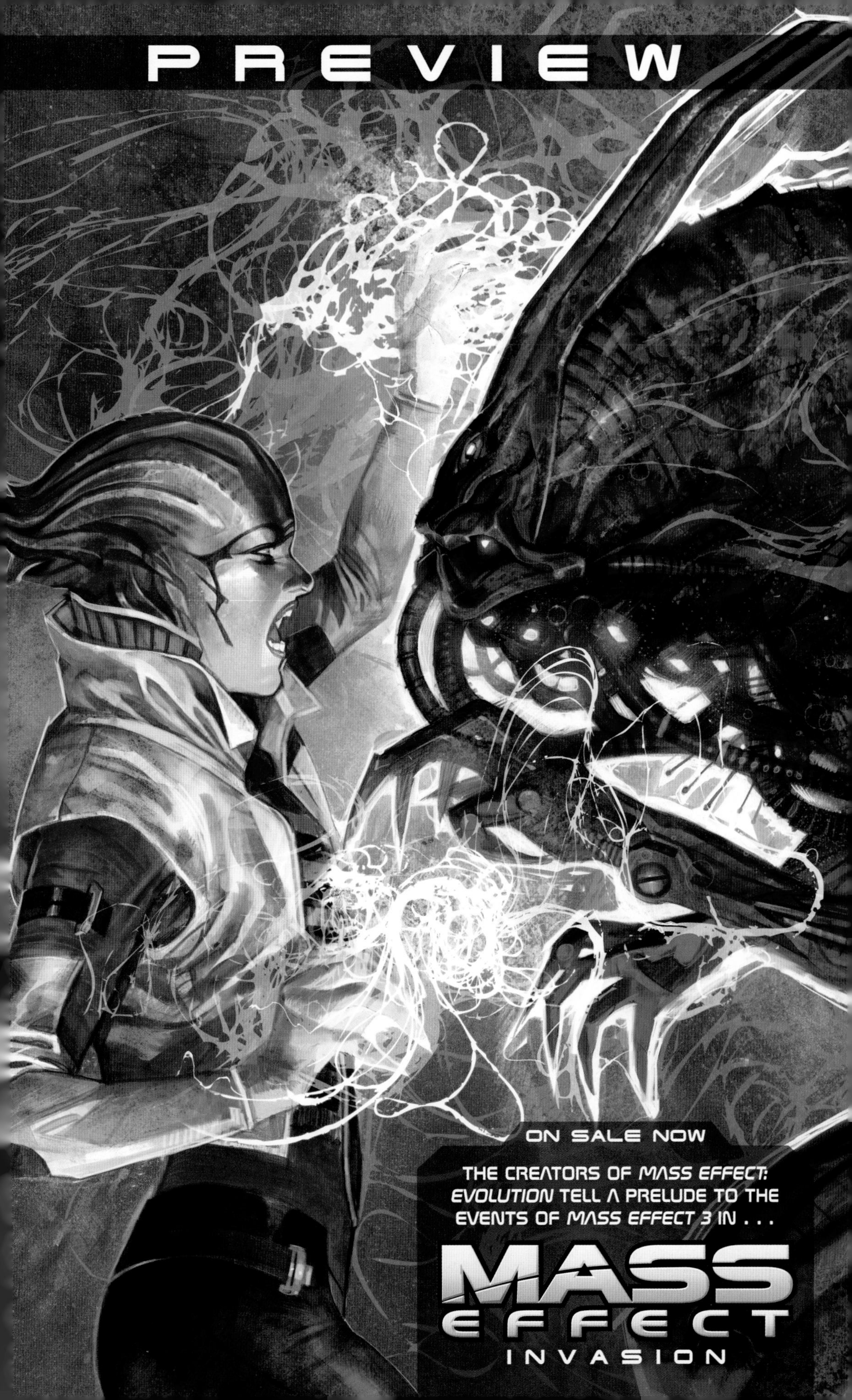
PREVIEW
ON SALE NOW
THE CREATORS OF *MASS EFFECT: EVOLUTION* TELL A PRELUDE TO THE EVENTS OF *MASS EFFECT 3* IN . . .
MASS EFFECT
INVASION

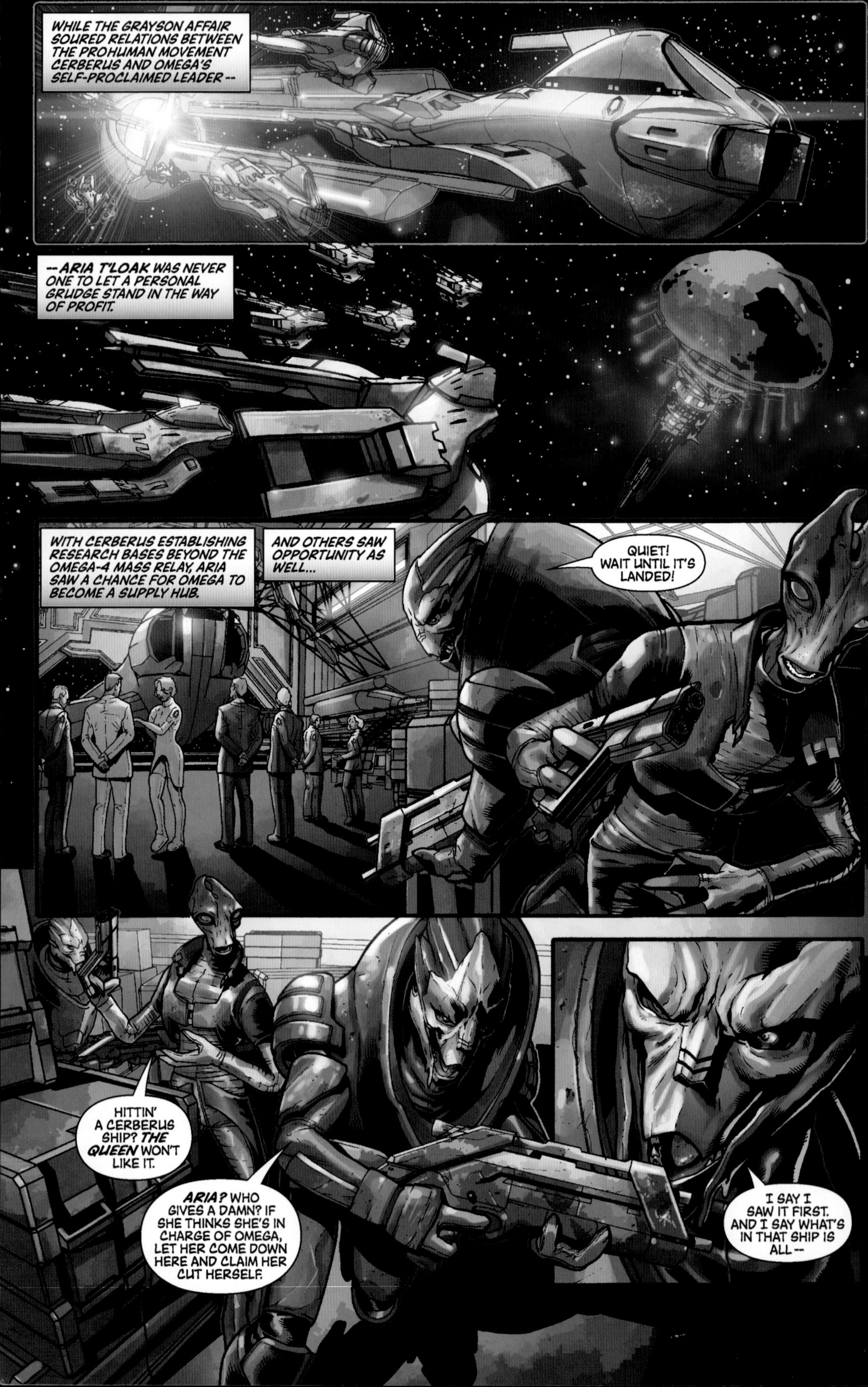
WHILE THE GRAYSON AFFAIR SOURED RELATIONS BETWEEN THE PROHUMAN MOVEMENT CERBERUS AND OMEGA'S SELF-PROCLAIMED LEADER --
--ARIA T'LOAK WAS NEVER ONE TO LET A PERSONAL GRUDGE STAND IN THE WAY OF PROFIT.
WITH CERBERUS ESTABLISHING RESEARCH BASES BEYOND THE OMEGA-4 MASS RELAY, ARIA SAW A CHANCE FOR OMEGA TO BECOME A SUPPLY HUB.
AND OTHERS SAW OPPORTUNITY AS WELL...
QUIET! WAIT UNTIL IT'S LANDED!
HITTIN' A CERBERUS SHIP? THE QUEEN WON'T LIKE IT.
ARIA? WHO GIVES A DAMN? IF SHE THINKS SHE'S IN CHARGE OF OMEGA, LET HER COME DOWN HERE AND CLAIM HER CUT HERSELF.
I SAY I SAW IT FIRST. AND I SAY WHAT'S IN THAT SHIP IS ALL --

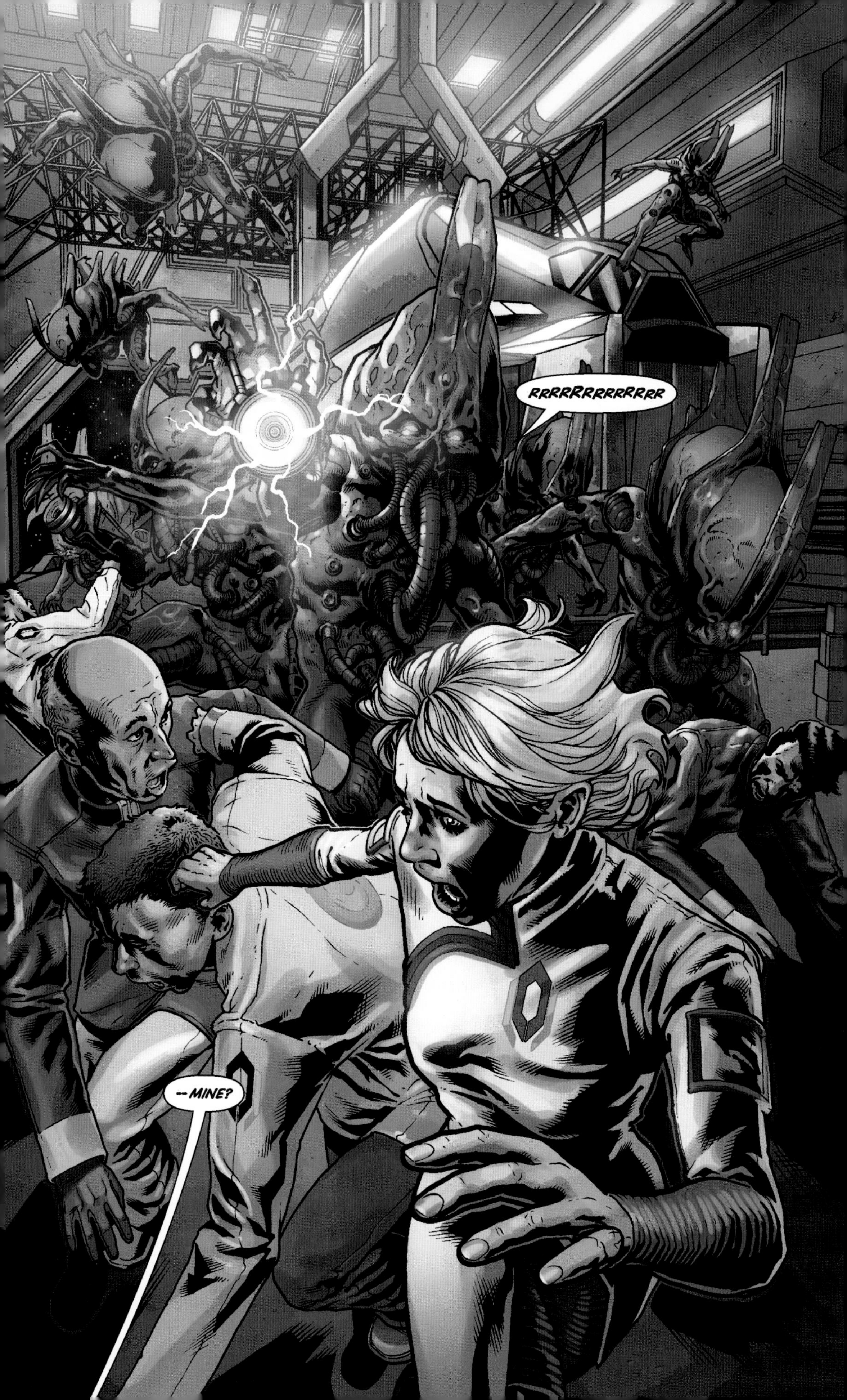
RRRRRRRRRRRRR
--MINE?

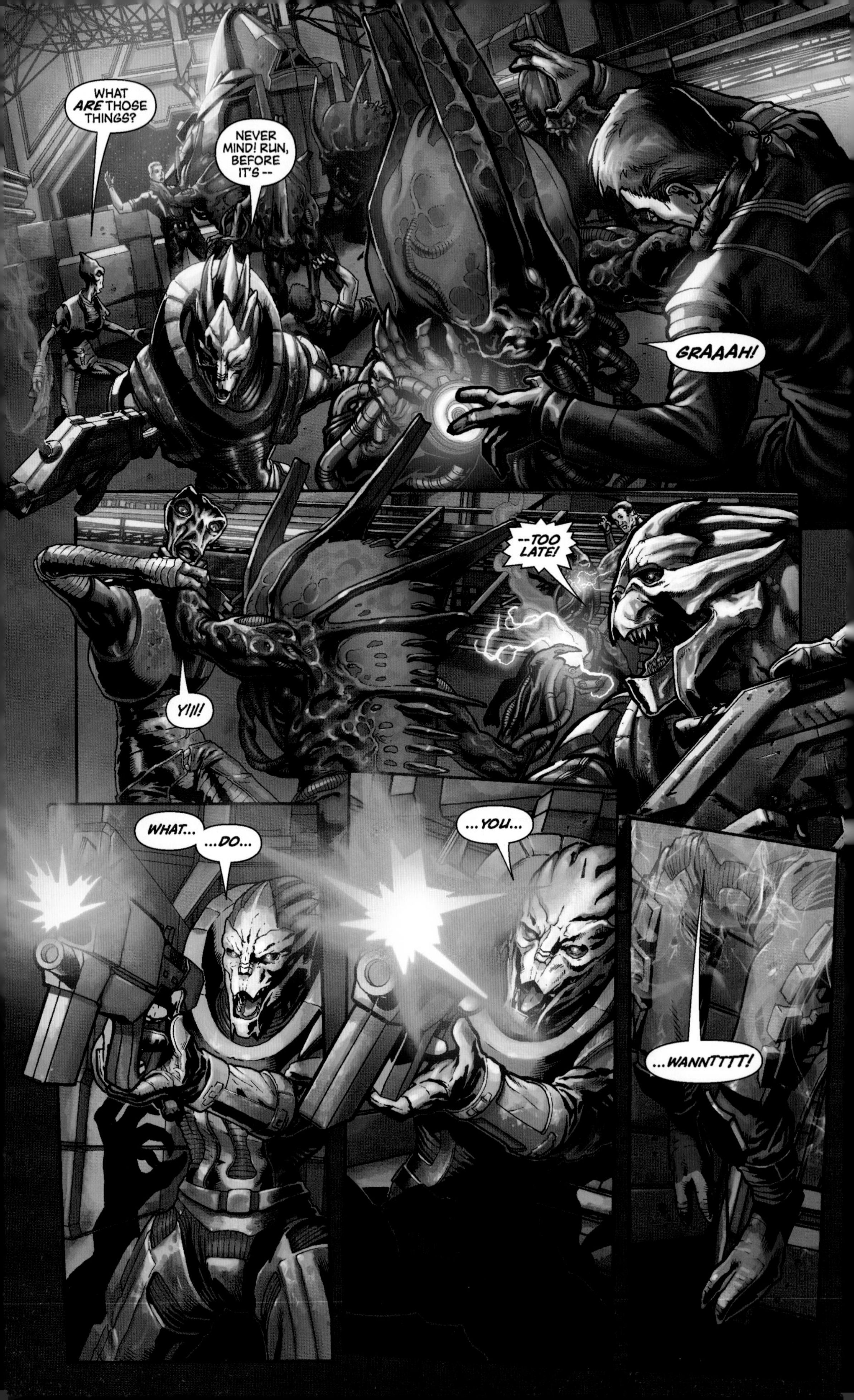
WHAT ARE THOSE THINGS?
NEVER MIND! RUN, BEFORE IT'S --
GRAAAH!
--TOO LATE!
YIII!
WHAT...
...DO...
...YOU...
...WANNTTTT!

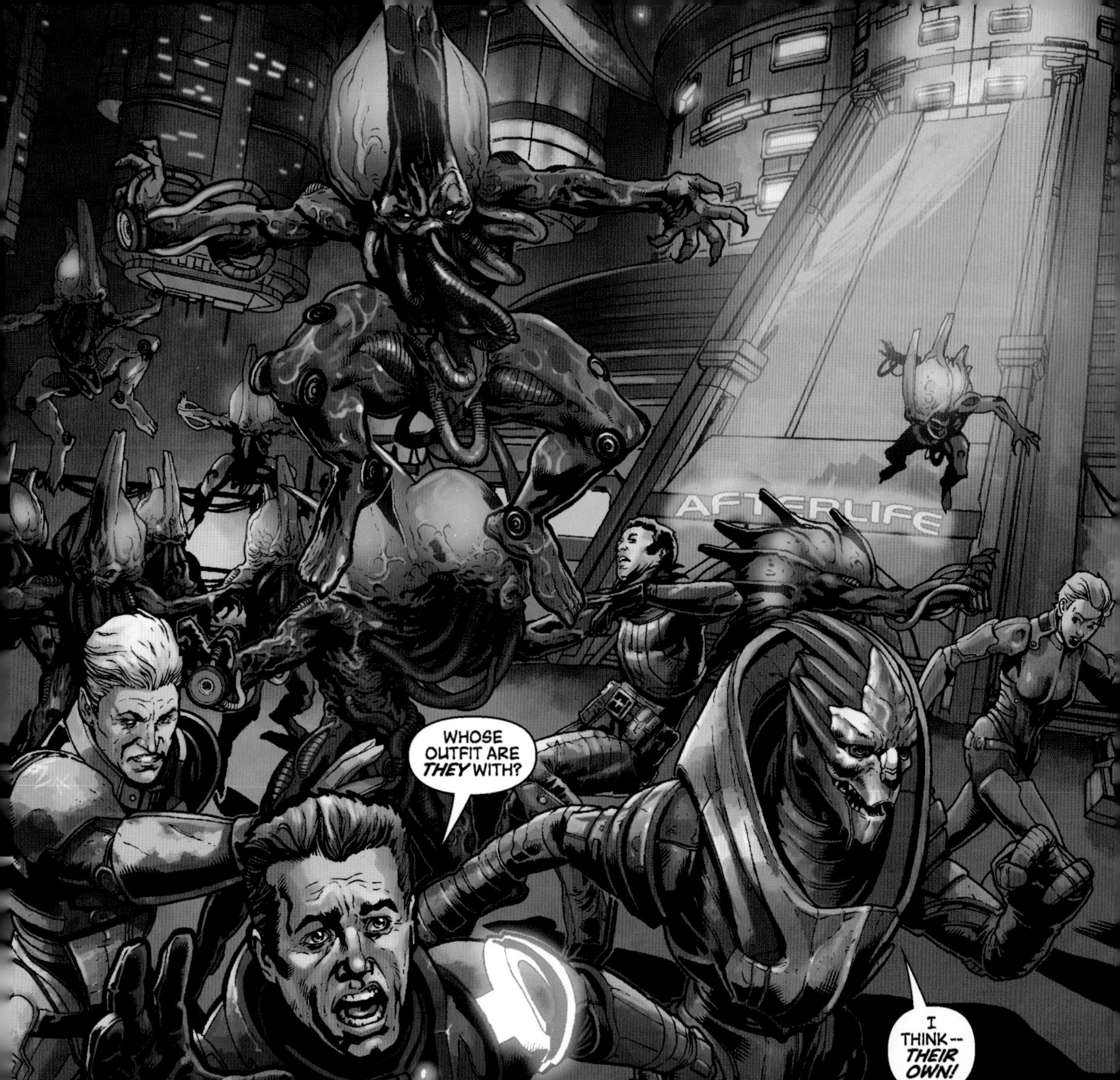

WHOSE OUTFIT ARE *THEY* WITH?
I THINK-- *THEIR OWN!*

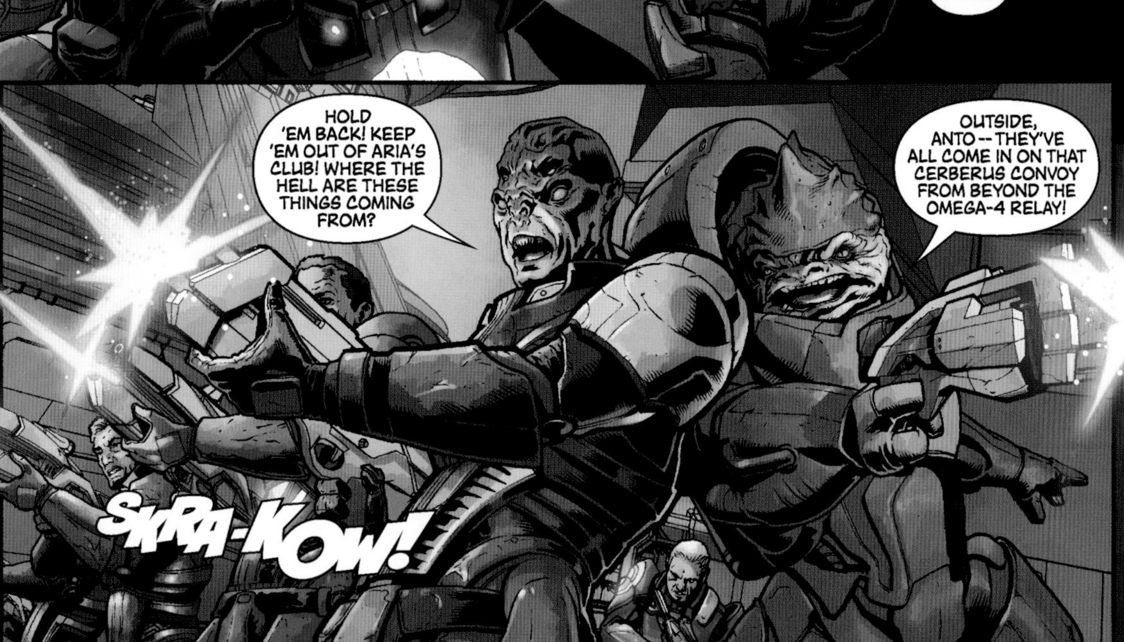

HOLD 'EM BACK! KEEP 'EM OUT OF ARIA'S CLUB! WHERE THE HELL ARE THESE THINGS COMING FROM?
OUTSIDE, ANTO -- THEY'VE ALL COME IN ON THAT CERBERUS CONVOY FROM BEYOND THE OMEGA-4 RELAY!
SKRA-KOW!
AFTERLIFE

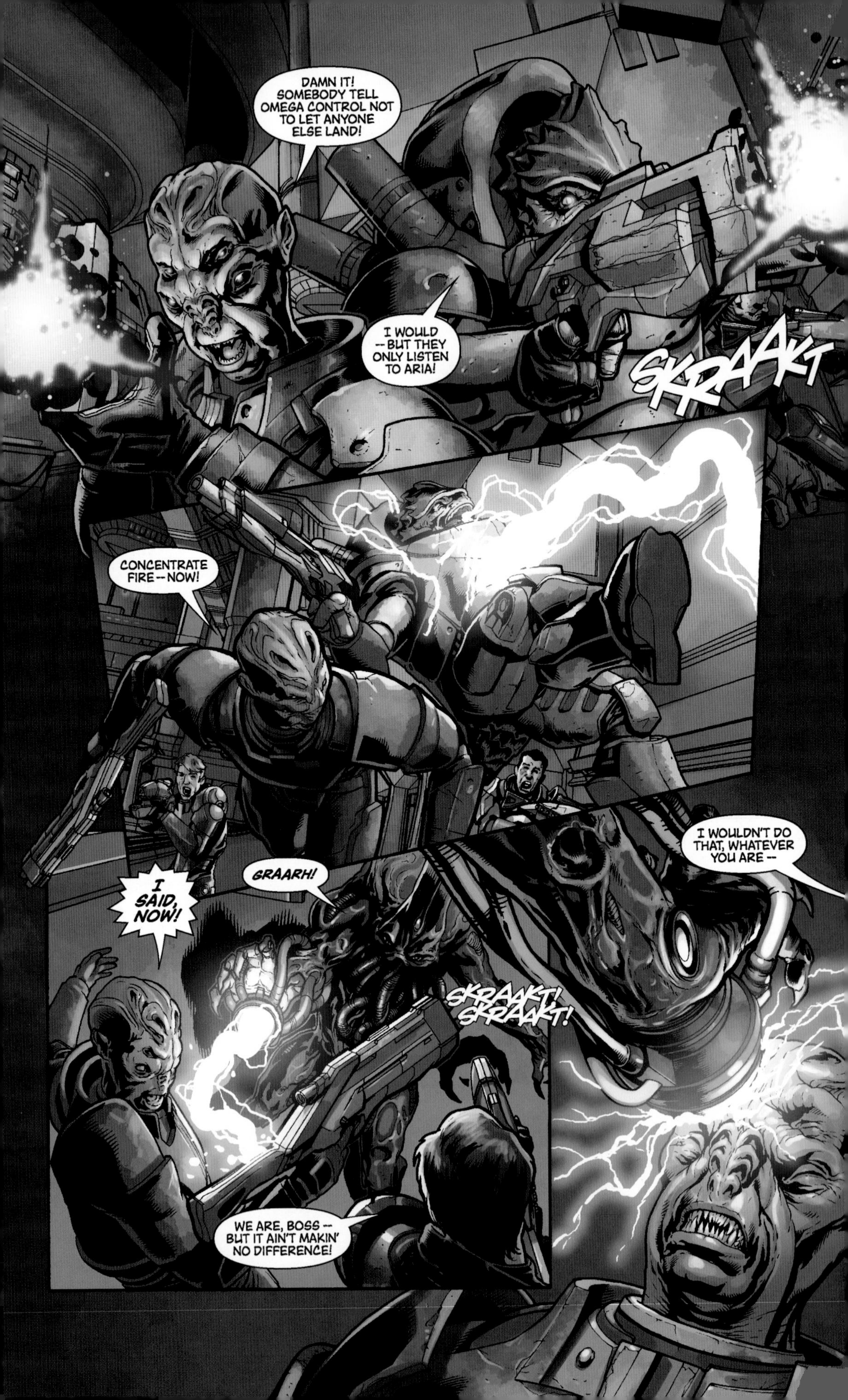
DAMN IT! SOMEBODY TELL OMEGA CONTROL NOT TO LET ANYONE ELSE LAND!
I WOULD --BUT THEY ONLY LISTEN TO ARIA!
SKRAAKT
CONCENTRATE FIRE--NOW!
I WOULDN'T DO THAT, WHATEVER YOU ARE--
I SAID, NOW!
GRAARH!
SKRAAKT! SKRAAKT!
WE ARE, BOSS -- BUT IT AIN'T MAKIN' NO DIFFERENCE!

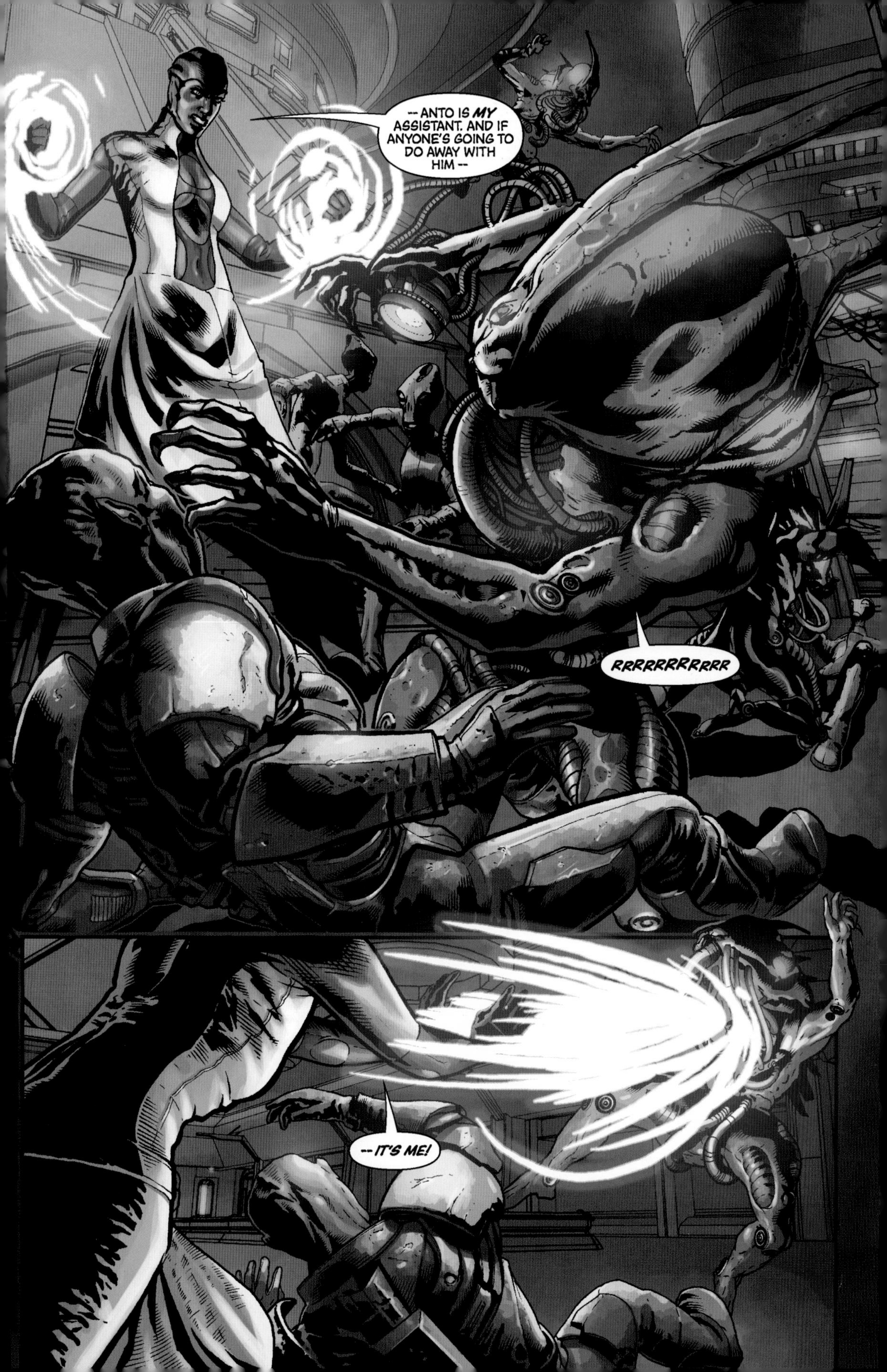
-- ANTO IS *MY* ASSISTANT. AND IF ANYONE'S GOING TO DO AWAY WITH HIM --
RRRRRRRRRRR
-- IT'S ME!

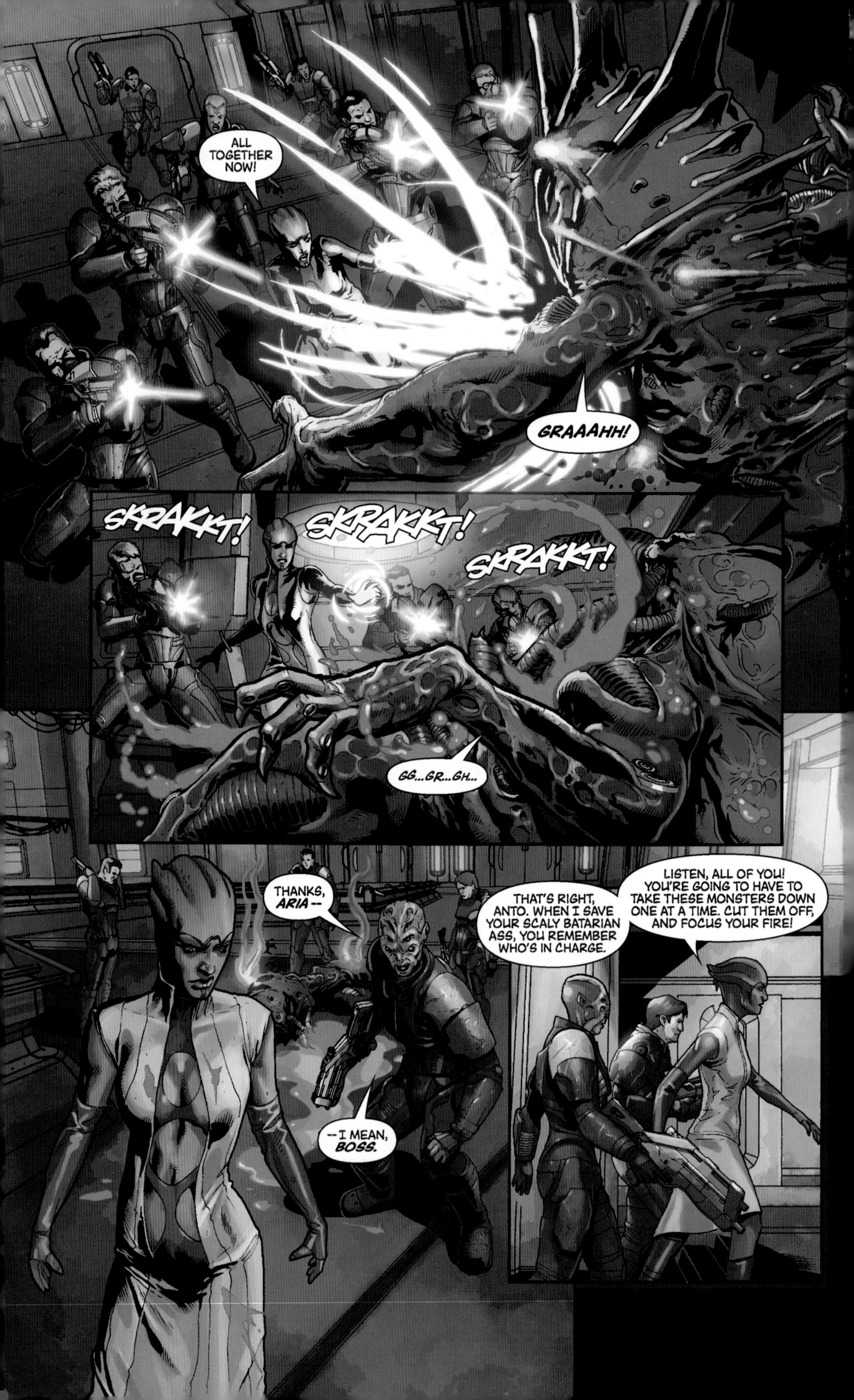
ALL TOGETHER NOW!
GRAAAHH!
SKRAKKT!
SKRAKKT!
SKRAKKT!
GG...GR...GH...
THANKS, *ARIA* --
-- I MEAN, *BOSS.*
THAT'S RIGHT, ANTO. WHEN I SAVE YOUR SCALY BATARIAN ASS, YOU REMEMBER WHO'S IN CHARGE.
LISTEN, ALL OF YOU! YOU'RE GOING TO HAVE TO TAKE THESE MONSTERS DOWN ONE AT A TIME. CUT THEM OFF, AND FOCUS YOUR FIRE!